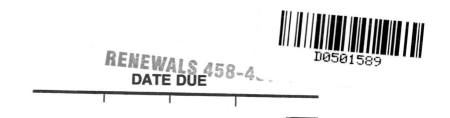

A Web of Prevention

A Web of Prevention

Biological Weapons, Life Sciences and the
Governance of Research

Edited by
Brian Rappert and Caitríona McLeish

London • Sterling, VA

First published by Earthscan in the UK and USA in 2007

ISBN-13:   978-1-84407-373-3
Typeset by FiSH Books, Enfield, Middx.
Printed and bound in the UK by TJ International Ltd, Padstow
Cover design by Susanne Harris

For a full list of publications please contact:

Earthscan
8–12 Camden High Street
London, NW1 0JH, UK
Tel: +44 (0)20 7387 8558
Fax: +44 (0)20 7387 8998
Email: earthinfo@earthscan.co.uk
Web: **www.earthscan.co.uk**

22883 Quicksilver Drive, Sterling, VA 20166-2012, USA

Earthscan publishes in association with the International Institute for Environment
and Development

A catalogue record for this book is available from the British Library

Library of Congress Cataloging-in-Publication Data
A web of prevention : biological weapons, life sciences, and the governance of
research/edited by Brian Rappert and Caitriona Mcleish
     p. cm.
  ISBN-13: 978-1-84407-373-3 (hbk.)
  ISBN-10: 1-84407-373-4 (hbk.)
 1. Biological weapons. 2. Life sciences–Research–Government policy.
3. Biotechnology–Research–Government policy. 4. Bioterrorism–Prevention.
I. Rappert, Brian. II. McLeish, Caitriona.
  UG447.8.W43 2007
  623.4'594–dc22   2007021164

FSC
Mixed Sources
Product group from well-managed
forests and other controlled sources
Cert no. SGS-COC-2482
www.fsc.org
© 1996 Forest Stewardship Council

The paper used for this book is FSC-certified and totally chlorine-
free. FSC (the Forest Stewardship Council) is an international
network to promote responsible management of the world's forests.

Contents

List of Contributors

Ronald M. Atlas served as president of the American Society for Microbiology and is graduate dean, professor of biology, professor of public health and co-director of the Center for Health Hazards Preparedness at the University of Louisville, US.

Brian Balmer is a reader in science policy studies in the Department of Science and Technology Studies, University College London, UK. His research interests focus on the nature of scientific expertise and the role of experts in science policy formation. He continues to work on this topic, and is also involved in research on the role of volunteers in biomedical research and the history of the 'brain drain' debate in the UK.

Malcolm Dando is professor of international security at the University of Bradford. A biologist by original training, his main research interest is in the preservation of the prohibitions embodied in the Chemical Weapons Convention and the Biological Weapons Convention.

John L. Finney has been professor of physics at University College London, UK, since 1993. Previously professor of crystallography at Birkbeck College London, he was seconded to the Rutherford Appleton Laboratory for five years as head of neutron science and as ISIS chief scientist, and was the science coordinator of the European Spallation Source Project from 1993 to 1997. He was the founding editor of *Euroscience News* and a past vice-president of Euroscience, a grassroots organization aiming to raise the profile of science in Europe. He is currently treasurer of the British Pugwash Group and chairs the Weapons of Mass Destruction (WMD) Awareness Programme.

Daniel Feakes is a fellow at SPRU – Science and Technology Research at the University of Sussex, UK. Since 1997 he has worked with the Harvard Sussex Program on Chemical and Biological Weapons (HSP), including spending three years working as the HSP researcher in the Organization for the Prohibition of Chemical Weapons in The Hague.

Elisa D. Harris is a senior research scholar at the Center for International and Security Studies (CISSM) at the University of Maryland, US. From 1993 to 2001, she was director for non-proliferation and export controls on the US National Security Council staff, where she had primary responsibility for coordinating US policy on chemical, biological and missile proliferation issues. This chapter was written while she was a visiting fellow at the Robert Schuman Centre for Advanced Studies at the European University in Florence, Italy.

Thomas V. Holohan M.D. has been a medical officer in the US Navy and the Public Health Service. He was director of the Office of Health Technology Assessment, and from 1996 to 2004 was the associate deputy chief medical director of the Veterans' Health Administration. He was the first executive director of the National Science Advisory Board for Biosecurity at the National Institutes of Health. He currently directs and conducts clinical research in the private sector.

Jez Littlewood is an assistant professor at the Norman Paterson School of International Affairs, Carleton University, Ottawa, Canada. He has over six years of experience on international diplomacy in the Biological Weapons Convention (BWC) field both as a member of the secretariat of the BWC meetings and conferences (1998 to 2002) and as an adviser to the UK government on the BWC (2005 to 2007). Between 2002 and 2006 he was a research fellow at the Mountbatten Centre for International Studies, University of Southampton, UK, and since 2006 he has also been a research associate at the Canadian Centre for Treaty Compliance, Carleton University, Canada.

Caitrìona McLeish is a fellow at SPRU – Science and Technology Research at the University of Sussex, UK. Since 1996 she has been attached to the Harvard Sussex Program on Chemical and Biological Weapons, where she has undertaken projects on the governance of dual use technologies in both the chemical and biological warfare environments, and conducted assessments on the impact of dual use controls on innovation within scientific and industrial communities.

Brian Martin is a professor in the School of Social Sciences, Media and Communication at the University of Wollongong, Australia. He has written a dozen books and numerous articles on non-violent action, dissent, scientific controversies, information issues and strategies to oppose justice.

Robert J. Mathews is head of nuclear, biological and chemical weapons arms control in Australia's Defence Science and Technology Organization. He is also principal fellow/associate professor in the Faculty of Law, University of Melbourne, Australia.

The Royal Society is the UK's national academy of science and is the world's oldest scientific academy in continuous existence having been founded in 1660. The Society is committed to delivering the best independent advice, drawing upon the expertise of the Society's Fellows and Foreign Members and the wider scientific community.

Brian Rappert is an associate professor of science, technology and public affairs in the Department of Sociology and Philosophy at the University of Exeter, UK. His long-term interest has been the examination of how choices can be and are made about adopting and regulating security-related technologies, particularly in conditions of uncertainty and disagreement.

Catherine Rhodes is a post-doctoral research fellow in the Bradford Disarmament Research Centre within the Peace Studies Department at Bradford University, UK. She completed her PhD on the coherence of the international regulatory response to the biotechnology revolution in August 2006 and continues to work on this area.

Margaret Somerville is Samuel Gale professor of law, professor at the Faculty of Medicine and founding director at the Centre for Medicine, Ethics and Law, McGill University, Montreal, Canada. Her most recent book is *The Ethical Imagination: Journeys of the Human Spirit* (House of Anansi Press, 2006).

Emmanuelle Tuerlings is a scientist to the Programme for Bio-risk Reduction for Dangerous Pathogens in the Department of Epidemic and Pandemic Alert and Response at the World Health Organization in Geneva, where she is currently working on the project Life Science Research and Development and Global Health Security. Prior to this appointment, she was a researcher at the Harvard Sussex Program based at the University of Sussex, UK, and also worked as a consultant for several international and non-governmental organizations (NGOs).

Foreword

The 21st century is the century of the life sciences. The speed and exponential development of the biological sciences are comparable with the rapid developments that have taken place in the field of information technology during recent decades. Great advances have been steadily made, especially in molecular biology and genetics. While we have benefited vastly from these developments in terms of combating diseases, fighting hunger, improving health conditions and increasing agricultural productivity, each of these great advances also bears the danger of being misused.

As a result, the problem of biological research is its potential dual use character. While it is essential to conduct research into vaccines and medications, the very same research can be applied to develop biological weapons. As biological research advances and technologies become more accessible, the potential for accidental or intentional harm grows exponentially. Significant challenges for future work stem from the need to improve global standards and increase international cooperation in addressing the challenge of biological risks. The current lack of a shared global language on this issue, as well as of shared risk assessment methodologies and standard settings in biosafety, biosecurity and best practices, needs to be addressed.

The emergence of terrorism using biological agents has led to greater international cooperation on preventive measures. The 2001 US anthrax attacks gave rise to serious policy concern about the possible misuse of the life sciences. The fear of further deliberate use with micro-organisms or toxins for harming people, plants and livestock has led to intensified efforts on how to prevent such events in the future. Legal, scientific, security, public health and law enforcement experts from around the world have worked together to explore ways of improving coordination and cooperation to increase security, without limiting the research necessary for the development of medication and vaccines. They have explored how know-how can be protected from being exploited for malicious purposes, which approaches are needed for better protection, and what are effective barriers to prevent misuse and to help build a culture of responsibility and accountability among the scientific community.

It is noteworthy that, in the context of the inter-sessional meetings before the Sixth Review Conference of the Biological Weapons Convention (BWC), the issue about codes of conduct for scientists was raised, among other topics. The main goal for such codes would be to raise awareness of the convention and of the potential risks inherent in scientific activity, and to help scientists and others to fulfil their legal, regulatory, professional and ethical obligations. The BWC provides the legal basis to prohibit the development, production, stockpiling, retention and acquisition of bacteriological (biological) agents in quantities that have no justification for prophylactic, protective or other peaceful purposes. The BWC is as relevant today as it was at the time of its entry into force, over 30 years ago. It covers biological weapons of any kind, whether targeted at humans, animals and/or plants. A legal framework, such as that provided by the BWC, remains the best protection against bio-proliferation. Currently, there are 156 member states to the convention and the goal is universal adherence. Only universal adherence to international/multilateral disarmament and non-proliferation agreements and full and effective implementation of their provisions by the state parties can provide assurance of an effective prohibition of biological and chemical weapons, and can contribute to the non-proliferation of weapons of mass destruction, while reducing the risk of their use by states and non-state actors.

However, the BWC does not have a verification regime, unlike in the nuclear and chemical areas, where international organizations exist to handle matters of safeguarding, inspection and verification, as well as disarmament. In the absence of such a body, the international community has to initiate concrete steps to connect the dots and cooperate in improving the already existing synergies of different activities.

The provisions of the convention need to be translated into domestic laws and national legislation to criminalize illicit biological science activities and to establish enforcement mechanisms, as well as to undertake measures to strengthen import/export and transit and border controls. Finally, the universality of the convention is a common goal.

International activities in the area of non-proliferation have complemented existing treaties to strengthen national implementation. Security Council Resolution 1540 (2004) is the first comprehensive strategy on the non-proliferation of weapons of mass destruction. It required all states to refrain from providing any form of support to non-state actors who attempt to develop, acquire, manufacture, possess, transport, transfer or use nuclear, chemical and biological weapons and their means of delivery, as well as to adopt and enforce appropriate effective laws to this effect. The resolution also required states to take and enforce effective measures to establish domestic controls to prevent the proliferation of such weapons and their means of delivery.

In relation to this wider context, *A Web of Prevention* provides a timely contribution to the current debate about life science research and its implications for security. It is an informative guide for both experts and the public. It especially addresses the need to help prevent accidents and deliberate misuse in biological research, as well as how to increase biosecurity and biosafety measures without hampering life science research. It is a forward-looking contribution covering both ends of the equation and creates momentum for the current discussion on effective preventive and control measures. The authors examine multiple check points leading to a synergistic and complementary network of steps for the web of prevention of different types and at different levels, from the individual to the international.

While there are no guarantees for preventing misuse, there are, nonetheless, crucial steps that the world community can take towards the overarching goal of a global protective network for the life sciences. This book sheds light on concrete steps to achieving this worthy goal.

Dr Gabriele Kraatz-Wadsack
Chief, Weapons of Mass Destruction Branch
Office for Disarmament Affairs
United Nations
June 2007

Acknowledgements

Our thanks to all those who contributed to this book through their chapters and suggestions. A grant from the Alfred P. Sloan Foundation enabled Brian Rappert to undertake much of the editorial work in preparing this volume.

List of Acronyms and Abbreviations

AAHSC	Aquatic Animal Health Standards Commission
AChE	acetylcholinesterase
AEC	activity of extreme concern
AIDS	acquired immune deficiency syndrome
AMC	activity of moderate concern
APC	activity of potential concern
APEC	Asia–Pacific Economic Cooperation
ASM	American Society for Microbiology
ATCSA	Anti-terrorism, Crime and Security Act
BSC	Biological Standards Commission
BWC	Biological Weapons Convention
BTWC	Biological and Toxin Weapons Convention
CAC	Codex Alimentarius Commission
CBD	Convention on Biological Diversity
CBM	confidence-building measure
CBW	chemical and biological weapons
CBW/SAG	Chemical and Biological Weapons Scientific Advisory Group (WHO)
CDC	Centers for Disease Control and Prevention
CeCalCULA	Centro Nacional de Calculo Cinetifico
CIA	Central Intelligence Agency (US)
CISSM	Center for International and Security Studies at Maryland
CoCOM	Coordinating Committee on Multilateral Export Controls
COP	Conference of the Parties
COSHH	Control on Substances Hazardous to Health
CPC	Counter-Proliferation Committee
CPIC	Counter-Proliferation Implementation Committee
CWC	Chemical Weapons Convention
DCI	Director of Central Intelligence
DFID	Department for International Development (UK)
DHHS	Department of Health and Human Services (US)
DHS	Department of Homeland Security (US)
DNA	deoxyribonucleic acid

DoD	Department of Defense (US)
DSTL	Defence Science and Technology Laboratory (UK)
DTI	Department of Trade and Industry (UK)
ECO	Export Control Organization (UK)
EU	European Union
FAO	United Nations Food and Agriculture Organization
FBI	Federal Bureau of Investigation (US)
FCO	Foreign and Commonwealth Office (UK)
FIOCRUZ	Fundação Oswaldo Cruz in South Africa
GAP	Government Accountability Project (US)
GCE	General Certificate of Education
GM	genetically modified
HIV	human immunodeficiency virus
HMRC	Her Majesty's Revenue and Customs (UK)
HSE	Health and Safety Executive (UK)
HSP	Harvard Sussex Program
IAEA	International Atomic Energy Agency
IAP	InterAcademy Panel on International Issues
IBC	International Bioethics Committee
IBC	Institutional Biosafety Committee
ICGEB	International Centre for Genetic Engineering and Biotechnology
ICRC	International Committee of the Red Cross
IGBC	Intergovernmental Bioethics Committee
IHR	International Health Regulation
IUPAC	International Union of Pure and Applied Chemistry
MDG	Millennium Development Goal
MoD	Ministry of Defence (UK)
MRC	Medical Research Council
MTCR	Missile Technology Control Regime
NaCTSO	National Counter Terrorism and Security Office
NAM	Non-Aligned Movement
NATO	North Atlantic Treaty Organization
NBC	nuclear, biological and chemical weapons
NGO	non-governmental organization
NIH	National Institutes of Health
NPRA	National Pathogens Research Authority
NPT	Nuclear Non-Proliferation Treaty
NSABB	National Science Advisory Board for Biosecurity
NSG	Nuclear Suppliers Group
NTI	Nuclear Threat Initiative
OECD	Organisation for Economic Co-operation and Development
OIE	Office International des Epizooties
OPCW	Organization for the Prohibition of Chemical Weapons
OSC	Office of Special Counsel (US)
PAMP	pathogen-associated molecular pattern

PSI	Proliferation Security Initiative
RAC	Recombinant DNA Advisory Committee
R&D	research and development
REU	Restricted Enforcement Unit (UK)
RNA	ribonucleic acid
SAB	Scientific Advisory Board
SANBI	South African National Biodiversity Institute
S&T	science and technology
SAP	Scientific Advisory Panel
SARS	severe acute respiratory syndrome
SBSTTA	Subsidiary Body on Scientific, Technical and Technological Advice (*of the* CBD)
SCAD	Scientific Commission for Animal Diseases
siRNA	short interfering RNA
STS	Science and Technology Studies
TAHSC	Terrestrial Animal Health Standards Commission
TSA	Transportation Security Administration (US)
UK	United Kingdom
UN	United Nations
UNESCO	United Nations Educational, Scientific and Cultural Organization
UNMOVIC	United Nations Monitoring, Verification and Inspection Commission
UNSCOM	United Nations Special Commission
UNSCR	United Nations Security Council resolution
US	United States
USDA	United States Department of Agriculture
VEREX	Ad Hoc Group of Government Experts to Identify and Examine Potential Verification Measures from a Scientific and Technical Standpoint
WHO	World Health Organization
WMD	weapon of mass destruction

Introduction: A Web of Prevention?

Daniel Feakes, Brian Rappert and Caitríona McLeish

In June 2006, an ominous article titled 'Dark materials' appeared in the UK newspaper the *Guardian*. In it, the author warned about future dangers to the human population and the planet as a whole because of developments in science. He stated:

> *We are collectively endangering our planet, but there is a potential threat from individuals too. 'Bio' and 'cyber' expertise will be accessible to millions. It does not require large, special-purpose facilities as do nuclear weapons. Even a single person will have the capability to cause widespread disruption through error or terror.*

Among the many areas of science identified as raising serious questions, biotechnology was said to be enabling 'qualitatively' novel forms of human intervention. The article went on to state: 'There is an ever-widening gap between what science allows, and what we should actually do. There are many doors science can open that should be kept closed, on prudential or ethical grounds.'

While highlighting the significant potential for societal benefit associated with scientific developments, the author also called for meaningful forms of restraint. He advocated that scientists:

> *... should forgo experiments that are risky or unethical. More than that, they should foster benign spin-offs, but resist dangerous or threatening applications. They should raise public consciousness of hazards to environment or health.*

Furthermore, claims were made that the choices in the application of science were too important to be left to scientists alone to handle.

What made this contribution particularly noteworthy was its author: Lord Martin Rees, then also serving as the president of the British Royal Society, one of the world's oldest academies of eminent scientists.

The article received a number of responses, including one from Professor Ross Anderson at Cambridge University (Anderson, 2006). This professor of security engineering said that the system of 'worldwide surveillance and regulation' proposed by Lord Rees was both 'foolish and wicked'. Further to this, he argued:

> *Controls on biological technologies are particularly foolish. The diseases that kill millions are not biowar lab nasties, but naturally occurring pathogens such as HIV, Sars and flu. If the US and Europe won't let Sudanese students do PhDs in pathology, then Khartoum won't have capable public health services – which could be bad news for us next time a virus starts making its way down the Nile.*

Instead of embracing the sorts of controls identified by Martin Rees, Professor Anderson proposed that 'The scientist's job is to shine light in the darkness, and if we occasionally burn our fingers on the candle, so be it. Lord Rees can choose the darkness if he wants. I'm not going to.'

The account of the exchange raises many questions: What destructive possibilities are enabled by modern science? Are these bringing hitherto novel capabilities for causing death or disruption? What are the chances that such potentials turn into actualities? To what extent might science need to be controlled because of security fears? Who should determine what measures are prudent?

In response to concerns regarding biological weapons, during recent years a number of individuals and organizations have proposed the need for a 'web of prevention'. While such a web is not intended to block out all light, so to speak, the various appeals made for it do suggest that something should be done to reduce the likelihood that biological weapons are developed or employed. This book provides an examination of the possible elements of such a web, one *specifically* focused on the governance of scientific research. The contributors do so while also giving critical attention to the assumptions – regarding the nature of threats and the possible effects of responses – underlying such a call.

Origins

The concept of a 'web' of measures to address biological weapons overall has a relatively recent pedigree, with its origins in the early 1990s. However, a similar concept, that of a 'regime', was used during the 1980s to describe international measures adopted against chemical weapons. Today, while both web and regime are still frequently used, another term that has come into common currency in relation to efforts to deal with the problem of chemical and biological weapons is 'network'. Although each term has different origins and different implications, they all have, at root, the idea that there is no single 'solution' to the challenges posed by chemical and biological weapons, that multilateral arms control conventions are only a part of the response, albeit a very significant one, and that in order to effectively counter chemical and biological weapons, other complementary measures are required.

Over the decades since the entry into force of the 1972 Biological Weapons Convention (BWC), the attention paid to the complementary elements of the web has waxed and waned. However, the concept appears to be undergoing something of a resurgence in recent years, stimulated by the re-emergence of international terrorism, dramatic advances in science and technology, changes in the nature and conduct of diplomacy, and the rise of significant new actors. Tracing the evolution and connection between notions of webs, regimes and networks will sharpen our focus about the prospects for a web and help situate the contribution of the authors to this volume. It will also be used here to recount policy and conceptual developments during recent years regarding the prohibition of biological weapons.

Webs

In 1993, Graham Pearson, then the Director-General of the Chemical and Biological Defence Establishment at Porton Down in the UK, introduced the concept of the 'web of deterrence' into the debate on chemical and biological arms control (Pearson, 1993, p150). Pearson wrote that it has 'become evident that no arms-control regime is guaranteed to be wholly effective' and that what was therefore needed was 'a strategy that complements arms control with a range of other measures to form a web of deterrence'. He identified the key elements of such a web as comprehensive, verifiable and global chemical and biological arms control; broad export monitoring and controls; effective defensive and protective measures; and a range of determined and effective national and international responses to the acquisition and/or use of chemical and biological weapons (Pearson, 1993, p151).

The 'web of deterrence' concept has also been reflected in national policy. The 1993 Defence White Paper stated that 'it is likely that worthwhile deterrence [of biological weapons] could be achieved by a web of measures restricting potential violators' room for manoeuvre' (UK Ministry of Defence, 1993, p58); a 1999 Ministry of Defence publication stated that 'our policy rests on four inter-related pillars: arms control, preventing supply, deterring use and defending against use' (UK Ministry of Defence, 1999); and three years later, a UK Foreign and Commonwealth Office (2002, p5) paper stated that this four-pillar approach 'remains at the heart of our policy'.

And yet, the origin of the term 'web of deterrence' goes back further than the 1990s in relation to security discussions as a whole. It can be found in the doctrine of 'flexible response', which had been adopted by the North Atlantic Treaty Organization (NATO) in 1967 in place of its earlier strategy of massive nuclear retaliation. Flexible response sought to deter aggression by the maintenance of conventional, theatre nuclear and strategic nuclear forces that would enable the alliance to respond to any attack at an appropriate level (Legge, 1983, p9). Lawrence Freedman (1981) wrote that 'flexible response offered the notion of a seamless web of deterrence', and Williams (1983, p198) wrote that the

NATO decision in 1979 to deploy cruise and Pershing missiles in Western Europe 'will not necessarily restore the "seamless web" of deterrence as was initially hoped'. For their part, the Soviet Union also referred to its combination of strategic and theatre nuclear weapons as the 'seamless web of deterrence' (USA National Intelligence Council, 1999).

The 'web of deterrence' description was appropriate for biological weapons in the early 1990s when the Warsaw Pact was only just unravelling and when such weapons were seen mainly in the context of military conflict between the East and West. However, by the late 1990s, Pearson, by then a visiting professor at the University of Bradford, had adjusted his terminology to reflect 'an age of regional or local conflicts' and demands from the public for reassurance that governments would protect them from biological weapons, whether possessed by rogue states or non-state actors (Pearson, 2001, p8). For this reason, Pearson instead called for a 'web of reassurance' with similar but broader constituent elements, compared to his earlier 'web of deterrence': a strong international and national prohibition regime reinforcing the norm that biological weapons are totally prohibited; broad international and national controls on the handling, storage, use and transfer of dangerous pathogens; preparedness, including both active and passive protective measures and response plans that have been exercised; and determined national and international response to any use or threat of use of biological weapons, ranging from diplomatic sanctions through to armed intervention (Pearson, 2001, p8).

Today, the notion of a web of measures is often evoked in discussions on the control of biological weapons. A 1999 British Medical Association publication – *Bioweapons, Technology and Humanity* (primarily written by Pearson's Bradford colleague Malcolm Dando) – focuses on the concept of a 'web of deterrence' to prevent the acquisition and use of biological weapons (British Medical Association, 1999). In 2002, the International Committee of the Red Cross (ICRC) launched an initiative on Biotechnology, Weapons and Humanity, calling for a reaffirmation of norms against biological weapons and for better controls on potentially dangerous biotechnology (Kellenberger, 2002). Central to the initiative are awareness-raising and education activities directed at life scientists in order to contribute to what the ICRC calls a 'web of prevention'. In a 2003 publication, the ICRC stated:

> *Those in a position to help prevent biotechnology being used for hostile purposes too often focus on only one aspect of the solution, such as the Biological Weapons Convention, bio-safety rules, disease surveillance or countering 'bio-terrorism'. Seldom is synergy of action achieved between the different entities concerned. (ICRC, 2003, p6).*

Therefore, the ICRC envisages the 'web of prevention' as a 'broad and integrative approach that should be taken by all those concerned to minimize the risk'. It uses the analogy of fire prevention to explain the intention behind the web.

Interestingly, the same analogy is used in a recent report by the US National Academies (2006, p4), *Globalization, Biosecurity and the Future of the Life*

Sciences, which calls for a 'web of protection'. According to the report, 'the committee could not envision any sort of "silver bullet" capable of providing absolute protection against the malevolent application of new technologies' (US National Academies, 2006, p16). Instead, the actions and strategies recommended in the report are described as 'complementary and synergistic'.

Regimes

The notion of creating a broad and synergistic array of measures to address the problem of biological and chemical weapons is not a recent innovation. One important source of earlier thinking can be found in the international relations field of regime analysis, which emerged during the mid 1970s as scholars sought to understand the dramatic increase in cooperative arrangements between states (see Ruggie, 1975; Keohane and Nye, 1977). A widely accepted definition of a regime was put forward in 1982 by a group of American scholars: 'sets of implicit or explicit principles, norms, rules and decision-making procedures around which actors' expectations converge in a given area of international relations' (Krasner, 1982, p186).

The first scholar to apply regime analysis to the problem of chemical or biological weapons was Robinson (1985). Since then, the regime has been further extended by the coordination of national export controls among a group of like-minded countries within the Australia Group; the empowerment of the United Nations (UN) Secretary-General to investigate allegations of the use of chemical and biological weapons; the 1993 Chemical Weapons Convention (CWC); and, most recently, UN Security Council resolution 1540. In 1988, Nicholas Sims described a 'treaty regime of biological disarmament' centred on the BWC (Sims, 1988, p5) and, in a later publication, described how this regime was 'defined and developed by a process of cumulative diplomacy and accretion' (Sims, 2001, p18). Sims also illustrated how the concept of a 'treaty regime' was used by diplomats, particularly Ambassador Winfried Lang of Austria (Lang, 1990), and by academics, such as Falk (1990) and Meselson and colleagues (1990).

An attempt was made during the 1990s to develop a CWC-style comprehensive regime for biological weapons through the negotiation of a supplementary protocol to the BWC. According to the most comprehensive account of the BWC protocol negotiations, the conceptual approach taken was of a 'single treaty silver-bullet "solution" to the biological weapons problem' (Littlewood, 2005, p203). The approach adopted was modelled closely on the CWC, with a system of declarations and inspections overseen by an international organization. This has since been acknowledged by two of those who participated in the Ad Hoc Group established in 1994 with a mandate to negotiate the BWC protocol (Randin and Borrie, 2005, p101; Lennane, 2006, p7).

However, it is interesting to note that this single-treaty model was not the only possible option for creating a regime. As already mentioned above, even before the entry into force of the CWC, a fragmented regime existed against chemical weapons. Bernauer (1993, p375) noted how there were two basic options for resolving the chemical warfare problem: the comprehensive 'once-and-for-all' solution that was eventually adopted, or an incremental approach based upon partial agreements of varying formality. Outlining possibilities for the latter, Bernauer (1993, p378) mentioned the following: expanding the Australia Group; amending or supplanting the Geneva Protocol; strengthening the Geneva Protocol by developing its existing investigation and enforcement mechanisms; establishing chemical weapon-free zones; reducing chemical weapons stockpiles; or imposing chemical disarmament obligations on specific states through coercion. A similar incremental approach would also have been possible for the BWC during the 1990s. However, state parties chose to follow the single-treaty approach modelled on the CWC.

This approach ultimately failed in 2001 at the Fifth Review Conference when the 'vision text' which the Ad Hoc Group chairman had drafted was rejected by the US, with a number of other state parties more quietly not in favour. The US additionally rejected the approach taken by the Ad Hoc Group since 1995, arguing that 'the traditional approach that has worked well for many other types of weapons is not a workable structure for biological weapons' (Mahley, 2001). During the 1990s, international action against biological weapons had been focused on strengthening the BWC almost to the exclusion of everything else (see Littlewood, 2004, p14). This imbalance was evident both internationally and nationally. Within states there were few individuals or agencies with a comprehensive overview of all measures aimed at addressing biological weapons.

Networks

The sudden loss of what had been the guiding ambition for six years was quickly followed by the terrorist attacks on the US in September 2001. The dramatic rise of the combination of international terrorism and weapons of mass destruction as the main threat facing developed nations has led to much greater emphasis on building collaboration and improving synergy. Moodie (2004) notes that 'the combination of politics, science and technology, and the treaty language of the CWC and BWC ensures that these conventions will be insufficient on their own' to deal with the threat posed by international terrorism. He goes on:

> What is needed is an approach that goes beyond the traditional modalities of arms control to new ways of thinking about how to strengthen the conventions and the norms against CBW that these conventions embody. (Moodie, 2004, p48)

In that spirit there has been an explosion in the number of initiatives, measures, efforts and activities either directly or indirectly aimed at addressing the biological weapons problem (e.g. the Proliferation Security Initiative, the Global Health Security Initiative, the G8 Global Partnership and UN Security Council resolution 1540).

Nowhere is this more apparent than in efforts to prevent the misuse of the life sciences. Stimulated, in part, by the ICRC's Biotechnology, Weapons and

Humanity initiative, but also by the decision of BWC state parties to examine the issue of codes of conduct for life scientists in 2005, the past five years have witnessed a significant rise in the engagement with those in the life sciences. For example, in 2005 representatives of 23 international, regional and national scientific and professional bodies were allowed to participate in the BWC Meeting of Experts as 'guests of the meeting', an innovation described by one observer as 'a considerable step for a convention that had hitherto permitted only states and – with limitations – intergovernmental organizations to participate in its meetings' (Lennane, 2006). In many ways, though the initial expectations were very low, the work programme adopted by BWC state parties in 2002 has proved a significant innovation and has, in fact, shifted the BWC into a different mode of action. The annual meetings organized between 2003 and 2005 have seen the active involvement of private industry, international organizations and a wide range of civil society actors. They have also demonstrated the need for approaches across a range of areas; according to a European Union (EU) paper, this range 'goes well beyond the "national only" approach and also well beyond the "multinational" agenda as traditionally understood' (EU, 2006, p5).

Further, prior to the Sixth BWC Review Conference in November 2006, BWC President Masood Khan actively encouraged attendance by international organizations; as a result, six international organizations addressed the conference, as well as the UN Secretary-General himself. Also attending was a record number of 33 non-governmental organizations (NGOs). The review conference ended successfully with agreement on another inter-sessional work programme modelled on the 2003 to 2005 meetings and on the need to establish a small Implementation Support Unit in Geneva and to encourage state parties to create national contact points for interaction with this unit and each other. Therefore, although it is only early days, the review conference sowed the seed for a potentially significant new set of interactions.

Whether the framework of regime analysis is still adequate to conceptualize and understand this plethora of activity is debatable. Although regime analysis was, in part, intended as a shift away from realist conceptions of international relations with its acknowledgement of normative factors and of the influence of domestic politics on state behaviour, regime analysis is still a largely state-centred framework. However, the biological weapons problem is no longer (if, indeed, it ever was) one that is solely confined to or manageable by states.

As demonstrated by Rischard (2003), the world is witnessing the emergence of 'global issue networks' on topics that cannot be dealt with by one state alone. The existence of networks between governments is not novel. However, while government networks themselves are not new, a number of factors distinguish contemporary networks from their predecessors. As identified by Slaughter (2004, pp10–11), these include the 'scale, scope and type' of transgovernmental ties, the 'wider array of functions' performed than in the past, and the fact that they have 'spread far beyond regulators to judges and legislators'.

Reflecting the complexity of countering biological weapons and the rise of networks in other areas of international relations, in 2006 the UN Secretary-General proposed the creation of:

> *... a forum that will bring together the various stakeholders –*
> *Governments, industry, science, public health, security, the public writ large*
> *– into a common program, built from the bottom up, to ensure that biotech-*
> *nology's advances are used for the public good and that the benefits are*
> *shared equitably around the world. (UN, 2006)*

Such a forum would be a true 'global issue network' as conceptualized by Rischard (2003). The forum has been endorsed by UN member states; but at the time of writing it has yet to be formally constituted.

The nature of diplomacy itself has also changed in recent years, meaning that diplomats themselves are now not so wedded to concepts and methods of the past. This is partly a response to the changing nature of the challenges that modern diplomats face. A key facet of the varying nature of diplomacy is the emergence of civil society as a significant actor in world politics. In its 2004 report, the Panel of Eminent Persons on United Nations–Civil Society Relations stated that 'the rise of civil society is, indeed, one of the landmark events of our times. Global governance is no longer the sole domain of governments' (UN, 2004). Another key factor is the role now played by private industry and the 'increased contemporary significance of an upward trend in the management of global affairs by economic actors' (Cutler et al, 1999, p4).

Taken together, all of these factors have led to the emergence of 'multi-stake-holder diplomacy'. Hocking (2006, p13) argues that:

> *... actors, including states – commonly identified as the generators of diplo-*
> *macy – are no longer able to achieve their objectives in isolation from one*
> *another. Diplomacy is becoming an activity concerned with the creation of*
> *networks, embracing a range of state and non-state actors focusing on the*
> *management of issues that demand resources over which no single partici-*
> *pant possesses a monopoly.*

One small example is the way in which a Geneva-based NGO, the BioWeapons Prevention Project, has been entrusted with the implementation of an outreach and assistance programme adopted by a regional organization, in this case the EU. The examples given above, such as the shift in approach demonstrated by the 2003 to 2005 work programme, the UN Secretary-General's 'bio-forum' proposal and the decisions at the Sixth BWC Review Conference, all suggest that 'multi-stakeholder diplomacy' is another vital element in international efforts to address the biological weapons problem complementary to webs, regimes or networks.

What is apparent today is that countering the development or use of biological weapons is not a matter that can be solved for all time, nor is it one that can be managed by states alone, nor can it be addressed simply through a single treaty or some other instrument of international collective action. What is required is a broad array of measures at all levels, from the individual to the international, that are complementary and synergistic. What this array is called – web, regime or network – is, in many respects, largely immaterial. The main thing is that its constituent elements are in place and are able to manage an issue that is only likely to get more complex.

Outline of the book

While the previous section provided an overview of policy and conceptual developments in relation to webs, regimes and networks to address the development and use of biological weapons overall, this book focuses on a specific and emerging priority area: the governance of life science research. A central justification for exploring this area in isolation from other elements of the web of responses initiatives is that because international law has outlawed these weapons, much of the attention needs to be placed on the components for weapons – this includes the scientific and technological components.

Because much of the same knowledge, tools and techniques needed to develop and produce biological weapons are also used in activities such as scientific research, drug and vaccine production, agriculture and industrial processing, it is essential to bring in all those who work upon, trade in, move, finance and regulate in their respective domains. A web-based approach that broadens the horizon of security concerns to incorporate technology governance, allowing relevant initiatives, measures, efforts and activities initiated for a variety of reasons by a range of stakeholders, often with no security agenda, to be linked together in the name of reducing the potential for science and technology, can be diverted to malign applications.

The need and potential for such an expansive approach is argued for in Chapter 1. During recent years, particularly because of the 2005 meetings held as part of the BWC, renewed attention has been given to the role of professional and workplace codes of conduct. Against the backdrop of existing legal rules and ethical norms proscribing the development of bioweapons, Chapter 1 argues for the importance of establishing codes to further ethical reflection, formulate agreed standards and facilitate deliberation. More than just considering the role of codes, Atlas and Somerville provide a useful background on a range of initiatives, regulations and laws currently being considered to prevent the destructive use of the life sciences.

When the application of standards of conduct is mooted, then a frequent response is the need to enact protections for those so-called 'whistleblowers' that point out carelessness, ignorance or intent. In a wide-ranging analysis of the experiences of past whistleblowers in Chapter 2, however, Martin contends that such official channels rarely provide the type of protection so often expected of them. Rather, much more attention needs to be given to improving the knowledge, skills and contacts of would-be whistleblowers.

Many of the options covered in this book depend upon knowledgeable and cognizant individuals or they aim to enhance individuals' thinking. In Chapter 3, Rappert assesses what functions can be fulfilled by educating those associated with the life sciences in preventing the accidental or deliberate spread of disease. As contended, because practical attempts to educate require deciding just who needs to know what and how that understanding should come about, they can often generate contention. This is all the starker in the case of educating highly trained and specialized scientific and technical experts who are often said to be best left to govern themselves. Following on from these points about education, in Chapter 4, Finney, a practising physicist, offers his reflections on the social responsibility of scientists and the state of discussions within the physicist community to address the destructive applications of their research.

One set of responses to prevent this and the accidental spread of disease in relation to the life sciences has been to propose national and international oversight systems for research. In Chapters 7 and 8, the prospects for such systems are examined. In Chapter 7, Harris surveys prominent existing proposals for formal oversight and, in particular, outlines the rationale for the Biological Research Security System developed by her and colleagues at the Center for International and Security Studies in Maryland, US. In Chapter 8, Holohan, formerly executive director of the US National Science Advisory Board for Biosecurity, assesses the Maryland system and situates it within wider national and international considerations about oversight.

The contribution of expert advice is a well-established means by which members of the scientific community seek to shape government decision-making. Two chapters in this book address expert advice. The first, in Chapter 5, is an account by the British Royal Society of the conclusions of an international workshop of scientists, policy analysts, officials and others held at the Royal Society from 4 to 6 September 2006. Building on similar activities under the Chemical Weapons Convention, this workshop intended to identify scientific and technological developments most relevant to the BWC in order to inform deliberations at the Sixth Review Conference. In Chapter 6, Rhodes and Dando provide a wider examination of the potential for scientific expert advice in furthering the BWC and thus furthering a web.

Denying technology transfers in order to reduce the risks of proliferation and terrorism involving biological weapons is a central policy response to the problem of biological weapons. In Chapter 9, Littlewood examines the role and function of export controls in managing the threat posed by biological weapons and considers whether or not export controls represent a boundary to international science. In Chapter 10, Mathews considers the role played by the Australia Group and reflects upon the growing acceptance of the Australia Group export-control lists as an international benchmark in relation to export controls directed at CBW proliferation. In his opinion, a national export licensing system based on the Australia Group lists should be regarded as an essential component of the 'web of prevention'.

Although controls on the transfer of technology, the dissemination of information and associated monitoring of scientists to prevent harmful information being made public has been flagged positively as part of a web of prevention, Balmer notes in Chapter 11 that the spectre of undue censorship and excessive secrecy can follow rapidly in its wake. Contributing to contemporary debates about transparency and secrecy and the dissemination of certain forms of scientific research, Balmer reflects on the operation of secrecy in the British biological weapons programme, noting that secrecy can be constructed, lost and restored through the use of rumour and gossip.

In Chapter 12, McLeish offers reflections on the issue of dual use. Exploring the differing conceptualizations of dual use found in regulatory responses to the biological weapons problem and governance initiatives, McLeish details three distinct models of dual use that are currently evident. Complementary to an extent, she reflects on whether such differing conceptualizations might lead to lost governance opportunities through the exclusion of stakeholders and unhelpful competition. McLeish calls for an intellectual space to be opened where relevant security, technology and innovation experts, together with all interested stakeholders, can work together to strengthen the foundations of the web of prevention.

One example of the sort of innovative work that can be generated when traditional and non-traditional security stakeholders come together is when governance of dual use research is considered as an international health security issue. In Chapter 13, Tuerlings relates the work of the World Health Organization (WHO) and, in particular, the work being conducted as part of the Life Science Research and Development and Global Security project. This includes details of the work performed by a specially convened scientific working group consisting of a mix of public health workers, academicians, researchers, policy-makers, security experts and representatives from international organizations.

These chapters then attempt to reflect key parts of the web of prevention. Although it is recognized that many more chapters could have been included (particularly to include reflections on initiatives centred outside of the West), the topics covered span a wide-ranging set of issues that should give an illustration of what might be done.

References

Anderson, R. (2006) 'We cannot allow the terrorists to terrorise us', *Guardian*, 20 June

Bernauer, T. (1993) *The Chemistry of Regime Formation*, Geneva, UNIDIR and Dartmouth Publishing Company

British Medical Association (1999) *Biotechnology, Weapons and Humanity*, London, Harwood Academic Publishers

Cutler, C., Haufler, V. and Porter, T. (1999) 'Private authority and international affairs', in Cutler, C., Haufler, V. and Porter T. (eds) *Private Authority and International Affairs*, Albany, NY, SUNY Press, pp3–28

EU (European Union) (2006) *The Intersession Programme of Work: Its Utility and Contribution to Fulfilling the Object and Purpose of the Convention between 2003–2005 and a Case for further Intersessional Work after 2006*, Sixth Review Conference Document, BWC/CONF.VI/WP.8, 20 November

Falk, R. (1990) 'Inhibiting reliance on biological weaponry: The role and relevance of international law', in Wright, S. (ed) *Preventing a Biological Arms Race*, Cambridge, MA, MIT Press

Freedman, L. (1981) 'NATO myths', *Foreign Policy*, vol 45, pp48–68

Hocking, B. (2006) 'Multistakeholder diplomacy', in Kurbalija, J. and Katrandjiev, V.

(eds) *Multistakeholder Diplomacy: Challenges and Opportunities*, Malta and Geneva, Diplo, pp13–29

ICRC (International Committee of the Red Cross) (2003) *Biotechnology, Weapons and Humanity*, Geneva, ICRC

Kellenberger, J. (2002) 'Biotechnology: An appeal to governments and scientists', *International Herald Tribune*, 27 September

Keohane, R. and Nye J. (1977) *Power and Interdependence*, Boston, MA, Little Brown

Krasner, S. D. (1982) 'Structural causes and regime consequences', *International Organization*, vol 36, no 2, pp185–205

Lang, W. (1990) 'The role of international law in preventing military misuse of the biosciences and biotechnology', *Politics and the Life Sciences*, vol 9, no 1, pp37–45

Legge, J. (1983) *Theater Nuclear Weapons and the NATO Strategy of Flexible Response*, Santa Monica, Rand Corporation

Lennane, R. (2006) 'Blood, toil, tears and sweat', *Disarmament Forum*, no 3, pp5–15

Littlewood, J. (2004) *Managing the Biological Weapons Problem*, Stockholm, Weapons of Mass Destruction Commission

Littlewood, J. (2005) *The Biological Weapons Convention: A Failed Revolution*, Aldershot, UK, Ashgate

Mahley, D. (2001) *Statement by the United States to the Ad Hoc Group of Biological Weapons Convention States Parties*, 24 July, US Department of State, Washington DC

Meselson, M., Kaplan, M. and Mokulsky, M. (1990) 'Verification of biological and toxin weapons', in Calogero, F., Goldberger, M. and Kapitza, S. (eds) *Verification, Monitoring Disarmament*, Boulder, CO, Westview Press

Moodie, M. (2004) 'Confronting the biological and chemical weapons challenge: The need for an "intellectual infrastructure"', *The Fletcher Forum of World Affairs*, vol 28, winter, pp43–55

National Research Council (2006) *Globalization, Biosecurity, and the Future of the Life Sciences*, Washington, DC, National Academies Press

Pearson, G. (1993) 'Prospects for chemical and biological arms control', *Washington Quarterly*, vol 16, pp145–162

Pearson, G. (2001) 'Why biological weapons present the greatest danger', Seventh International Symposium on Protection against Chemical and Biological Warfare Agents, Stockholm

Randin, V. and Borrie, J. (2005) 'A comparison between arms control and other multilateral negotiation processes', in Borrie, J. and Randin, V. (eds) *Alternative Approaches in Multilateral Decision Making: Disarmament as a Humanitarian Action*, Geneva, United Nations

Rees, M. (2006) 'Dark materials', *Guardian*, London, 10 June

Rischard, J.-F. (2003) *High Noon: 20 Global Problems, 20 Years to Solve Them*, New York, Basic Books

Robinson, J. P. (1985) *Chemical Warfare Arms Control*, London, Taylor and Francis

Ruggie, J. G. (1975) 'International responses to technology: Concepts and trends', *International Organization*, vol 29, pp557–583

Sims, N. (1988) *The Diplomacy of Biological Disarmament: Vicissitudes of a Treaty in Force, 1975–85*, Basingstoke, UK, Macmillan Press

Sims, N. (2001) *The Evolution of Biological Disarmament*, Oxford, Oxford University Press

Slaughter, A.-M. (2004) *A New World Order*, Princeton, NJ, Princeton University Press

UK Foreign and Commonwealth Office (2002) *Strengthening the Biological and Toxins Weapons Convention*, London, HMSO

UK Ministry of Defence (1993) *Defending our Future*, London, HMSO

UK Ministry of Defence (1999) *Defending Against the Threat of Chemical and Biological Weapons*, London, HMSO

UN (United Nations) (2004) *We the Peoples*, Note by the Secretary-General, General Assembly Document A/58/817, 11 June

UN (2006) *Uniting against Terrorism*, Report by the Secretary-General, General Assembly Document, A/60/825, 27 April

US National Academies, Committee on Advances in Technology and the Prevention of Their Application to Next Generation Biowarfare Threats (2006) *Globalization, Biosecurity, and the Future of the Life Sciences*, Washington, DC, National Academies Press

USA National Intelligence Council (1999) *China and Weapons of Mass Destruction*, Washington, DC, National Intelligence Council

Williams, P. (1983) 'The United States' commitment to Western Europe', *International Affairs*, vol 59, no 2, pp195–209

1

Life Sciences or Death Sciences: Tipping the Balance towards Life with Ethics, Codes and Laws

Ronald M. Atlas and Margaret Somerville

The search for ethics to govern the life sciences and the threats to public health their misuse could entail is part of a complex ongoing process which is forcing us to confront diverse and sometimes strongly conflicting viewpoints. To successfully reduce the threat from biological weapons, and to protect public health, especially on a global level, we all will need to engage across boundaries that have separated us in the past. Only by doing so can the promise of our unparalleled discoveries of new knowledge in the life sciences be fulfilled and the potential for unprecedented harm averted. Certainly, no one measure will be sufficient to ensure that science is not misused, or public health put at risk, or people's rights not unjustifiably breached, but in conjunction with other measures, ethics and law properly used can contribute to the protection of people, the reduction of risks of serious harm, and the deterrence of bioterrorism and biowarfare. 'Ethics and law are related, but they are not the same. Law draws the line we cannot cross without becoming "outlaws". Even if we do not like it, we must nonetheless follow it (while working to change it) or risk ... being prosecuted for being an outlaw... Americans can go to jail for violating the law, but not for violating codes of ethics. We aspire to uphold ethics – we deserve praise (at least some) for behaving "ethically"; whereas we deserve none for simply following the law, some of which is, in fact, made up of "legal technicalities".' (Annas, 2006) Breaches of ethics can, however, have consequences ranging from disapproval or shunning by colleagues, to loss of research funding or unemployment and de-licensing or other professional penalties. We argue that both ethics and law, in a wide variety of institutional forms, are needed to help to ensure the life sciences do not become the death sciences.

In general, ethics is used to govern relationships between intimates and law is used to govern relationships between strangers. Today's relationship between science and society is a mixture of trusted friends whom we depend upon for health and well-being, and distant strangers whose motives are often unknown and, sometimes, malicious. Thus, we require new paradigms that encompass laws establishing which activities are prohibited, regulations that safeguard how an inherently acceptable activity is to be carried out in order to avoid foreseeable harm or unreasonable risk, and ethical codes which articulate what may and must not be done if shared societal values are to be honoured (Somerville, 2002).

As we consider the legal and ethical approaches that can be employed to help protect against the misuse of science for bioterrorism or biowarfare purposes, we should recognize the challenges in developing these measures if they are to be effective and ethical. There is no 'one-size-fits-all' approach to the governance of life sciences research and biotechnology, and the measures we choose to utilize will need to reflect a balance between the necessary certainty (to know what may and what must not be done) and flexibility to be open to universal applicability. This will, of necessity, involve opening up a critical international dialogue that will help to define the boundaries that science must respect in order to protect against its misuse and to implement the safeguards needed to protect public health throughout the world.

Legal prohibitions

The Geneva Convention of 1925 banned the use of bacteriological weapons. Yet France reserved the right to arm itself with biological weapons for retaliatory purposes (Guillemin, 2006), invoking the biblical concept of 'an eye for an eye'. The Biological Weapons Convention (BWC) of 1972, however, is exceptional in having established an absolute ban on biological warfare and the development of biological weapons (States Parties to the Convention, 1972). We could regard these prohibitions as a contemporary example of the ancient concept of a taboo. A taboo is one side of a coin; the other side is the sacred. We can postulate that in our contemporary world we need to develop a concept of the 'secular sacred' that protects that which we hold most precious: life, especially human life (Somerville, 2006a).

Despite the BWC norm against the development of biological weapons, there are several problems that arise from its necessary allowance for activities that are prophylactic, protective or otherwise for peaceful purposes. Many of the activities that would form the basis for biological weapons development are identical to those that could be carried out for permitted purposes. This has allowed several countries, including the former Soviet Union, South Africa and Iraq, to cloak their biological weapons programmes within seemingly legitimate facilities – that is, facilities that could have dual uses (Atlas and Dando, 2006). In effect, the BWC bans a given activity if the intent is to develop biological weapons, but allows that same activity to be carried out if the intent is for peaceful purposes. We allow the production and 'stockpiling in warehouses' of large quantities of botulinum toxin intended for cosmetic uses as 'botox' (i.e. large quantities of potential bio-threat agents can be and are produced for peaceful purposes).

Although the BWC established the international 'legal' norm against the development of biological weapons, it does not include provisions specifying the consequences for failing to meet the obligations of the treaty. As pointed out by Guillemin (2006):

> *When considering the potential threat of biological weapons in the hands of rogue states or terrorist groups, security experts tend to assume that scientists will always lend a hand to prevent such nefarious use of their research.*

Yet every programme to develop biological weapons – including those by the US, Canada, the UK, Japan and France (prior to the signing of the BWC in 1972), the former Soviet Union (even after their becoming a signatory to the BWC), Iraq (prior to the first Gulf War) and others – included scientists who were willing to engage in such activities. Despite such violations of the convention and the international norm against biological weapons development, efforts to establish legally binding verification measures and specific penalties for violating the provisions of the BWC have failed. Essentially, it is an international legal agreement without 'teeth' since it lacks investigatory powers and specified penalties for violators.

The BWC, however, requires that each state party implement national legislation to ensure compliance – that is, each state party to the convention is obliged to enact laws that prohibit activities in breach of the convention and specify penalties for breach. A number of nations, including the UK and the US, have enacted legislation codifying the prohibitions of the BWC. The UK adopted the 1974 Biological Weapons Act and the US enacted the 1989 Biological Weapons Anti-Terrorism Act to meet their obligations under the BWC.

While such national statutes are necessary to implement international conventions in domestic law and are useful in deferring the prohibited conduct, they present daunting problems of harmonizing their various provisions with domestic law regarding the definition of crimes, rights of the accused, dispute resolution and judicial assistance, amongst other matters. One response to these obstacles has been calls for an international law that would criminalize bioterrorism and the development of biological weapons, and allow for extradition (Meselson and Robinson, 2004).

Legitimate research that could be misused: Dual use research

Beyond the issue of legally banned activities, there is the dilemma of trying to inhibit the potential misuse of knowledge resulting from legitimate research intended to advance scientific knowledge for the public good for biowarfare or bioterrorism:

> *Because the differences between research on offensive biologic weapons and research on defensive biologic weapons are a matter of degree, not kind, and because biotechnology research is an international activity, any evidence that such research is doing more to put the public at risk than to protect the public will (and should) be especially damaging to the entire enterprise. (Annas, 2006)*

There is legitimate concern that research in the life sciences permitted by the BWC (i.e. research for prophylactic, protective or peaceful purposes) could be dangerous and, in particular, could lead to the development of biological weapons. Such concern raises the inevitable debate as to whether the pursuit of scientific knowledge is value free and, thus, without bounds, or whether there is 'dangerous research' that should not be done and knowledge that should not be openly shared. The consensus now, although still opposed by some scientists, is that ethics must be applied to science from its inception: the pursuit of knowledge is not value free and must conform to ethical norms and the requirements of society.

Not surprisingly, there have been recurring debates since 11 September 2001 concerning what research should and should not be conducted and what information should and should not be disseminated in the open literature (House of Commons, 2003; Journal Editors and Authors Group, 2003; NRC, 2004; Campbell, 2006). As Scholze (2006) notes:

> *From the Hippocratic Oath to the Russell–Einstein Manifesto, from Maimonides's Oath to the Declaration of Geneva (the Physician's Oath), human history reveals an abundance of pledges, guidelines and laws to regulate the relationship between professionals and society. However, increasing concerns about the new and emerging ethical aspects of biomedical research, and its potential for abuse, have led to a surge of ethical debates and their translation into a new, globally accepted codification.*

But not everyone will buy into that codification and even if we had a globally agreed-upon oath for life scientists, the debate over the boundaries for ethically legitimate scientific enquiry will be the subject of ongoing debate.

This is not a new issue. In fact, the concern of how to protect scientific knowledge from misuse dates back to the very beginnings of science. Sir Francis Bacon (1626) wrote in his essay 'The New Atlantis':

> *And this we do also: we have consultations, which of the inventions and experiences which we have discovered shall be published, and which not; and take all an oath of secrecy, for the concealing of those which we think fit to keep secret; though some of those we do reveal sometime to the State, and some not.*

So, from the inception of modern science, the community of scientists acknowledged that it needed to act responsibly to protect the public against the abuse of scientific knowledge to do harm.

The Committee on Advances in Technology and the Prevention of Their Application to Next Generation Biowarfare Threats in its report *Globalization, Biosecurity and the Future of the Life Sciences* (2006) says:

> ... *as with all scientific revolutions, there is a potential dark side to the advancing power and global spread of these and other technologies. For millennia, every major new technology has been used for hostile purposes, and most experts believe it naive to think that the extraordinary growth in the life sciences and its associated technologies might not similarly be exploited for destructive purposes. This is true despite formal prohibitions against the use of biological weapons and even though, since antiquity, humans have reviled the use of disease-causing agents for hostile purposes.*

This report, as well as others, such as the Fink committee report *Biotechnology Research in an Age of Terrorism* (NRC, 2004), raise the spectre that research in the life sciences, especially in molecular biology and informatics, may be misused for biological weapons development, bioterrorism, and biowarfare – the so-called 'dual use' dilemma.

The InterAcademy Panel on International Issues (IAP), which is a global network of science academies, echoes this view:

> In *recent decades, scientific research has created new and unexpected knowledge and technologies that offer unprecedented opportunities to improve human and animal health and environmental conditions. But some science and technology can be used for destructive purposes, as well as for constructive purposes. Scientists have a special responsibility when it comes to problems of 'dual use' and the misuse of science and technology. (IAP, 2005)*

The security concerns about dual use research reflect a growing awareness that the rapid advances in knowledge and technology occurring in the life sciences that offer great potential benefits can, by accident, produce unexpected results or be misused to cause deliberate harm through bioterrorism or even biowarfare – for instance, biowarfare waged through 'planned epidemics'. The life sciences tragically could become the death sciences.

But how does one define what research should be done and what should be prohibited, or what research findings should be subjected to restrictions or restraints on communication? And who should make these decisions and on the basis of what criteria? The difficulties in developing sound approaches for limiting the potential for misuse of research in the life sciences occur, in part, because virtually all of the research that is aimed at protecting humankind from disease or otherwise improving quality of life could theoretically be misused. Legally binding measures could do harm by constraining research that would improve future human health and well-being.

Additionally, research in the life sciences is a global endeavour:

Enhancing public health and safety [and protecting public health] against biological threats arising from natural or man-made causes is an over-whelming challenge for traditional governance structures. (Taylor, 2006)

Laws and regulations would help to reduce these threats; but to be most effective, there is a need for international accord and widespread concerted national legislation. If we were only concerned about the actions of nations, we would not need to be as diligent to achieve wide-scale buy-in internationally. But we are thinking in terms of terrorist acquisition of bio-threat agents, which means that safety will only come from globally implemented protective mechanisms. What we have in mind, ultimately, is to make bioterrorism a taboo internationally. This will require the buy-in of many nations, preferably by enacting laws and adopting regulations that prohibit activities which could reasonably facilitate bioterrorism, thereby reducing the threat of it and expressly prohibiting bioterrorism itself. And we must do all of this while keeping in mind that unless the scope of research of concern can be defined in such a way that only research of the greatest concern is legally constrained, there inevitably will be a severe impact on the advancement of biomedical knowledge, detrimental to humankind.

Against the backdrop of this concern, the Fink committee of the National Academy began to map out a strategy for responsible action within the scientific community – an effort that it hoped would spread worldwide. The committee attempted to narrow the sphere of concern of dual use research for the scientific community by elucidating classes of experiments that it said should be subject to review and discussion by informed members of the scientific and medical communities before they are undertaken or, if carried out, before they are published fully in order to ensure that the likely benefits outweighed the likely risks of misuse (NRC, 2004). The seven classes of experiments of concern that were identified focus on the near-term threats of microbial pathogens and toxins. In the longer term, it is likely that other types of threats, including direct human genetic modification and human behaviour biological modifiers, will need to be considered as well (Relman, 2006). The development of synthetic biology has increased fears about such potential threats. And humans are not the only potential targets. Modification or destruction of plant and animal species could wipe out food supplies and have devastating ecological consequences.

Recognizing that some research could result in severe harm if misused, but that most research in the life sciences contributes to the advancement of knowledge for the betterment of humankind, the Fink committee (NRC, 2004) endorsed the approach recommended earlier for the physical sciences by the Corson Report (NRC, 1993) and embodied in National Security Presidential Directive 189, issued by President Reagan and, post-11 September 2001, supported by Assistant to the President for National Security Condoleezza Rice that:

... to the maximum extent possible, the products of fundamental research [should] remain unrestricted ... [and] where the national security requires control, the mechanism for control of information generated during feder-

*ally funded fundamental research in science, technology and engineering at
colleges, universities and laboratories is classification. (White House, 1985)*

Classifying research findings places a legally binding barrier around the knowledge that is generated. Classifying knowledge in the life sciences would mean
that high walls restricting the use of the knowledge generated can be established
at the onset of research, but not at a later stage. However, research in the life
sciences, unlike nuclear research, is not born classified and, in life sciences
research, most 'novel and unexpected findings' are made at a later stage. This
means that most information of concern from life sciences research would fall
into the area of 'sensitive but unclassified' (i.e. information that might be dangerous, but is not legally constrained). It is difficult to use the law to govern this
situation because of the unpredictability that is present as to when the law should
be used to prohibit or restrict certain conduct and when not. To be valid, the law
must be reasonably certain in its definition and application, especially in the
form of coercive or punitive legal measures, or it will be invalid on the grounds
that it is void for uncertainty or for being overly broad.

An international response is also needed because no single country, not even
the US with its leadership role in biotechnology, has a monopoly on research in
the life sciences that might be misused.

Thus, the means of constraint, if they are to be effective to protect scientific
knowledge in the life sciences from misuse, might need to come, at least in part,
from voluntary efforts within the global scientific community. Establishing
effective voluntary constraint would require the development of a culture of
ethical behaviour that takes into consideration national and global security.
'Scientists are, in principle, no more or less responsible than any other citizen,
but they are certainly expected to act responsibly by their public paymasters'
(Campbell, 2006). A self-policing approach leaves open the issue of
enforceability, and how high levels of compliance are ensured and how
compliance requirements are uniformly interpreted. The Fink committee
envisaged a living system overseen by a committee of scientists and members
of the national security community, which would continually be charged with
assessing the scientific knowledge that could contribute to biological weapons
development, bioterrorism or biowarfare, and which would seek means of
protecting that knowledge from misuse.

The National Science Advisory Board for Biosecurity (NSABB) at the
National Institutes of Health was established to undertake this task for the US
and as a model that could be extended internationally. The NSABB is supposed
to reach out to the international community so that others will establish similar,
if not identical, systems for oversight – much as had occurred following the
Asilomar meetings and the development of the Recombinant Advisory
Committee for the oversight of recombinant DNA research:

*The NSABB is charged specifically with guiding the development of: A
system of institutional and federal research review that allows for fulfill-
ment of important research objectives while addressing national security*

> *concerns; Guidelines for the identification and conduct of research that may require special attention and security surveillance. (Office of Biotechnology Activities National Institutes of Health, 2004)*

The NSABB has established a committee on 'dual use' that is considering defining dual use research of concern for the life sciences as:

- research with agents that posses a high biological threat potential;
- research that could increase the potential of an agent to do harm;
- research that could enhance the susceptibility of a host to harm; and/or
- research in enabling technologies and facilitating information that may be misused to pose a biologic threat to public health and/or national security (Kasper, 2005).

The NSABB, as well as many international bodies, has also begun to consider the role of ethics and responsible conduct in science to help protect against the misuse of the life sciences for biowarfare or bioterrorism.

Towards professional codes of conduct

Recognizing that deplorable past breaches of ethics have occurred despite the presence of a code relevant to the conduct in question also presents another challenge – namely, guarding against the cynicism or despair that breaches may evoke in relation to the capacity of a code of ethics to have any, or at least some, worthwhile protective effect. But there is new reason for optimism in this respect. Research in the philosophy of science shows that as long as a small clustered nucleus of ethical voices remains, despite a majority of people acting only in self-interest, ethics has a high probability of reasserting itself; however, if those voices are lost, so is ethics – at least from that source (Nowak et al, 1995; Malinas and Bigelow, 2004; Somerville, 2006a). Consequently ethics requires that we continue to try to be ethical ourselves, and to encourage and help others to do likewise, even when (or especially when) we are in a minority.

In our view, there is an urgent need for an international consensus on the steps that must be taken to realize the goal of protecting against the misuse of science in the cause of bioterrorism or biowarfare. One such step is that throughout the world all persons and institutions associated with or involved in science or medicine – especially scientists, physicians, scientific institutions, international institutions (in particular, the World Health Organization) and others engaged in research and development in the life sciences – must be aware of their ethical obligations to prevent a horrific transformation of the life sciences to the death sciences. To promote such awareness we need to understand, in a very general way, what 'doing ethics' requires; what the role of people, whose job it is to implement ethics in practice, is (whether ethicists or ethics committees); and what instruments (e.g. codes of ethics or laws) might help to ensure ethical behaviour. A code of ethics would help to set the normative standards for the behaviour that we must strive to have implemented as one of the necessary, although not alone sufficient, protections against bioterrorism.

The international scientific community, in particular, has a key role to play in ensuring that efforts to manage the risks improve security and strengthen international collaboration to ensure non-malicious use of scientific advances. The development of professional codes of conduct is of paramount importance for protecting science and the global public against the potential misuse of the life sciences. Adopting a code could be an important way of promoting the necessary international consensus and of raising levels of awareness to confront the dual use dilemma. Consequently, the idea of developing codes of conduct to prevent the misuse of the life sciences has become an important topic of discussion at many international scientific and governmental meetings, including the Meeting of Experts of the States Parties to the BWC meeting in Geneva in June 2005.

In constructing a code of ethics, it needs to be recognized that language is not neutral and nowhere is the choice of language more important and difficult than in drafting provisions that can touch on some of our most profound and dearly held moral values and beliefs. Codes of ethics unavoidably do that with the result that we may not always agree with each other about their provisions. But society cannot afford simply to walk away from a search for ethics in science because people cannot agree on what should or should not be included in a code of ethics. Rather, there is a need to establish a code and then use it as a basis to engage in an ongoing debate (i.e. as a means of fostering 'ethics talk') because that is an important way in which ethics can move forward in conjunction with science as it advances (Somerville, 2000). A code not only raises awareness of the need for ethics and provides some guidelines against which to judge the ethical acceptability of any given conduct, but also functions as a teaching tool and provides less senior people, including students, with a means of raising ethical concerns, especially with respect to the conduct of those in authority. By actively supporting the creation and implementation of norms to govern the conduct of research and the communication of scientific information in the life sciences – including behavioural norms established through public discourse – national and global security can be enhanced.

The ancient Hippocratic Oath consists of particular provisions that apply in specific circumstances and, contrary to popular belief, does not explicitly articulate the mandatory injunction 'First, do no harm.' This is, however, the underlying general ethical principle upon which all of the provisions of the oath are based and for which the oath now stands. To reiterate its overall message: physicians and scientists must today, even more crucially than in the past, first do no harm – *primum non nocere*. And to paraphrase a provision in the modern Hippocratic Oath: physicians and scientists shall remember that they have a pact with society to advance knowledge and to apply that knowledge for the good of humanity. Scientists and scientific institutions must act responsibly to limit the potential misuse of scientific materials and information by potential bioweaponeers. In particular, Revill and Dando (2006) see value for a Hippocratic-style oath for the life sciences as a means of helping to educate researchers about the dangers of dual use research.

Basic presumptions of a code for protecting the life sciences against misuse

Basic presumptions are the foundation stones from which we start an ethical analysis, or any other analysis or decision-making. We cannot avoid such a starting point; but if we think about that reality at all, we usually take whatever basic presumption we use to ground our ethical analysis and decision-making as self-evident. There is, in fact, a choice to be made and that choice has a major impact on whether our decisions go one way or the other. These basic presumptions are important because they establish the decision-making framework, including the ethical decision-making framework, upon which we ground our arguments.

There are four possible basic presumptions:

1   '*No*': we must not do this.
2   '*Yes*': we may do it; there are no restrictions or conditions on what we want to do.
3   '*No, unless …*': no, we must not do it unless we can justify it and these are the requirements for justification.
4   '*Yes, but …*': yes, we may do it, but not if certain circumstances prevail.

Most ethical analysis involves situations where we must choose to use either a 'no, unless' or a 'yes, but' analysis. You might think that it does not matter which of those we favour, and that is true where the ethical answer is relatively clear. But where we are equally doubtful about which of two courses of action to take, these two presumptions give polar opposite results. In such situations, a 'no, unless' presumption means that we may not proceed. In contrast, a 'yes, but' presumption in the same circumstances means we may proceed until it becomes obvious that, for example, it is not reasonably safe to do so.

In democratic Western societies, the basic presumption has been a 'yes, but' one, including in relation to science. This is consistent with those societies having 'open legal systems' (anything that is not prohibited is permitted) compared with 'closed legal systems' (anything that is not permitted is prohibited). One question now is whether certain science – for instance, that with serious dual use potential – should remain subject to a 'yes, but' approach. Once again, it will be difficult to find consensus.

Rappert (2004) points out that attempts to establish codes must address demanding questions about their goals and audience – questions whose answers depend upon potentially contentious issues regarding arms control, science, ethics and politics. A common theme of the discussions to develop a code for the life sciences is a principle we discussed previously: 'First, do no harm' (Royal Society and Wellcome Trust, 2004). But beyond that principle, which is widely fostered within the medical community, it is proving difficult to achieve consensus, although efforts to do so continue. For instance, the InterAcademy Panel recently issued a statement on biosecurity aimed at providing principles to guide the life sciences community in developing codes of conduct to reduce the risks that research in the life sciences could be misused for bioterrorism or biowarfare. These principles were awareness; safety and security; education and information; accountability; and oversight (IAP, 2005).

Elements of a code to counter bioterrorism

So, what are the critical elements that a code of ethics for the life sciences should be based on, and should recognize and include? The code needs to be built upon ethically relevant facts and should articulate the substantive and procedural principles of ethics that govern its interpretation and application in any given circumstances and the provisions needed to implement them. Consequently, we propose that such principles and provisions should include recognition of the following:

- The power of science to result in harm – if it is not governed by strong ethical standards – has been vastly augmented, in particular, by advances in molecular biology and informatics, especially in the context of the life sciences.
- Society has entrusted all people and institutions engaged in all aspects of science to undertake it in such a way as to show respect for life, particularly human life.
- Safeguards are needed to ensure the fulfilment of the public trust in relation to science and the fiduciary obligations that it engenders, and to protect against breach, in particular, in order to ensure that science is not used in the cause of bioterrorism or biowarfare.
- Ethics must be embedded in all aspects of scientific research from its inception.
- The standards of behaviour embodied in a code of ethics will help to protect against the misuse of science, especially the life sciences.
- Compliance with a code of ethics and adherence to its principles is both the individual and collective responsibility of all people engaged in all aspects of science.
- A code of ethics will underline the importance of ethics reviews of proposed scientific research and the monitoring of ongoing research, including by ensuring the ethics of involving humans or animals as research subjects.
- A code of ethics can establish a basic presumption of openness and transparency of scientific information and knowledge, but can allow for exceptions, the use of which must be justified by the persons relying on them to maintain secrecy when there is a real risk that such information or knowledge could be used to do serious harm.
- A code of ethics will support the protection of people who act in accordance with its requirements to bring breaches of ethics in scientific research or the misuse of science to the attention of relevant authorities or the public.
- Scientists, physicians, other researchers and scientific institutions who fail to act ethically are at high risk of losing the respect of their peers and the respect and trust of society as a whole, which would have harmful consequences not only for them, but also for scientific research and for all people and institutions engaged in science and society.
- Some breaches of ethics can concurrently constitute contravention of existing

law. Because codes of conduct and ethical principles that are broadly accepted by one's peers are often used by courts to establish legal standards, violations of this code could also result in legal penalties, as well as censures for breaches of ethics.

- Individuals with ethical or moral objections to participation in certain research need protection and support.
- A code of conduct based upon strong ethical principles will facilitate transmitting the values that must govern scientific research to trainees and students, and will provide them with guidance for themselves and benchmarks against which to assess the conduct of their teachers and mentors.

Proposed codes of ethics for the life sciences

There have been various proposals for a code of ethics or guidelines to govern the life sciences. As expected, these proposals have considerable overlap, which can be seen from the ones we include here. We have included this repetition in order to provide the reader with easy access to the contents of several proposals and to examine which provisions are common to all and which are not.

We, Somerville and Atlas (2005), proposed a Code of Ethics for the Life Sciences as a way of engaging the scientific community and the broader public in a discussion of the actions needed for responsible conduct that could help to protect against the potential catastrophic impacts of biological weapons. Given the potential harm that could be done to humanity by biological weapons, we considered such responsible conduct by the scientific community essential and therefore proposed that the life sciences community have a mandatory obligation to follow the proposed code. As such, the code could well have legal implications since failure to abide by the code could be viewed as negligent or even reckless behaviour.

Under the proposed code, all individuals and institutions engaged in any aspect of the life sciences would have to:

- Work to ensure that their discoveries and knowledge do no harm by:
  - refusing to engage in any research that is intended to facilitate or that has a high probability of being used to facilitate bioterrorism or biowarfare; and
  - never knowingly or recklessly contributing to the development, production or acquisition of microbial or other biological agents or toxins, whatever their origin or method of production, of types or in quantities that cannot be justified on the basis that they are necessary for prophylactic, protective, therapeutic or other peaceful purposes.
- Work for the ethical and beneficent advancement, development and use of scientific knowledge.
- Bring activities that are likely (based on reasonable grounds) to contribute to bioterrorism or biowarfare to the attention of the public or appropriate authorities (including unethical research).
- Allow access to biological agents that could be used as biological weapons

only to individuals about whom there are reasonable grounds to believe that they will not misuse them.

- Restrict dissemination of dual use information and knowledge to those who need to know in cases where there are reasonable grounds to believe that the information or knowledge could readily be misused through bioterrorism or biowarfare.
- Subject research activities to ethics and safety reviews and monitoring to ensure that:
  - legitimate benefits are being sought and that they outweigh the risks and harms; and
  - involvement of human or animal subjects is ethical and essential for carrying out highly important research.
- Abide by laws and regulations that apply to the conduct of science unless doing so would be unethical, and recognize a responsibility to work through societal institutions to change laws and regulations that conflict with ethics.
- Recognize, without penalty, all individuals' rights of conscientious objection to participation in research that they consider ethically or morally objectionable.
- Faithfully transmit this code and the ethical principles upon which it is based to all who are or may become engaged in the conduct of science (Somerville and Atlas, 2005).

Yet another approach is to impose very strict standards on laboratories conducting research in the life sciences. In a recent move:

> *Biological research labs working with the most dangerous pathogens face stiffer city oversight under new rules approved by the board of the Boston Public Health Commission. Under the regulations, labs doing work at biosafety level 3 and 4 must obtain a permit from the commission, set up a safety committee that includes two outside community members and submit regular reports on research and safety procedures. In addition, Boston labs can't try to create weapons or conduct classified research and must hold public meetings to disclose research being done. Labs that fail to comply with the new rules could face fines of [US]$1000 per day, per violation and a suspension of their research. (Pearson, 2006)*

Regardless of which approach or code is adopted or whether a code is viewed as mandatory or voluntary, it is important that the scientific community assumes responsibility for preventing the misuse of its science and that it works with legal authorities, when appropriate, to achieve this end. Inevitably, there will be an important interface between any professional code of conduct and codified laws and regulations. Whistleblowing is, for example, an important ethical responsibility; but establishing a system of responsible authorities to whom concerns can be revealed and ensuring that the whistleblower can be protected from retribution remain major challenges. Also, as evidenced in the Thomas Butler case (Enserink and Malakoff, 2003), there is a divide between the law enforcement and regulatory communities, which seek to ensure compliance with laws and regulations that have been enacted to prevent dangerous micro-organisms from being acquired by terrorists, and a well-intentioned scientific community which is trying to find cures for diseases. Peer pressure within the scientific community is needed to ensure full compliance with anti-terrorism laws and biosafety/biosecurity regulations, which are viewed by many researchers as excessively restrictive and impeding legitimate science, but the establishment of a code of conduct to reduce the threat of the misuse of the life sciences has yet to be achieved.

Responses to proposed codes of ethics to govern the life sciences

The proposal for professional codes of ethics and the contents of the code proposed by Somerville and Atlas (2005) have both met with strongly conflicting views. Van Aken (2006) doubts that any system based solely on responsibility and self-regulation will be sufficiently comprehensive and effective. According to Van Aken (2006), 'first and foremost, any such system must be able to cast legally binding verdicts, even if scientists favour non-binding systems based on their own individual or collective responsibility'. He proposes that an international standard-setting body should be responsible for defining experiments of concern and for reviewing those that are most critical. This is also the view of Steinbruner and Okutani (2004). They propose that certain lines of scientific enquiry should be prevented and that there should be an international body empowered to make such legally binding determinations. Similarly, Corneliussen (2006) questions the value of self-regulatory codes of conduct unless they are accompanied by other measures, including mandated regulatory measures that are backed by sanctions and real threats of serious penalties.

The scientific community increasingly recognizes that science itself is not a value-free activity and that the choice of what research to undertake and how to undertake it must be governed by ethical principles. But there is still a nucleus of scientists who oppose that concept, arguing that there must be no restrictions on the search for new knowledge and that ethical principles only become relevant in the application of that knowledge. Scientists' reasons for holding such a view can range from cognitive (ethics requirements will not work), to emotional (fear that they will shut down science), philosophical (science is value free; it is only its applications that need ethical guidance), misguided (scientists are ethical people and all that ethics requires is that they act in good conscience), monetary (the ethics requirements will bankrupt our company) and personal (they will ruin my career).

Letters sent to *Science* in response to the publication of the code of ethics to govern the life sciences that we proposed (Somerville and Atlas, 2005) attested that the code had caused people to think about the value of ethics and the need to act to protect science from misuse. These letters enriched the original discussion and opened up further major issues. The majority confirmed the view that codes are valuable and that 'ethics talk' involving the broadest possible range of participants is even more valuable.

Matters that were raised included that the values and ethical standards enshrined in a code of ethics must be reflective of a very broad spectrum of people that stretches well beyond those of a given profession and that the public must have a strong voice in deciding on these values and ethical standards. Ethics requires more than scientists just acting in good personal conscience, and the same is true of them acting collectively as a profession in good professional conscience. Rather, the broadest possible range of people and institutions must be involved in ethics decision-making in relation to science in order for that decision-making to be ethically acceptable.

Some of the ways in which we can engage people outside science, particularly the public, in setting values and ethical standards for the life sciences include the following:

- An ethics review of all research, as is now the norm, must be undertaken by ethics committees that have a very broad-based membership.
- Recognizing that the scientific professions hold science on trust for society establishes that society has the final say as to what will and will not be allowed in terms of ethics.
- Adopting a basic presumption of openness and transparency of scientific knowledge and information allows the public to monitor the ethics of science on an ongoing basis, as does the protection of 'whistleblowers'.
- An express duty to bring to the attention of the public or appropriate authorities activities that are unethical or could contribute to bioterrorism or biowarfare engages public participation in decision-making about these activities.
- Likewise, requiring protection and support for individuals with ethical or moral objections to participating in certain research, and protecting their freedom of conscience, promotes public knowledge and involvement in the ethics of science.
- Finally, we must encourage an ongoing debate about contested values and beliefs as a means of stimulating 'ethics talk', an important way in which ethics is developed and implemented in practice. It is widely accepted in ethics that this 'talk' must include the public, and it merits stating that the 'ethics talk' we need must go beyond any one country to include broad international participation.

More specifically, as indicated above, providing protection for whistleblowing is an essential element in implementing ethics in science. Occasionally, difficulties can arise because the person or body to whom one would normally report has a conflict of interest. For example, one's own government could (and would, unless procedures were put in place to avoid it) have a conflict of interest in receiving information about its own wrongdoing. In such cases, it would not be an appropriate authority to which to report. Who would be the appropriate authority must be determined on a case-by-case basis and might include a role for other national authorities or international ones, as well as the public.

We do not need to reinvent the ethical wheel. For instance, medicine has considerable experience in developing ethical guidance in relation to both research and practice, and we should use these developments as models. It is important to identify and build on all currently existing relevant resources. And those resources may also benefit from comparison with others. Moreover, ongoing monitoring of ethics as the research evolves is not only instructive ethically, but is also required as part of 'doing ethics'.

Even those who question the value of a code agree that research in the life sciences, including bio-defence research, must be conducted in a safe and ethical manner. Such assurance is essential in maintaining public trust, which, in turn, is essential for the continued support of research. Bodies speaking out publicly about this need for ethics include the General Assembly of the World Medical Association in adopting the Washington Declaration on Biological Weapons (World Medical Association, 2002); the British Medical Association (British Medical Association, 1999); the US National Research Council (NRC, 2004); the UK Parliament (House of Commons, 2003); and the Asia–Pacific Economic Cooperation (APEC) leaders (APEC, 2003), among others (Rappert, 2006). Most recently, in October 2006, the World Health Organization convened a working group consultation in Geneva on research and development in life sciences, public health and global security. The Working Group's first report is now being broadly circulated for discussion. Many of the ethics issues we discuss in this chapter were also raised in that context.

Conclusions

One way to raise the awareness of people in the life sciences to their ethical obligations is through the national and international adoption of a code of ethics to govern research in the life sciences. Experience has shown that professional specificity of ethical requirements is needed for scientists to personally identify with them and, as a result, apply them in practice. Consequently, we need statements about ethics and ethics research specific to the life sciences.

It must be recognized that a code of ethics alone is not a complete solution – that some, possibly even many, people will not comply with the code and that other measures will also be required. But to ask whether a code will provide complete protection is the wrong question. The right question is whether society is better off with a code than without one. The argument we put forward (Somerville and Atlas, 2005) is that society is better off with one. A code can foster 'ethics talk' in a way that other means might not. Its 'opportunity costs' are very low – that is, the resources (economic, human effort and educational) invested in it will not detract from other measures in any major way. And it is likely to augment the effectiveness of other measures to counteract bioterrorism with which it operates conjunctively.

Critics of the formal implementation of ethics believe, for instance, that 'imposing ethical standards … will demonize the scientific community'; that scientists will not inadvertently 'develop weapons through their benign research efforts'; and that 'aggressive law enforcement and intelligence efforts' are the only ways of countering bioterrorism and are not complemented by implementing ethics (Perman, 2005). It can be argued that such views are counterproductive in terms of ensuring ethical science and must be challenged. Ethics is integral to science, which means that unethical science is bad science, not just bad ethics. Like all elements of good science, ethics must be intentionally included. Scientists need support to fulfil their ethical responsibilities to help protect against the misuse of science by those who would do harm.

The basis on which societal-level trust is established has shifted in postmodern Western societies from *blind trust* – 'trust me to make all the decisions because I have knowledge, power and status that you don't have, and I know what is best for you and will act in your best interests' to *earned trust* – 'trust me because I will show that you can trust me and thereby earn your trust' (Katz, 1984). Earning trust requires openness, honesty and integrity. It is a continuing process, not an event, and, in particular, requires the sharing of information and the informed consent of those who give their trust. All of this means that the public has a critical role in deciding on the ethics that should govern the life sciences, and that structures must be put in place to ensure and to show the public that those ethics are consistently applied by scientists in practice. Dialogue and 'ethics talk' with constituencies within and beyond the scientific community are critical to achieving this goal. Scientists must develop a manifest culture of responsibility to maintain the public trust upon which not only science, but also public safety and public health, now depend.

Finally, life sciences research promises great benefits from new knowledge and technologies, but it also creates potential risks for public health. We must avoid being hysterical or fear mongering; but we would be very remiss to underestimate the harm that could be unleashed. Let's hope that with coordinated, international and sustained efforts we can ensure a future in which everyone can feel that ethics prevail, that public health is protected and, as a result, that fear of an 'accidental, negligently caused or planned epidemic' can be realistically reduced to a minimum (Somerville, 2006b).

References

Annas, G. J. (2006) 'Bioterror and "bioart" – a plague o' both your houses', *The New England Journal of Medicine*, vol 354, pp2715–2720

APEC (Asia–Pacific Economic Cooperation) (2003) *Asia–Pacific Economic Cooperation (APEC) Leaders' Statement on Health Security*, www.apecsec.org.sg/apec/leaders__declarations2003/2003_StmtHealthSecurity.htm, accessed October 2006

Atlas, R. M. and Dando, M. (2006) 'The dual use dilemma for the life sciences: Perspectives, conundrums, and global solutions', *Biosecurity and Bioterrorism*, vol 4, no 3, pp276–286

Bacon, F. (1626) 'The New Atlantis', http://oregonstate.edu/instruct/phl302/texts/bacon/atlantis.html, accessed October 2006

British Medical Association (1999) *Biotechnology, Weapons and Humanity*, London, Harwood Academic Publishers

Campbell, P. (2006) 'Empowerment and restraint in scientific communication', *EMBO*

Reports, Science and Society, vol 7, ppS18–S22

Corneliussen, F. (2006) 'Adequate regulation, a stop-gap measure, or part of a package?', *EMBO Reports, Science and Society*, vol 7, ppS50–S54

Enserink, M. and Malakoff, D. (2003) 'The trials of Thomas Butler', *Science*, vol 302, pp2054–2063

Guillemin, J. (2006) 'Scientists and the history of biological weapons', *EMBO Reports, Science and Society*, vol 7, ppS45–S49

House of Commons (2003) *Security of Research: Select Committee on Science and Technology Eighth Report*, www.publications.parliament.uk/pa/cm200203/cmselect/cmsctech/415/41515.htm, accessed October 2006

IAP (InterAcademy Panel on International Issues) (2005) *Statement on Biosecurity*, www.royalsoc.ac.uk/displaypagedoc.asp?id=17463, accessed October 2006

Journal Editors and Authors Group (2003) 'Statement on scientific publication and security', *Proceedings of the National Academies of Sciences*, vol 100, p1464

Kasper, D. (2005) *Criteria for Identifying Dual Use Research and Results: Progress Report to the 2nd Meeting of the NSABB*, 21 November, Washington, DC, www.biosecurity-board.gov/meetings/200511/Criteria%20Slides%20for%20Nov%2005%20Meeting%20(18nov).pdf, accessed October 2006

Katz, J. (1984) the *Silent World of Doctor and Patient*, New York, Free Press

Malinas, G. and Bigelow, J. (2004) 'Simpson's paradox', in Zalta, E. N. (ed) *The Stanford Encyclopedia of Philosophy*, Stanford, California, The Metaphysics Research Lab, http://plato.stanford.edu/archives/spr2004/entries/paradox-simpson/, accessed October 2006

Meselson, M. and Robinson, J. (2004) 'A Draft Convention to Prohibit Biological and Chemical Weapons under International Criminal Law', *The Fletcher Forum of World Affairs*, vol 28, no 1, pp57–71

Nowak, M., May, R. M. and Sigmund, K. (1995) 'The arithmetics of mutual help', *Scientific American*, vol 272, issue 6, pp76–81

NRC (National Research Council) (1993) *Research to Protect, Restore and Manage the Environment*, Washington, DC, National Academies Press, http://darwin.nap.edu/books/0309049296/html, accessed October 2006

NRC (2004) *Biotechnology Research in an Age of Terrorism*, Washington, DC, National Academies Press, http://darwin.nap.edu/books/0309089778/html, accessed October 2006

Office of Biotechnology Activities National Institutes of Health (2004) National Science Advisory Board for Biosecurity, www.biosecurityboard.gov/, accessed October 2006

Pearson, A. (2006) 'Analysis of Boston Public Health Commission's proposed biological laboratory regulations', Washington, DC, Center for Arms Control and Non-Proliferation, www.armscontrolcenter.org/archives/002246.php/, accessed October 2006

Perman, B. (2005) 'Using ethics to fight bioterrorism', *Science*, vol 309, pp1012–1017

Rappert, B. (2004) 'Responsibility in the life sciences: Assessing the role of professional codes', *Biosecurity and Bioterrorism: Biodefense Strategy, Practice, and Science*, vol 2, pp164–174

Rappert, B. (2006) *Biological Weapons and Codes of Conduct*, www.ex.ac.uk/codesofconduct/Chronology/, accessed October 2006

Relman, D. (2006) 'Bioterrorism – preparing to fight the next war', *New England Journal of Medicine*, vol 354, pp113–115

Revill, J. and Dando, M. R. (2006) 'A Hippocratic Oath for life scientists', *EMBO Reports, Science and Society*, vol 7, ppS55–S60

Royal Society and Wellcome Trust (2004) *Do No Harm: Reducing the Potential for the Misuse of Life Science Research*, www.royalsoc.ac.uk/displaypagedoc.asp?id=13647, accessed October 2006

Scholze, S. (2006) 'Setting standards for scientists', *EMBO Reports, Science and Society*, vol 7 (special issue), ppS65–S67

Somerville, M. (2000) *The Ethical Canary: Science, Society and the Human Spirit*, Toronto, Viking, pp1–21

Somerville, M. (2002) 'The question behind the question: More rules or voluntary compliance?', Biotechnology Conference Department of Justice of Canada, Ottawa, Ontario, 21–22 February

Somerville, M. (2006a) *The Ethical Imagination: Journeys of the Human Spirit*, Toronto, Canada, House of Anansi Press

Somerville M. (2006b) 'Public Health, Biosecurity and Ethics', Working paper, Scientific Working Group on Life Science Research and Global Health Security, Geneva, World Health Organization

Somerville, M. and Atlas R. M. (2005) 'Ethics: A weapon to counter bioterrorism', *Science*, vol 307, pp1881–1882

States Parties to the Convention (1972) 'Convention on the Prohibition of the Development, Production and Stockpiling of Bacteriological (Biological) and Toxin Weapons and on Their Destruction', Washington, DC, London, and Moscow, 10 April, www.fas.org/nuke/control/bwc/text/bwc.htm/, accessed June 2007

Steinbruner, J. and Okutani, S. (2004) 'The protective oversight of biotechnology', *Biosecurity and Bioterrorism: Biodefense Strategy, Practice, and Science*, vol 2, pp273–280

Taylor, T. (2006) 'Safeguarding advances in the life sciences', *EMBO Reports, Science and Society*, vol 7 (special issue), ppS61–S64

Van Aken, J. (2006) 'When risk outweighs benefit', *EMBO Reports, Science and Society*, vol 7 (special issue), ppS10–S13

White House (1985) *National Security Decision Directive 189: National Policy on the Transfer of Scientific, Technical and Engineering Information*, www.fas.org/irp/offdocs/nsdd/nsdd-189.htm, accessed October 2006

World Medical Association Policy (2002) *Declaration of Washington on Biological Weapons*, Document 17.400, www.wma.net/e/policy/bl.htm, accessed October 2006

2

Whistleblowers: Risks and Skills

Brian Martin

Whistleblowing means speaking out in the public interest, and in bioweapons research there are many potential reasons for doing this. Perhaps a rogue researcher is pursuing dangerous experiments, or defensive research is being subtly oriented in offensive directions. Perhaps someone is releasing sensitive information without authorization; safety systems are being neglected; data are being forged; or the lab is pursuing research, under government instructions, that the government is denying publicly.

But is it wise to speak out? What are the risks? Consider these examples.

On 22 July 2005, Charles de Menezes, having just entered a train, was shot in the head seven times by London police. The police claimed he was wearing a bulky coat and had jumped over the ticket barrier and had run to the train. But Lana Vandenberghe knew the police were lying. She worked for the Independent Police Complaints Commission and had access to evidence presented at the commission's inquiry into the shooting. She leaked information to a television journalist – and then was subject to reprisals by the police. In a dawn raid on 21 September 2005, ten police officers broke down her door and arrested her. She was kept in a cell without access to a lawyer for eight hours and threatened by police that she could go to prison. She said: 'It never crossed my mind that I would be treated as if I was a criminal for telling the truth. Unlike the police, I hadn't killed an innocent person' (Sanderson, 2006).

Teresa Chambers was chief of the US Park Police, like a municipal police department but with responsibility for national parks and monuments, mainly in the Washington, DC, area. It had over 600 officers. In the aftermath of 11 September 2001, the US Park Police were given additional anti-terrorism responsibilities, but no additional funding. Chambers spoke regularly to the media; it was part of her job. In December 2003, she spoke to a *Washington Post* journalist, saying anti-terrorism duties meant less services in regular park functions and asking for a greater budget to cover all the service's tasks. Soon after, she was stripped of her gun and badge – a tremendous humiliation – and put on leave, and was later terminated (Katovsky, 2006, pp231–244).

Thomas Bittler and Ray Guagliardi worked for the US Transportation Security Administration (TSA). In 2003, while serving as training coordinators at Buffalo Niagara International Airport, they noticed numerous violations of regulations for inspecting baggage – for example, inadequate inspections following alarms. They reported their concerns to their boss, which led nowhere, so they wrote to the TSA headquarters. The result: they lost their jobs two months later, officially due to a staff restructure. However, 'both men say TSA officials told them that they should never have complained. According to Bittler, one supervisor said: "If you people would just learn to shut your mouths, you would still have your jobs"' (Scherer, 2004).

Richard Levernier was a nuclear security professional with 23 years' experience. After 11 September 2001, he raised concerns with the Department of Energy about the vulnerability of US nuclear power plants to terrorist attack – pointing out that contingency plans assumed terrorists would both enter and exit facilities, therefore not addressing the risk of suicide attacks. His security clearance was withdrawn and he was relegated to a basement office coordinating departmental travel, his career in nuclear security terminated. Levernier went to the Office of Special Counsel (OSC), the body responsible for US federal whistleblower matters. Four years later, the OSC vindicated Levernier and ruled that the Department of Energy's retaliation was illegal – but the OSC had no power to restore Levernier's security clearance, which remained revoked (GAP, 2006).

Whistleblowing definitely is a risky business. These examples are just a sample of thousands of similar cases, although each one is far more complicated than can be conveyed by a short summary.

The typical whistleblower is a conscientious employee who believes the system works. When such an employee sees something wrong, their natural response is to report it. This is often a serious mistake.

Some of the common methods used against whistleblowers are ostracism, harassment, spreading of rumours, reprimands, punitive transfers, threats, referral to psychiatrists, demotion, dismissal and blacklisting. To simply list these methods gives only a faint indication of the tremendous damage that they do. Ostracism is a common experience: bosses shun the whistleblower and so do most other workers out of fear for their own jobs. Because validation by peers and supervisors is vital for a worker's self-esteem, ostracism is extremely hard to handle. Yet, this is just one of many reprisals commonly suffered by whistleblowers.

Many whistleblowers trusted the system. That, after all, is why they spoke out: they expected to be treated seriously, perhaps even lauded for their efforts. Indeed, many thought they were just doing their job: reporting a discrepancy in accounts, pointing out a conflict of interest, reporting on a hazard at work. They assumed people in authority would look into the matter, decide whether their concerns were valid and, if so, take appropriate action. Often they do not think of themselves as whistleblowers.

When, instead, they come under attack, this shakes them to the core of their being: because the system turns against them for being public spirited, their world is turned upside down. The system turns out to be unfair rather than just, and this is psychologically devastating (Alford, 2001).

The damage to whistleblowers is extensive. Many lose their jobs and have huge legal bills: the economic impact is enormous. Health and relationship problems are common. Many are forced out of their field and are unable to begin a new career (Glazer and Glazer, 1989; Miceli and Near, 1992; Vinten, 1994; Hunt, 1995, 1998; De Maria, 1999; Miethe, 1999; Alford, 2001).

Reprisals against whistleblowers usually involve attacks on reputation, working conditions and employment – physical attacks are relatively rare. But in a few areas, there is a greater risk of assault, frame-ups and imprisonment, including whistleblowing about police corruption, organized crime, military abuses and national security issues. Because bioweapons are linked to national security, speaking out about problems and violations is likely to be especially risky. Hence, exceptional caution and care are needed.

In my reading about suppression of dissent over several decades and my discussions with hundreds of whistleblowers, I have come across cases in just about every field: government, corporations, professions, indigenous organizations, police, military, churches, and feminist and environmental groups, among others. There seem to have been few prominent bioweapon-related whistleblowers – but that does not mean there are no problems to expose. For every public case, there are probably 10 or 100 known only to insiders. The most reasonable assumption is that suppression of dissent occurs in bioweapons research at about the same rate as other scientific fields (Martin, 1999b). The treatment of whistleblowers is remarkably similar across diverse occupations. This chapter presents general insights and advice concerning whistleblowing, which is almost certainly relevant to exposing problems related to bioweapons.

In attacking a whistleblower, there is also great damage to the organization. A talented employee is damaged or lost. There may be extensive legal or compensation costs. Reprisals against whistleblowers send a powerful message to other employees: speak out and you too will suffer. The result is often greater acquiescence to managerial directives. And this may be the biggest cost of all.

Whistleblowers can be considered a part of a warning system for society to fix problems before they become worse. Pain is one of the body's warning systems: it can signal danger. Sometimes the pain is superficial and it is sensible to take a few painkillers. But pain can also signal something deeper: ignore it and the problem gets much worse.

Whistleblowers can cause a sort of pain to organizations. Sometimes their warnings are misguided, at others, their concerns point to deeper problems. Think of Enron, in which massive fraud persisted without checks, leading to the firm's demise, which also brought down Enron's accountants, Arthur Andersen.

It is easy to sympathize with whistleblowers when one agrees with their concerns. Enron bit the dust and therefore has few supporters today. But matters are seldom so clear cut at the time. Managers, co-workers and others often see whistleblowers as both misguided and as serious threats to a worthwhile enterprise. For these managers and co-workers, 'whistleblower' is too complimentary a term: these individuals are malcontents and traitors.

Daniel Ellsberg worked for the US Defense Department during the Indochina war, helping to write a massive inside history. He gradually became disillusioned with the justifications for the war and leaked the history, called the Pentagon papers, to the media. He could easily have gone to prison; but by the time the Pentagon papers were published, in 1971, there was sufficient public opposition to the war that imprisoning Ellsberg would have been counterproductive. But there was no way that he could have retained his job with the government (Ellsberg, 2002).

It can be hard to appreciate the power of loyalty within organizations. Anyone who goes against the group may be treated as the enemy. Stepping out of line may mean ending one's career. Few individuals are able to break such a big story as Ellsberg and create a new network of support.

So what should be done? The instinctive response of most whistleblowers is to seek justice somewhere else: from a higher-level boss, an internal grievance procedure or an outside agency, such as an ombudsman or the courts. Whistleblowers who speak out because they believe the system works, but experience reprisals instead, often assume that the problem is local and that justice can be found somewhere else. Unfortunately, this is usually misguided.

Official channels

Surely, if whistleblowers suffer reprisals for speaking out, the solution must be laws protecting whistleblowers. It seems straightforward. But the reality is disturbingly different.

What is a reprisal? Dismissal, certainly. But what if there is a restructure in the workplace several months down the track – as in the case of Bittler and Guagliardi – and the whistleblower, perhaps along with a few others, is pushed to take a redundancy payment or accept a less attractive post? An employer could easily argue, perhaps sincerely, that the restructure was unrelated to anything that the employee did.

There are other, more insidious, ways of getting at whistleblowers. Ostracism is potent but easily denied, as is petty harassment. In a workplace, quick acceptance of changes to working hours might be standard; a slower and less helpful response might be within the rules, but is incredibly frustrating, although it may not seem like much to outsiders. Damaging rumours are similarly difficult to attribute to reprisals.

Another problem is that the whistleblower, usually a lone individual, has to confront the full power of the organization. A dismissed whistleblower who takes the employer to court for wrongful dismissal has to spend large amounts of money on lawyers while surviving without a salary, confronting an organization with virtually unlimited funds and time. The scales are heavily tilted against the whistleblower.

Official channels tend to be very slow. Court cases can take months or years; even if a court judgment is favourable to the whistleblower, the organization can appeal, spinning out the process. Ombudsmen, auditors-general, anti-corruption bodies and the like are also slow to move. As the months pass, the whistle-blower may suffer further reprisals or be out of a job.

Official channels are procedural: cases are often decided on technicalities. Whistleblowers usually seek moral justice; but courts and agencies are seldom in a position to provide it (Rosenbaum, 2004).

Worst of all, the slow procedural and reactive processes of official channels put all attention on the treatment of the whistleblower, neglecting the organizational problems that the whistleblower originally spoke out about. Even when the whistleblower is successful (e.g. in obtaining a generous compensation payment), the original problems are unaddressed.

These problems with official channels – reprisals under the radar of laws, an imbalance of power in the whistleblower–organization conflict, slowness, a procedural orientation and lack of attention to the original organizational problem – explain their appalling record in helping whistleblowers. The shortcomings are well known to experienced advisers of whistleblowers (Devine, 1997; Martin, 1999a). Jean Lennane, for many years president of Whistleblowers Australia, says that the only thing you can rely on concerning official channels is that they will not work. William De Maria, in the most significant study of whistleblowers' experiences with official bodies, found that they reported being helped in less than one out of ten approaches, and in many cases they were worse off (De Maria, 1999).

Tom Devine (1997), in *The Whistleblower's Survival Guide,* the most comprehensive advice manual for US whistleblowers, finds serious flaws with even the most effective laws and agencies. The US has by far the longest experience with whistleblower protection, beginning during the 1970s. The pattern is that laws are passed but dodged by employers, unenforced by agencies and subverted by courts.

The Office of the Special Counsel, set up to receive whistleblowing disclosures from federal employees, seldom exercises its power to demand investigation of charges made by whistleblowers: 'The OSC's annual report for fiscal 1995 reveals that out of 333 whistle-blowing disclosures, the office forwarded only two for agency investigation' (Devine, 1997, p68).

Devine (2004, pp83–84) paints a gloomy picture:

> *On balance, in practice U.S. statutory whistleblower laws have been Trojan horses, creating more retaliation victims than they helped achieve justice … the system has been rigged so that realistically it routinely endorses retaliation.*

After the US Congress passed a stronger law in 1989 and bolstered it with amendments in 1994, the problems continued, according to Devine:

> *… the pattern of futility persists. Between passage of the 1994 amendments and September 2002, whistleblowers lost 74 of 75 decisions on the merits at the Federal Court of Appeals, which has a monopoly on judicial review of administrative decisions. (Devine, 2004, p85)*

The law is filled with loopholes and the court regularly interprets the law to favour the government. Meanwhile, in the private sector, there is seldom any legal protection to start with.

One explanation for governments' enthusiasm for whistleblower protection is that laws give the appearance of dealing with the problem without any substantive change in the way that organizations deal with dissent (Martin, 2003). Several governments have considered or passed whistleblower laws without any consultation with whistleblowers.

Most whistleblowers know nothing about the track record of laws and agencies. With their belief in the system, many of them approach one agency and, after an unsatisfactory response, go on to another, sometimes trying half a dozen bodies in a futile quest for justice. Some of them eventually get in touch with a whistleblowers' group and find, to their surprise, that others have had identical experiences.

The faith in official channels runs deep. It is to be expected that politicians and agency officials believe in them; but so do quite a few whistleblower activists who argue for stricter laws, better funded agencies and stronger enforcement.

Ethics codes

What about codes of professional ethics, such as the Hippocratic Oath for doctors? Promoting such codes seems like a good idea; but do they work? This is a difficult question because there seems to be virtually no research on the effectiveness of codes. Codes seldom feature in whistleblower stories: I do not recall any case in which codes played a significant role except for one in which a whistleblowing engineer was charged with violating the professional code.

A code of professional ethics is most likely to be effective when it is well established and there are consequences for those who violate it. The Hippocratic Oath therefore should be the standard bearer; but in many cases it has been inadequate to prevent grievous abuses. The most famous example is the behaviour of Nazi doctors in carrying out gruesome experiments (Lifton, 2000). More recently, doctors overseeing the treatment of prisoners at Guantánamo Bay and other US prisons – said by many to involve torture – have come in for criticism (Nicholl et al, 2006).

Engineers commonly subscribe to codes of professional ethics. But this seems not to have discouraged engineers from designing and building nuclear weapons, land mines, cluster bombs and other anti-personnel weapons. There is no record of engineering bodies reprimanding or expelling members for involvement in such activities. The suspicion is that codes of ethics are, in practice, more about protecting the status of the profession than encouraging ethical behaviour in any wider sense.

For example, one analyst of professional codes says: 'Almost every code of professional ethics includes a provision imposing a responsibility on members of the profession to report violators. Yet, professionals have a poor track record in this regard.' The main reason is that maintaining harmony in the profession is a priority. The likelihood of reprisals is also important in discouraging reporting (Frankel, 1989).

The *process* of promoting and implementing a code of ethics may be a useful one if it involves intense discussions among those concerned. But until there is solid evidence that codes work in practice, it would be unwise to rely on them.

A number of statements about bioweapons work put trust in codes – and some of the codes promote whistleblowing. For example, the InterAcademy Panel on International Issues (IAP, 2005) put out a statement on biosecurity. One of its five points, accountability, states: 'Scientists who become aware of activities that violate the Biological and Toxin Weapons Convention or international customary law should raise their concerns with appropriate people, authorities and agencies.' Somerville and Atlas (2005) advocate a 'code of ethics for the life sciences', and urge that individuals and institutions should 'Call to the attention of the public, or appropriate authorities, activities (including unethical research) that there are reasonable grounds to believe are likely to contribute to bioterrorism or biowarfare.' The International Committee of the Red Cross put out a statement on 'Preventing hostile use of the life sciences' (ICRC, 2004). The statement's principle of 'voicing concern' includes two action points: 'Encourage people who work in the life sciences to voice concern about issues relating to poisoning and the deliberate spread of infectious disease' and 'Ensure that adequate mechanisms exist for voicing such concerns without fear of retribution.' The International Centre for Genetic Engineering and Biotechnology, in a working paper on a code of conduct for biological scientists, states: 'Whenever any suspicion about the possible hostile use of their research arises, the involved scientists must raise the issue at the appropriate level' (ICGEB, 2005). Such statements (for a general discussion, see Rappert, 2004) sound good on paper; but as I have outlined, the practical reality for those who speak out is grim, and formal systems give only an illusion of protection.

Skills

Rather than relying on codes of ethics, laws and official bodies to prevent or address problems, an alternative is to mobilize support through alliances and publicity. The basic idea is to win over people who will apply pressure to deal with the problem (Martin, 1999a).

Which people? It could be members of the general public who have no particular concern about the issues involved. It could be particular groups or movements with commitments to relevant goals. It could be co-workers.

Before proceeding further, it is best to step back a bit and ask: 'What is my goal?' A person who speaks out thinks there is a problem and reports it, assuming that authorities will investigate and, if necessary, act. But if it is naive to trust the authorities, then the alternative is to find some other way of addressing the problem – either that, or sit back and do nothing.

The fundamental flaw in the idea of whistleblowing is the assumption that a single person, by speaking the truth, can bring a powerful organization to account. But organizational elites are unlikely to change unless there is a coun-tervailing power. That means that some other people, and the resources that they can bring to bear, need to believe, along with the whistleblower, that something must be done. The whistleblower's task, then, is to win allies: to convince them that something is wrong and they should act.

It may be that the problem is a rogue scientist who is violating protocols with-out management's awareness. Speaking out about this may not seem risky. But what if managers actually know about the activity? Even if they oppose it, they may not appreciate being shown up for poor oversight.

A scientist, working in the lab, comes across documents suggesting the illicit use of biomaterials. Report it immediately, and the consequence could well be denial, destruction of evidence and reprisals. So, pause and think: how can I convince others that this is serious? Which others should I approach? Whom can I trust?

To convince others, three crucial components are evidence, personal credibil-ity and packaging. Evidence needs to be ample, solid and convincing. The best evidence is physical: letters, emails, recordings and samples. It is unsafe to rely on people's verbal testimony. The boss may have clearly stated at the meeting that the experiment is going ahead regardless; but it is unwise to rely on the other dozen people present to back up your account – they might all lie, fearing the consequences of stating the truth.

Another problem is that perpetrators will say that the documents have been superseded or that they are being misinterpreted – in other words, they will claim that the documents do not indicate what is really happening. In a straight credibility context, most people will believe the director of a lab over a single employee. As a result, it is important to have plenty of documents: enough to show convincingly what is going on. It is commonly recommended to whistle-blowers to obtain ten times as many documents as they think they will need.

The second crucial component in convincing others is personal credibility. A person known for telling lies, getting drunk, shouting abuse or undermining colleagues will have much less credibility than one known for honesty, sobriety, politeness and generosity.

There are ways around a bad reputation. One of the best is anonymity. Instead of speaking out, leak documents to those who will act on them (Flynn, 2006). The documents will need to be good enough to stand on their own, with-out personal recommendation and interpretation. Leaking has the great advantage of lowering the risk of reprisals. Nevertheless, it is not easy to be an effective 'leaker' because employers have so many ways of tracking them down. Some photocopiers leave distinctive marks: taking photocopies of photocopies is a wise precaution. Even without a direct physical link, the leaker can sometimes be identified by the documents revealed. A nasty employer will retaliate by dismissing one or more people, even if they are not responsible, making the leaker feel guilty for causing damage to the careers of co-workers.

An intermediate option is to be a leaker and be known to a few individuals who are in receipt of the leaked documents. In this case, personal credibility is again important, as is secrecy when communicating with contacts. The other option is to go public. This can lead to dismissal or denial of privileges, which reduces or terminates access to documents. As a result, it is vital to collect all possible documents first.

Once whistleblowers are identified, it is almost certain that efforts will be made to tarnish their reputation. Any blemish will be uncovered and publicized. School principals have been known to go through personal files of whistleblowing teachers and unearth and make known pupil complaints against the teacher dating five or ten years earlier. Having a totally unblemished record is not full protection because damaging documents may be manufactured and fictitious stories created to discredit the whistleblower. But such attempts are less likely to be successful if the person has a good reputation and good relationships.

The third crucial element in convincing others is packaging – namely, putting relevant information into an accessible and appealing form. All too often, whistleblowers send off a pile of printed material or giant electronic files. The likely recipient – a journalist, politician or activist – seldom has the time or energy to go through a large volume of material to figure out what it's all about. Therefore, a crucial skill for mobilizing support is to summarize the case clearly and briefly, preferably in a single page. This sounds easy enough, but can be extraordinarily difficult for someone very close to the issue. The temptation is to give chapter and verse of every sordid incident. Far better is something written for an outsider, assuming no prior knowledge and highlighting only essential, well-documented points.

Another temptation is to pass judgement – for example, accusing others of malign motivations and unsavoury conduct. A simple recitation of facts is far more effective, leaving it for the reader to make judgements.

In summary, in order to convince others, a substantial body of sound evidence is needed. This needs to be packaged with a short and simple outline of the key issues, and it must be conveyed by someone with a reasonable degree of credibility in terms of who they are and how they present themselves.

The next question is who to approach. This is where good judgement is at a premium. For something trivial, it is best to use the usual channels – it looks silly to go straight to the auditors about a missing UK£10. But something seemingly trivial is occasionally linked to something bigger: the missing £10 might be part of a long-running scam.

The general rule is that it is unwise to trust anyone who has a vested interest in hiding the truth. This means that the safest people to approach are the ones right outside the organization. But rather than rule anyone out automatically, it is worth considering all possible allies.

Co-workers are an obvious possibility. Half a dozen workers making a claim are far more powerful and convincing than a single one; finding even a single other person as an ally is far better than going it alone. Who to approach? This is the tricky part. Approaching the wrong person could be disastrous: the boss is quietly informed and suddenly all your access to materials is denied, your co-workers stay away and your security clearance is withdrawn. On the other hand, finding the right person can make an enormous difference, with access to additional information, contacts and wise advice.

In such situations, caution is advisable. If there are one or two people whom you trust implicitly, you can confide in them and share ideas about whom else to approach. But if you do not have a good sense of who is trustworthy, it may be worth seeking advice. Often there are some experienced members of the organization who have a good sense of people and organizational dynamics. Getting to know these experienced members is worthwhile. You can start by asking some innocent questions, such as how to help a colleague who is having difficulties with an experiment or a dispute over co-authorship – some sort of dilemma that is different from, but with structural similarities to, the one that concerns you. In this way, you can learn about who is trustworthy, who is self-seeking and who should be avoided.

If one or more co-workers can be brought into a circle of concern, this is a great beginning. If not, you will have to operate alone in the organization. The next step is whether to approach anyone else.

One possibility is unions and professional associations. Logically, they should be allies against abuses at work; but the available evidence suggests that unions are unreliable allies for whistleblowers. Sympathetic union officials can be tremendous supporters: they typically have experience and skills to manage conflict situations well. However, in many cases, union officials are useless or worse: sometimes they are tools of management or are aspiring managers themselves and will undermine or sacrifice the whistleblower. The best way of assessing a union is by its track record. Is it mainly concerned about wages and conditions, or does it also tackle civil liberties issues? Does it support unpopular employees or only mates of union officials? Has it ever stood up for whistleblowers in the past?

Professional associations are even less likely to be helpful. Associations for engineers, chemists, biologists and the like are mainly concerned about professional status, not taking stands on contentious issues. During the cold war, US scientific organizations were outspoken about the suppression of dissident Soviet scientists, but were silent about the suppression of US scientists. It is almost certainly futile to write a letter to a national society.

Scientists who report fraud by other scientists – in other words, whistleblowers about scientific fraud – often are treated as the guilty parties, suffering the usual set of reprisals (Martin, 1992; Sarasohn, 1993; Sprague, 1993; Couzin, 2006). In such situations, professional associations have not been valiant defenders of those who speak out. This is probably the best analogy to the situation faced by a scientist blowing the whistle on biosecurity hazards associated with bad laboratory oversight practices.

Rather than go to professional organizations, it is far more promising to approach social responsibility and whistleblower groups, where there are people with experience of similar situations. The UK group Freedom to Care is primarily made up of whistleblowers, as is Whistleblowers Australia. In the US, there is no equivalent national group; but there are quite a number of advocacy groups – most prominent is the Government Accountability Project (GAP) – and occupation-based social responsibility groups, such as Public Employees for Environmental Responsibility. Within such groups, there are experienced figures who can offer advice, although within limits: there are usually far more people needing help than there are advisers. The capacity of these groups to advocate on behalf of individuals is limited. GAP has enormous experience and expertise for using formal channels, but has the resources to support only a few of the many individuals who approach it for assistance. Whistleblowers Australia, as a voluntary organization, does not formally advocate on behalf of individuals: it can only offer information, contacts and advice. Outside of Australia, the UK and the US, there are even fewer groups dedicated to supporting whistleblowers. The upshot is that whistleblowers seldom have the luxury of having someone else to run with their case: usually they have to do most of the work themselves.

Another promising avenue for whistleblowers is to approach activist groups concerned with the issue. In relation to bioweapons, peace groups are an obvious possibility; environmental groups are another. But it would be unwise to appear at the offices of War Resisters' International or Women's International League for Peace and Freedom – two of the oldest peace groups – and expect to find ready support. Most peace groups are made up of volunteers, with only a few paid office staff. They are chronically under-funded and the staff are usually focused on a variety of immediate matters, such as answering correspondence, holding meetings, producing newsletters and organizing actions. It would be unusual to find someone on hand who is knowledgeable about bioweapons issues or with experience in handling inside information. But it is quite likely that activists could put you in touch with a good person with whom to talk about this.

Another valuable source of support for whistleblowers is media coverage or, more generally, publicity. The media relay stories to a wide range of people, most of whom have no connection with the organization. Therefore, the typical person hearing about the story through the media is likely to approach the matter with a relatively open mind – much more open, certainly, than bosses or watchdog agencies, who have a stake in what happens. If the whistleblower seems to have raised an important issue or has been unfairly treated, many people will be sympathetic or outraged. This is the reason why bureaucrats hate media coverage more than anything. They would much rather spend millions fighting a court case and settling out of court than suffer damaging publicity.

The mass media are big business and are often indifferent or hostile towards labour or other challengers to dominant groups. Major newspapers have business pages, but nothing equivalent for labour issues. In news reporting, some wars receive extensive coverage, but few peaceful protests ever do. Consumers of mainstream news know about Palestinian suicide bombers in Israel; but few are aware of peaceful protests in Palestine and Israel nearly every day by Palestinians, Israelis and international participants. Therefore, it might seem that whistleblowers – as challengers to organizational elites – would have a hard time in obtaining coverage.

But in the media, journalists and editors are constantly on the search for good stories. The standard news values emphasize factors such as prominence, conflict, proximity and timeliness. Stories about corruption and organizational malfeasance are attractive because they are manifestations of conflict and scandal that attract audience interest. They are not deeply subversive because the usual assumption is that a few individuals, or perhaps an entire organization, are corrupt, but not the entire system: a few apples are bad, not the barrel. Whistleblower stories add the spice of personality and can provide a disturbing story of a public-spirited person who is unfairly treated. In the past few decades, the idea of whistleblowing has become widely understood in the media and is routinely used to frame stories. This means that the media can provide tremendous support for whistleblowers.

But media coverage does not happen automatically. People who want to speak out need to know how the media operate and how to present their stories effectively. This includes being able to write a concise summary of one's case – as described above; knowing how to contact trustworthy journalists; knowing how much information to provide and when to provide it; being prepared for interviews (if one goes public); being prepared for the boom-bust pattern of coverage (with a burst of intense coverage typically followed by very little); understanding the interests of print, radio and television journalists; and much else. Most people have few regular interactions with the media except as consumers and therefore have little idea of how the media operate. As a result, it is worthwhile gaining tips from activists, sympathetic public relations staff, other whistleblowers and from journalists themselves.

It is important to realize that the media are not automatic supporters of whistleblowers. A good journalist will seek comment from both sides in a dispute, so no one can expect to have an entirely sympathetic story. On the other side, organizational elites are typically very unhappy about even a little negative coverage.

Sometimes the media turn against a whistleblower, joining organizational power-brokers in the attack. It's best to be prepared for this too. Far more likely, however, is a lack of interest from the mass media. The story may be too old, too complex or not considered important enough – or perhaps the whistleblower simply has not provided enough damning evidence. But it is still possible to take the story to a wide audience using alternative media, such as action group newsletters, community radio stations and internet news sites (e.g. Indymedia). Furthermore, dissidents can tell their own story through the internet by writing it up and putting it on a website, sending emails or writing blogs.

There are many options. One is to compose a sober message about the problems in an organization and to send it to all the staff using a standard list. Another is to put a substantial amount of information – summaries, documents and pictures – on a website (in another country for better security) and then send an email to interested parties.

Given the likelihood of reprisals, it is safest to leave the organization and find a new, sympathetic employer before making disclosures. And it is worth making sure that every single statement is factual, backed up by documents, in order to reduce the risk of being sued for defamation.

As well as the options of being a whistleblower – an open critic – and being a leaker, there is the possibility of being an open but anonymous dissident. It is possible to send an email to members of the organization – and perhaps to outsiders, as well, including journalists – revealing problems, using anonymous remailers to hide one's identity. There could well be a search though all employee accounts to find the sender, so it would be wise to use an internet café and a specially created email account for the single message.

The aim in this chapter is not to cover every possibility, but rather to point out that there are options and that having the knowledge and skills to pursue them is crucial to being an effective organizational dissident. Sadly, doing one's job, including reporting abuses and dangers, may require becoming a dissident.

A final skill of crucial importance is understanding oneself: one's motivations, strengths, weaknesses and goals. For example, it is vital to be able to separate a personal desire for recognition or revenge from a more altruistic concern about dangers to the public because speaking out in the public interest is far more likely to win support. Knowing that one is, for example, good at collecting documents, but poor in summarizing the arguments, is important and can guide one's search for allies.

An effective organizational dissident thus needs many skills for collecting information, writing coherent accounts, understanding organizational dynamics, liaising with groups, using the media and understanding oneself. Few of these skills are acquired in scientific, or, indeed, most other, jobs.

It is possible to imagine an enlightened management who decides to empower employees so that they are better able to document and expose organizational problems, and proceeds by distributing information about whistleblowing, running workshops on speaking and writing, and inviting speakers from activist groups. A skilled and networked workforce would be a powerful protection against abuses. But just to spell out this vision is to highlight how distant it is from the usual practice. Managements, instead, prefer to set up hotlines, grievance procedures and codes of ethics, all of which make employees dependent upon others, without any special skill development.

Therefore, the best hope for fostering the skills needed to address abuses lies with workers themselves and with outside groups, including whistleblower and activist groups.

Conclusions

The best people to expose problems within organizations are those who see them up close: the workers. But people who speak out often suffer reprisals. The normal solution to this problem is whistleblower protection: laws and procedures to protect those who make public interest disclosures. Unfortunately, the track record of whistleblower protection measures – whistleblower laws, hotlines, ombudsmen and the like – is abysmal. In many cases, these formal processes give only an illusion of protection. Codes of ethics seem similarly impotent in the face of the problems.

An alternative to whistleblower protection is fostering effective organizational action. This requires a shift in mindset. Rather than thinking: 'I observed a problem, so I'll speak out about it', the alternative is: 'I observed a problem, so I'll figure out the best way to be effective in dealing with it.' If there is a single rule for people wanting to address an organizational problem, it is to seek advice before acting, including advice from people who know a lot about how organizations operate and how to tackle social problems. Part of the likely advice is that just speaking out, without preparation, is unwise – in fact, it's likely to be disastrous. A lot of preparation is needed, including gathering information, recruiting allies, developing skills and planning a course of action.

Scientists are familiar with the discrepancy between everyday perceptions of the world and scientific understandings. The world may appear flat, the sun may appear to move across the sky and desks may appear to be solid; scientists, using their skills and tools, have arrived at more sophisticated and powerful understandings, some of which have become common knowledge.

Yet, when it comes to the social world, most scientists, like most other workers, are naive observers, treating social life in terms of surface understandings, including that a report about a problem will be investigated, that whistleblower laws protect whistleblowers and that courts and official agencies dispense justice. Research and the accumulated experience of whistleblower advisers point to different realities: workers who report a problem may be targeted with reprisals; whistleblower laws do not provide protection; and official channels do not dispense justice.

Whistleblowers often suffer a related misconception: their own case is different. Even when they hear about the treatment of other whistleblowers, they think their experience will be different because they know that they are right: they have truth on their side. Sadly, this is no protection. The key to progress in science, and in whistleblowing, is learning from the experience of others and developing the skills, acquiring the resources and building the networks to do better.

Acknowledgements

I thank Brian Rappert and Susan Wright for valuable comments.

References

Alford, C. F. (2001) *Whistleblowers: Broken Lives and Organizational Power*, Ithaca, NY, Cornell University Press

Couzin, J. (2006) 'Truth and consequences', *Science*, vol 313, 1 September, pp1222–1226

De Maria, W. (1999) *Deadly Disclosures: Whistleblowing and the Ethical Meltdown of Australia*, Adelaide, Wakefield Press

Devine, T. (1997) *The Whistleblower's Survival Guide*, Washington, DC, Fund for Constitutional Government

Devine, T. (2004) 'Whistleblowing in the United States: The Gap between Vision and Lessons Learned', in Calland, R. and Dehn, G. (eds) *Whistleblowing around the World*, Cape Town, Open Democracy Advice Centre; London, Public Concern at Work

Ellsberg, D. (2002) *Secrets*, New York, Viking

Flynn, K. (2006) 'Covert disclosures: Unauthorized leaking, public officials and the public sphere', *Journalism Studies*, vol 7, pp256–273

Frankel, M. S. (1989) 'Professional codes: Why, how, and with what impact?', *Journal of Business Ethics*, vol 8, pp109–115

GAP (Government Accountability Project) (2006) *OSC Vindicates Nuclear Security Whistleblower*, Government Accountability Project media release, 13 February, www.whistleblower.org/content/press1_detail.cfm?press_id=367

Glazer, M. P. and Glazer, P. M. (1989) *The Whistleblowers*, New York, Basic Books

Hunt, G. (ed) (1995) *Whistleblowing in the Health Service*, London, Edward Arnold

Hunt, G. (ed) (1998) *Whistleblowing in the Social Services*, London, Arnold

IAP (InterAcademy Panel on International Issues) (2005) *IAP Statement on Biosecurity*, IAP, 7 November, www.interacademies.net/?id=4909

ICGEB (International Centre for Genetic Engineering and Biotechnology) (2005) The Building Blocks for a Code Of Conduct for Scientists in Relation to the Safe and Ethical Use of Biological Sciences, Trieste, Italy, ICEGEB, June

ICRC (International Committee of the Red Cross) (2004) *Preventing Hostile Use of The Life Sciences*, ICRC, 11 November, www.icrc.org/Web/eng/siteeng0.nsf/html/biotechnology-principles-of-practice-111104

Katovsky, B. (2006) *Patriots Act*, Guilford, CT, Lyons Press

Lifton, R. J. (2000) *The Nazi Doctors*, New York, Basic Books

Martin, B. (1992) 'Scientific fraud and the power structure of science', *Prometheus*, vol 10, pp83–98

Martin, B. (1999a) *The Whistleblower's Handbook*, Charlbury, UK, Jon Carpenter

Martin, B. (1999b) 'Suppression of dissent in science', *Research in Social Problems and Public Policy*, vol 7, pp105–135

Martin, B. (2003) 'Illusions of whistleblower protection', *UTS Law Review*, vol 5, pp119–130

Miceli, M. P. and Near, J. P. (1992) *Blowing the Whistle*, New York, Lexington Books

Miethe, T. D. (1999) *Whistleblowing at Work*, Boulder, CO, Westview

Nicholl, D. J. et al (2006) 'Forcefeeding and restraint of Guantanamo hunger strikers', *The Lancet*, vol 367, 11 March, p811

Rappert, B. (2004) 'Towards a Life Sciences Code: Countering the Threats from Biological Weapons', Briefing Paper no 13 on Strengthening the Biological Weapons Convention', Department of Peace Studies, University of Bradford, UK, September

Rosenbaum, T. (2004) *The Myth of Moral Justice*, New York, HarperCollins

Sanderson, D. (2006) 'Police persecuted me, says de Menezes whistleblower', *The Times*, London, 8 May

Sarasohn, J. (1993) *Science on Trial*, New York, St. Martin's Press

Scherer, M. (2004) 'Flight risk', *Mother Jones*, July/August, pp15–17

Somerville, M. A. and Atlas, R. M. (2005) 'Ethics: A weapon to counter bioterrorism', *Science*, vol 307, 25 March, pp1881–1882

Sprague, R. L. (1993) 'Whistleblowing: A very unpleasant avocation', *Ethics and Behavior*, vol 3, pp103–133

Vinten, G. (ed) (1994) *Whistleblowing – Subversion or Corporate Citizenship?* London, Paul Chapman

3

Education for the Life Sciences: Choices and Challenges

Brian Rappert

The web of prevention is expressly designed to foster synergy of action among all people in a position to limit the risk of poisoning and the deliberate spread of disease. The idea is that if individual actors in the life sciences are properly informed of the risk, rules and their responsibilities, they will make better decisions. (ICRC, 2004)

Just to point out we are all thinking about education and we feel like that is the next stage, and at least our working group, and I am hearing the same thing from the others, feel like it is the next big thing we need to do. (Remark by Professor Paul Keim at the 30 March 2006 meeting of the US National Science Advisory Board for Biosecurity)

The education of those associated with the life sciences has gained a prominent place in considerations of how to prevent bioattacks. In many respects, this is hardly surprising or contentious. An understanding of the basis for, and the potential of, such weapons is a prerequisite for sound practices and effective policies. For an organization such as the US National Science Advisory Board for Biosecurity that is tasked with proposing procedures for researchers to define, evaluate and communicate dual use research, education has an obvious relevance.

And, yet, whatever the widespread and readily appreciated significance of education, when the question is asked: 'What should count as individuals being properly informed of risks, rules and their responsibilities?', then quiet agreement can give way to vocal questioning. Who needs to be properly informed? What should education consist of? Who should determine this? Education can be a source of disagreement, at least in part, because any idea of what it properly consists of is inexorably bound with the exercise of authority.

This chapter treats the topic of education as a window for examining many of the questions associated with determining what needs to be done in enacting a web. The next section begins by briefly reciting recent calls for professional education and awareness-raising – mainly those statements coming from Western countries. It notes that while such calls are frequently made, specifics about what that education should consist of are often absent. The third section examines some of the many choices and challenges associated with educational efforts; these relate to who should educate whom, and about what, how and why. The fourth section then briefly describes various activities currently under way. To illustrate some of the tensions in what gets done, the fifth section focuses on the possibilities and problems raised in seminars undertaken by Malcolm Dando and the author.

The pervasive call for education

The need for awareness-raising and education of one sort or another has long been recognized as part of efforts to prevent the development and use of biological weapons. For instance, the 1991 Final Declaration of the Third Review Conference and the 1996 Final Declaration of the Fourth Review Conference of the Biological Weapons Convention (BWC) appealed to the science community to adhere to the terms of the convention (see, as well, BMA, 1999). There is little doubt, though, that the urgency and extent of calls for education increased considerably after 11 September 2001 and the anthrax attacks in the US, in line with the overall boost in attention to biological weapons.

Such calls have taken a number of forms. The World Medical Association's (2002) *Declaration of Washington on Biological Weapons* underlined the responsibility of its national medical associations to educate the public and policy-makers, reinforce the norm against biological weapons, and instruct themselves about the health effects of biological weapons. With the passage into force of national legislation regarding the security of pathogens and laboratories (e.g. the US Public Health Security and Bioterrorism Preparedness and Response Act of 2002 and the 2001 UK Anti-terrorism, Crime and Security Act), researchers have been required to become familiar with their legal obligations.

Beyond these fairly traditional topics of concern, education has also been a strong theme in attempts by science and medical communities to establish systems of self-governance in response to heightened concerns about the 'dual use' potential of findings and techniques. As part of endorsing such an approach, the US National Academies report *Biotechnology Research in an Age of Terrorism* (NRC, 2003, p111) recommended that 'national and international professional societies and related organizations and institutions create programs to educate scientists about the nature of dual use dilemma in biotechnology and their responsibilities to mitigate its risks'. The US National Science Advisory Board for Biosecurity (NSABB), set up with the intention of taking forward many of the recommendations of *Biotechnology Research in an Age of Terrorism*, has a charge to develop recommendations for mandatory biosecurity education programmes for those working at federally funded institutions. While the NSABB had not yet taken up this charge by early 2007, as indicated by the quote from Professor Keim, concerns about education have come to underpin a variety of the board's deliberations. A meeting of British scientists, policy-makers and others in 2004, sponsored by the Royal Society and the Wellcome Trust, called for enhanced education and awareness-raising training for scientists regarding their legal and ethical responsibilities. This was done to further a system of self-governance.

At the international level, a variety of organizations have called for educational initiatives. This includes the International Committee of the Red Cross in its 2002 *Biotechnology, Weapons and Humanity* appeal, the UN Policy Working Group on the United Nations and Terrorism (2003), and the InterAcademy Panel in its *Statement on Biosecurity* (IAP, 2005), as well as the report of a Royal Society–InterAcademy Panel–the International Council for Science international workshop on science and technology developments (see Chapter 5 in this volume).

Many of the calls have received impetus from, and given impetus to, attempts to develop and promulgate codes of conduct. In 2005, States Parties to the BWC met to discuss and promote common understanding and effective action regarding the 'content, promulgation and adoption of codes of conduct for scientists'. Education figured as central in many of the codes papers and presentation by states and NGOs. Countries as diverse as Germany, China, Australia, Pakistan and Japan spoke about the need for scientists to be knowledgeable about laboratory safety procedures and cognizant of the ethical implications of their work. In relation to research relevant to dual use concerns, for instance, Germany argued that: 'Governments should therefore encourage universities to make [risk management] training obligatory in their biomedical and bioscience curricula' (Brasack, 2005, p3). It went further to promote a licensing system for those working in genetic engineering and pathogenic micro-organisms. Herein, a licence 'should be contingent upon proper training on the content of the Biological and Toxin Weapons Convention and the obligations incumbent on scientists under this treaty, as well as training on ethical decision-making and risk assessment'. The final *Report of the Meeting of States Parties* in 2005 contained a number of education-related points (see UN, 2005).

The predicaments of education

Many of the aforementioned calls and statements are largely just that: general declarations identifying sources of concern meant to encourage (more or less well-defined) future action. While forms of legislation and regulation related to laboratory security, as well as the vetting of researchers, generally stipulate obligations that are enforced by public agencies, much of the recent policy attention to education relates to more wide ranging concerns about the potential for the malign application of the life science findings and techniques. With regard to the latter, the attention to education is especially significant given the repeatedly expressed preference for research community self-governance mechanisms over the legislative approaches that often govern the transfer of materials and equipment (see Chapter 9).

In the initiatives mentioned so far, education is rarely portrayed as a problematic undertaking. Certainly, the extent of consensus regarding the inappropriateness of biological weapons suggests broad accord about the ultimate aim. The largely yet to be taken forward status of the educational calls mentioned in the previous section also contributes to the lack of explicit acknowledgement of knots and binds.

Even within the parameters of the general calls set out, though, it is possible to identify sources of likely tension. For instance, the IAP (2005) *Statement on Biosecurity* and the 2005 BWC final *Report of the Meeting of States Parties* (UN, 2005) suggest that scientists should consider the 'reasonably foreseeable consequences' of their work. But this poses the question of just what those consequences are, how far they extend into the future and who can foresee them. Related to this, general calls for those in the life sciences to consider the ethical implications of their work are likewise question begging about how those implications are to be determined.

This section examines some of the key questions about education in the web of prevention: what should that entail? How should it be done? Who should do it and for whom? Why is it necessary?

What?

The near universal denunciation of biological weapons provides the core component for educational messages seeking to foster a web of prevention. However, the consensus on this basic issue belies the potential for dispute elsewhere. While international agreements such as the BWC and the 1925 Geneva Protocol provide the cornerstone for the international legal prohibition of biological weapons, in certain key respects they leave standards of individual conduct ill defined. For instance, just what should count as justified for 'protective purposes' is not specified in the BWC. Since most, if not all, aspects of bio-defence activities have at least some offensive relevance, drawing lines about what can be done is often contentious. With the recent substantial expansion of bio-defence funding in the US, critical points have been made about the permissibility of certain activities and their effects on undermining international confidence in the convention (see Leitenberg et al, 2003; Rappert, 2006). While the ambiguity about central terms of the BWC was and probably remains essential in getting states to agree to it, this situation does make promulgating standards for individual conduct somewhat challenging.

The BWC not only entails elements of built-in ambiguity, but also of deferral. It is for States Parties to the convention to translate its general provisions into specific national measures and legislation. Nevertheless, the extent and nature of national implementation varies significantly, with a not inconsequential number of signatories having no implementation legislation (Pearson and Sims, 2006). Variation in how the convention is interpreted is particularly pronounced because of the lack of any verification and enforcement agency, as well as the absence of a negotiating mandate during recent years that might have facilitated more uniform practice. While variation in interpretation and implementation allows for individual nations to undertake actions in light of their respective resources and circumstances, it does mean that the make-up, emphasis and prioritization of any education activities are likely to differ in significant respects. The matter of how international agreements translate into national acts is not only an issue for formal arms control conventions. Just how (and whether) statements made by international groupings of national associations, such as those by the World Medical Association or the InterAcademy Panel, will translate into practical actions is far from clear. No doubt, determinations of the adequacy of an inconsistent approach depend upon assessments about the source of biological threat and just who is likely to be the target of it.

Such national variation is likely to affect what should be included in educational efforts. The aforementioned distinction between the safety and security of pathogens and the fairly novel emphasis on the dual use potential of research findings is relevant here. Undoubtedly, the latter receives greatest attention in the US. To the extent that questions about what gets done and how it is communicated are broached beyond its borders, contention related to national differences is likely to arise. Within the context of the BWC, for instance, many of those nations that make up the Non-Aligned Movement are likely to express fears that dual use responsive measures could restrict access to science and thus undermine Article X of the convention. This states that the BWC 'shall be implemented in a manner designed to avoid hampering the economic or technological development of States Parties to the Convention or international cooperation in the field of peaceful bacteriological (biological) activities'.

How?

The previous subsection pointed to likely differences in national appraisals of concerns that might well lead to significant dissimilarities in assessments of proper risks, rules and responsibilities. Noting such large-scale comparative variations raises the question of just how differences in assessments about the nature of threats and what should be done in response are to be handled through educational programmes. Is there an authoritative voice that can adjudicate between alternative assessments? Are there some ways of thinking that must be challenged? Who would do this on the international stage?

These issues, however, do not just pertain to what education should be *about*. Rather, the process *of* educating itself can entail a negotiation of what counts as authoritative knowledge. A key issue in this regard is whether the intention of education is to impart a particular authoritative understanding to an audience, or whether it is to elicit an understanding from individuals based on what they believe. The former is typically associated with traditional teacher-centred forms of education, the latter with more modern, progressive student-centred forms. The former is also perhaps much more prevalent in science education, whereas the latter is more so in ethics education. In relation to the topics under consideration in this chapter, this 'how' issue can be stated somewhat differently: is it the purpose of educational activities to confront certain (misconceived, poorly considered, etc.) ways of understanding the intersection of the life sciences and bioweapons, or is it to enable individuals (e.g. scientists, administrators, etc.) to make sense of these issues for themselves? The first would be consistent with a strategy of confrontation and conformity, the second with a strategy of dialogue and difference. The first would also be more appropriate to questions of laboratory safety and security, the second more appropriate to concerns about dual use knowledge.

As Billig et al (1989) argued, however, efforts to 'implant' and 'elicit' are not starkly opposed options; instead, the two often mix in complex ways, in practice. Consider this point in relation to one topic in current discussions. In the March 2006 meeting of the NSABB, attention was given to what procedures should be in place to communicate dual use research methodologies and results. This followed on from a previous agreement by a group of science journal editors to review manuscripts for their dual use potential. As noted in these deliberations, of the 16,000 manuscripts submitted to the journals of the American Society for Microbiology over a certain time period, only three were subjected to additional biosecurity peer review. Of those three, only one was modified.

What should these figures be taken to indicate? They might point out that the dual use problem – as it relates to the publication of scientific manuscripts – is 'largely one of perception' and therefore that any responses should be tempered (Casadevall, 2006). With this assessment there is a definite danger that policy responses may needlessly hamper research. Others, though, could contend that such low figures should be taken with caution because of the likelihood that there will be many more submissions of concern in the future and that past ones were missed (Osterholm, 2006). Here the potential lack of consistency in the way in which manuscripts are assessed is a major source of concern.

Given the widely expressed preference for self-governance by life science communities, in general, as well as self- and peer-vetting of manuscripts, whether one accepts the 3 in 16,000 figure is vital in justifying what needs doing. Should scientists and editors, for instance, be shaken out of their complacent mindset, or have the experts who have undertaken the reviews of manuscripts, to date, sufficiently taken everything into account? As an organization tasked with raising the existing profile of the dual use dilemma through devising mandatory educational activities, it would seem unavoidable that the NSABB will have to steer a complicated course between eliciting thinking by scientists, while seeking to influence that in some way.

Who?

These considerations regarding whether there is a proper understanding or not to be realized beg the question of just who is involved: who is the educator and who is the learner if, indeed, such a distinction is to be made. While much of the national regulations and legislation regarding the physical security of pathogens set down some parameters regarding just who needs to fulfil their obligations, in relation to concerns about the destructive use of results the issues at hand are much more complicated. Assessments of just who needs to be educated in relation to the latter could vary between those working with dangerous agents to a wider range of those (however peripherally) associated with the life sciences (e.g. including certain mathematicians, engineers and funders).

Determining who should be the audience and at what point in time depends upon assessments about where the problems lie. Are any likely dangers going to be associated with dangerous pathogens and toxins, or are there threats from areas of research, such as neuroscience and bioregulation (see Dando, 2003)? If one maintains the latter position, a considerable amount of research and development in large pharmaceutical companies and small biotech firms might merit scrutiny.

But making determinations of audience will also depend upon the desired end state of education. Is education merely to raise awareness of specific concerns or to bring about a particular collective understanding? Is the goal to get those with benign intent to recognize a potential or to compel particular forms of behaviour? If the audience is broadly conceived, then the first options would seem much easier.

As well, working with a relatively narrow pathogen-centred audience has the advantage of engaging with those much more likely to be aware of dual use concerns. The further that outreach goes from those familiar with the issues at hand, then the more likely any educator might need to be a proselytiser. In relation to the geographic breadth of an audience, for instance, there is now a considerable problem for those in the US most actively concerned about dual use knowledge: how can international attention to this topic be fostered without it appearing that it is an unacceptable expression of geopolitics?

Finally, the need for education is related to where threats are seen to come from: whether, for instance, they stem from those countries with the most active biotechnology activities, the most lax controls or the most frequent outbreaks of pathogenic diseases.

The matter of 'who' in certain education policy deliberation is not just an issue of 'who' in the science community. The rather wide ranging attention garnered by experiments, such as the artificial synthesis of polio virus, by the accidental release of pathogens from certain labs and by the recreation of the 1918 Spanish flu virus have led to concerns about 'the public's' reaction to past and future scientific pursuits. The spectre of further government legislation spurred on by public outcry haunts many policy debates (see, for example, Albright, 2003).

As a result, the education of *the public* has become a prominent matter for some (as in the deliberations of NSABB – see Keim, 2006). Such discussions have a rather distinctive flavour. Whereas earlier this chapter maintained that varying appraisals are given of what education *for* scientists should mean in terms of instilling and eliciting knowledge, education in relation to the public is routinely discussed in terms of educating the public *by* experts. The approach is one of transmitting knowledge in order to avoid misunderstanding. It is difficult to find any positive insights identified in policy discussions regarding what knowledge and insights members of the general public might bring to bear in responding to the destructive application of life science research.

Why?

As a final key area, the matter of why education is being pursued is highly germane. As an abstract call, the case for further education about bioweapons-related issues is rather uncontroversial. Once one becomes more hands on, however, the importance of education has to be weighed against other educational priorities. The question of why this particular topic is in need of greater attention then looms large. In the context of those countries with severe and chronic public heath problems, the reasoning for this question becomes all the more plain. In the context of dispute about where any bio-threats might stem from, this question becomes all the more complicated.

Education itself, furthermore, is often seen as way of spreading particular priorities and concerns. In its extreme formulation, education can be regarded as a type of propaganda. Why it is being done, then, is an important issue. In relation to bioweapons, this consideration can be perceived in different ways. The fact that significant attention is devoted to what gets funded, published and communicated might be interpreted by some as an imperious agenda. Education in the absence of other significant regulatory initiatives, however, might be seen by others as a cover to mask the absence of substantial action.

Educational initiatives

Against such considerations about what might be done, this section briefly mentions some of the educational activities being undertaken today. The purpose is not to provide a comprehensive account of all such efforts worldwide, but to illustrate something of the range of choices available. During recent years, educational activities in the area of biological weapons and the life sciences have included initiatives such as:

- Good laboratory practice. Under the World Health Organization's Biosafety Programme, various activities are being undertaken to reduce the accidental or inadvertent spread of disease from the handling of pathogens. This includes the provision of technical assistance and information, as well as the development of standards. In 2006, the WHO launched a laboratory guidance for biosecurity entitled Biorisk Management. US Sandia National Laboratories has an International Biological Threat Reduction programme centred on minimizing bio-risks from research. It undertakes workshops, lab consultations and conferences on such matters as assessing the risks with agents, laboratory biosecurity/biosafety procedures, transportation of agents, methods of pathogen and disease surveillance, means for reducing outbreaks, and export-control compliance.[1]
- Online education and training modules. The Southeast Regional Centre of

Excellence for Biodefense and Emerging Infections has established an online module intended for those engaged in biological research.[2] Its main focus is with the dual use potential of modern life sciences and the measures that scientists, technicians and others might undertake to minimize concerns stemming from their work. The Federation of American Scientists has produced a series of online educational modules designed to increase awareness of biosecurity and to promote enhanced self-regulation by scientists.[3] The Center for Arms Control and Non-Proliferation has also produced an online educational programme that includes information about the threat of biological weapons, the history of their use, the dual capability of modern biology, and national and international efforts to reduce bio-threats.[4]

- Summer courses. The Institute on Global Conflict and Cooperation within the University of California runs a two-week summer course for graduate students and junior professionals that examines the threat of bioterrorism and public policy responses.[5]
- Curriculum development. The Nuclear Threat Initiative compiled a listing of university and institute courses taught relevant to the area of biological weapons.[6] Middlebury College in Vermont, US, has convened a number of annual curriculum development workshops for those studying nuclear, chemical and biological weapons.[7]

With each of these activities, important questions can be posed about the what, how, who and why of education. Such a comprehensive analysis, however, is beyond the scope of this chapter. The remainder of it will, instead, examine one educational initiative in detail in order to suggest the choices and challenges at stake.

The life sciences, biosecurity and dual use research seminars

The dual use research seminars developed by Malcolm Dando at the University of Bradford, UK, and Brian Rappert (this author), from the Department of Sociology and Philosophy at the University of Exeter, UK, in 2004, comprise an interactive dual use seminar format, and are supported by grants funded by the UK Economic and Social Research Council as well as the Alfred P. Sloan Foundation. Originally, the seminars were undertaken with a view to informing policy deliberations in the UK in the build-up to the 2005 BWC codes of conduct meetings.

When we began thinking about what kind of educational activity to undertake, we thought it was vital to promote interaction *between* practising scientists. Because of the personally and professionally threatening nature of dual use concerns, we judged it essential to get peers to deliberate upon these issues with one another (rather than with us). In addition, the overall lack of professional attention to dual use issues in the past suggested that some researchers would not have well-thought out views about the issues posed. Encouraging interaction was one means of exploring how scientists and students defined the issues at stake. To this end, in a manner analogous to 'focus groups', we sought ways of bringing groups together and guiding them through questions in order to probe their reasoning and to encourage reflection.

Initial efforts to do so were made in the UK. The original plan was to convey seminars through the regional branch meetings of the Institute of Biology, a professional body for British biologists. However, due to a lack of interest in this topic and practical difficulties, this plan was abandoned. Instead, existing university faculty departmental seminar series were used. Rather than giving traditional presentations, where we would lecture for most of the time and then leave a few minutes for questions at the end, the seminars were designed as a question-and-answer session. We planned to talk about specific dual use cases and policies and then pose questions for group discussion.

As such, just what questions we asked and how became key concerns. At the start, it was difficult to know how to schedule the questions or what topics among the large range of possible relevant ones might be most appropriate. Three general issues were identified as central to current dual use knowledge debates: are there experiments or lines of work that should not be done? Are some results better left unpublished or otherwise restricted in their dissemination? Are the envisioned proposals for the oversight of research sensible? What we then did was to experiment with different orderings, contents and emphases to find ways of probing our emerging sense of participants' likely evaluations. For instance, prominent cases of dual use research in biosecurity discussions were introduced and the initial questions were posed about whether they should have been published or conducted. It was clear from the start that audience members were overwhelmingly in favour of publishing and conducting such experiments. The main arguments offered for this could be generalized as 'we need to know'. It was important to undertake research and disseminate its findings because this would provide beneficial health applications and also aid in devising defensive measures.

With an emerging sense of this initial prevalent evaluation, we transformed subsequent information and questions in order to encourage participants to elaborate upon the reasoning behind it (see Rappert, 2006). For instance, in response the prevalence of the contention that 'we need to know', Dando and I devised a follow-on slide that detailed how, in one particular case, the researchers involved did not just publish their results in a standard scientific journal, but communicated its possible dual use implications through the semi-popular magazine *New Scientist*. Here, then, was an attempt to flag concerns in an accessible way to a much wider audience. In contrast to the near unanimity regarding the publishing of experimental results in the scientific press, responders have almost always been sharply divided on the merits of 'popularly publishing'. This disagreement could then serve as a basis for generating discussion about more detailed questions, such as: who is the 'we' who needs to know? Is popular attention to an issue necessary to generate political action? Would raising attention to potential threats make biological weapons more attractive options because of heightened public anxiety? Would the failure to draw attention to concerns one day lead to allegations of the paternalistic attitude of scientists? Through such discussion, different models for thinking about the place of science in society could become topics for debate *between* seminar participants. As such, in facilitating the discussion, Dando and I not only had to attend to the current topic, but also to think about what should come next by way of intervention in order to encourage participants to elaborate upon their underlying and often unstated reasoning.

This transformative approach to questioning that began in late 2004 was extended beyond the UK to a number of other countries. By the beginning of 2007, 51 non-pilot seminars had been conducted in six countries: 23 in the UK; 1 in Germany; 4 in The Netherlands; 2 in Finland; 14 in the US; and 7 in South Africa. Detailed analysis of the content of the seminars has been given elsewhere (see Dando and Rappert, 2005; Rappert et al, 2006; Rappert, 2007) and has led to the production of interactive educational materials.[8]

Rather than reiterating the main conclusions of such analyses, the remainder of this section considers some of the choices and challenges associated with trying to conduct this specific form of outreach in relation to previous points in the chapter.

The brief account earlier of the transformative dynamics indicates the basic mechanism for generating discussion: based on our sense of likely responses, we were able to give additional information and ask follow-on questions that further probed individuals' thinking. Such an approach provided a way of confronting participants' thinking, but in an indirect manner. Thus, the seminars mixed both the 'implanting' and 'eliciting' goals of education insomuch as they challenged certain ways of thinking – while getting individuals to articulate their own (contrasting) reasoning to each other.

Relying on participants' responses in this manner was tension ridden – it provided the basis for discussion and also its limits. With regard to the latter, for instance, if no participant brought up what we might consider to be a pertinent perspective, then we, as facilitators, were left with an awkward choice. We could offer that perspective in the form of a question during the discussion ('What about the view that X?'). However, doing so (even in a way that was not directly backing such a position) may well make us appear to be advocating a certain way of thinking. This was especially the case because, as indicated previously, participants tended to respond to the central issues of the seminars in consistent ways ('We need to know'), and this meant that we would also be querying them in a consistent fashion. So, while the seminar design enabled us as facilitators to steer the basic course of the discussion, this was in a fairly coarse manner.

Following on from these points, in designing and conducting the seminars, there were important concerns regarding the extent to which we as presenters explicitly advanced our positions. While we attempted to gauge their thinking about certain issues, there were many possible options regarding how our own thinking entered that process. Instead of simply posing certain questions, we could have probed participants by explicitly challenging what they said in order to generate a response and then further discussion. While it was possible to design the seminar along the lines of a 'debate' rather than a 'question-and-answer session', it would have been more difficult interactively. For instance, an early attempt in the UK seminars to add a slide at the end that gave our assessment of participants' responses was abandoned because it repeatedly led to the closing down of discussion. Based on our experience in conducting the sessions, we decided to refrain from offering explicit positions on any of the questions unless asked.

However, it was exceptionally rare that we were asked for our thinking. While what would count as an instance of being asked is open to some interpretation, in all the seminars in the UK, I suggest that we were only directly asked about our evaluation of specific issues in the order of several times. More generally, except for South Africa, it was likewise exceptional that anyone queried our agendas in conducting the seminars beyond the explanation we provided. Such a lack of questioning had the advantage of helping to move the discussion along according to our design and concerns. It did, however, limit the types of exchanges and presumably in doing so led the participants to make incorrect attributions about why we were saying what we did. This is especially likely to be the case in our work in The Netherlands, Finland and South Africa, where the seminars were arranged with the cooperation of national organizations (the Finnish Ministry of Foreign Affairs, the Royal Netherlands Academy of Arts and Sciences, and the Institute for Security Studies (Africa) with Chandré Gould).

Our decision not to directly confront participants with our own thinking was somewhat necessitated by the division of expertise. With the exception of some of the US seminars, very few participants displayed knowledge of dual use policy discussions. Therefore, it was certainly more the exception than the rule that any participant at any time during a session would bring up biological weapons-specific considerations beyond what we as moderators presented. This meant that the points we raised by and large formed the basis for subsequent deliberation about biological weapons issues. It also meant that if we as moderators chose, we could have marshalled ever more information on policy discussions in order to advance our own evaluations. For instance, to suggestions that proposed initiatives that were infeasible or ill advised, we could have said: 'Perhaps, but what about … ?' Thus, we had to find ways of conducting ourselves in order to initiate and to perpetuate discussion.

It should also be noted that some participants were experts in the specialized scientific field of most concern (unlike us). They could have used this knowledge to dispute our ability to adequately comprehend the topics posed or to turn the sessions into narrow, highly specialized, debates that severely limit who can legitimately speak. However, such moves were exceptional. Thus, both they and we refrained from giving certain types of expert-based arguments as part of having a joint conversation.

Despite the overall limited display of knowledge of dual use policy deliberations, some participants were obviously highly knowledgeable about both the scientific and policy issues raised. Such individuals posed interactive questions. It would have been possible, for instance, to turn the seminars into detailed exchanges between them and us in order to achieve a robust treatment of the topics covered. It would also have been possible for us as moderators to let these individuals dominate the contributions from participants. However, we resisted both possibilities in order to achieve greater inclusiveness. We were able do this because our role as moderators posing questions gave us considerable control over the course of interactions, such as in determining who spoke next and for how long.

Conclusions

The account of the dual use seminars in the previous section illustrated some of the tensions that arise as part of educational efforts. Attempts to educate raise many difficult questions about who has claim to what expertise and how that is forwarded. In posing various challenges to realizing a web of prevention, the aim of this chapter has not been to issue a council of despair. Rather, it has sought to consider the many choices that demand measured attention. As argued, these choices are not matters that can simply be determined once and for all or that lend themselves to exclusive options and clear-cut answers because any educational initiatives require a negotiation of longstanding tensions.

As part of undertaking educational efforts, key questions include: is it expected that initiatives will lead individuals to act differently? Must researchers rethink the basic way in which they conceive their work? How likely is the potential for disagreement about the issues at stake and what needs to be built into the process of education? How are the aims of eliciting comprehension and providing knowledge balanced? Is education valuable in itself, or is it part of a process designed to aid some outcome?

Such questions and the general focus on the choices and challenges of education are of vital importance given current debates about the proper governance of dual use research. As noted in other chapters, many of the prevailing statements made on this topic stress the need for research community self-governance. Yet a basic prerequisite for the viability of such an approach is a knowledgeable community. There is a clear role for research into the effects of any educational initiatives, as well as the current knowledge base of those who self-govern; this is especially so in light of past experience of the difference between exceptions and practice in the governance of research (Sunshine Project, 2004). To the extent that the recommendations deriving from bodies such as the NSABB support systems are indebted to bureaucratic regulations, these matters are important in ensuring that the terms of regulations do not preclude necessary social and ethical reflection (see Rollin, 2006).

Acknowledgements

The author was aided in producing this chapter by a grant from the Alfred P. Sloan Foundation and a two-day workshop at Nuclear Threat Initiative (NTI) entitled Educating and Training the International Life Sciences Community on Dual Use Dangers, 25–26 July 2006.

Notes

1   See www.lanl.gov/orgs/chs/cbtr.shtml.
2   See www.serceb.org/modules/serceb_cores/index.php?id=3.
3   See www.fas.org/main/content.jsp?formAction=325&projectId=4.
4   See www.armscontrolcenter.org/resources/biosecurity_course/.
5   See www-igcc.ucsd.edu/cprograms/PPBT/PPBT.php.
6   See www.nti.org/h_learnmore/h5_teachtoolkit.html.
7   See https://segue.middlebury.edu/index.php?&site=nonproliferaton&section=12161 &page=50403&action=site.
8   See www.projects.ex.ac.uk/codesofconduct/BiosecuritySeminar/Education/index.htm.

References

Albright, P. (2003) ' "Sensitive" information in the life sciences', presented at the Meeting on National Security and Research in the Life Sciences National Academies and the Center for Strategic and International Studies, Washington, DC, 9 January

Billig, M., Condo, S., Edwards, D., Gane, M., Middleton, D. and Radley, A. (1989) *Ideological Dilemmas*, London, Sage

BMA (British Medical Association) (1999) *Biotechnology, Weapons and Humanity*, London, Harwood Academic Publishers

Brasack, B. (2005) *German Statement to Meeting of States Parties to the Biological Weapons Convention*, Geneva, 5 December

Casadevall, A. (2006) Comments made at National Science Advisory Board for Biosecurity, 20 March, Bethesda

Dando, M. (2003) 'Future incapacitating chemical weapons', in Lewer, N. (ed) *The Future of Non-lethal Weapons*, London, Frank Cass

Dando, M. and Rappert, B. (2005) 'Codes of Conduct for the Life Sciences', Bradford Briefing Paper no 16, 2nd series, www.brad.ac.uk/acad/sbtwc/briefing/ BP_16_2ndseries.pdf

IAP (InterAcademy Panel on International Issues) (2005) *Statement on Biosecurity*, Trieste, IAP

ICRC (International Committee of the Red Cross) (2004) *Responsibilities of Actors in the Life Sciences to Prevent Hostile Use*, Geneva, ICRC

Keim, P. (2006) Comments made at National Science Advisory Board for Biosecurity, 20 March, Bethesda

Leitenberg, M., Leonard, J., and Spertzel, R. (2003) 'Biodefense crossing the line', *Politics Life Sciences*, vol 22, pp1–2

NRC (National Research Council) (2003) *Biotechnology Research in an Age of Terrorism*, Washington, DC, National Research Council

Osterholm, M. (2006) Comments made at National Science Advisory Board for Biosecurity, 20 March, Bethesda

Pearson, G. and Sims, N. (2006) 'Successful Outcomes for the BTWC Sixth Review Conference', Review Conference Paper no 16, March, Bradford

Rappert, B. (2006) 'The life sciences, biosecurity and dual-use research', in Conference Proceedings of the 10th PIIC Beijing Seminar on International Security, 25–28 September, Beijing

Rappert, B. (2007) *Biotechnology, Security and the Search for Limits: An Inquiry into*

Research and Methods, London, Palgrave

Rappert, B. Dando, M. and Chevrier, M. (2006) 'In-depth Implementation of the BTWC: Education and Outreach', November, Bradford, Bradford Review Conference Paper no 18, www.brad.ac.uk/acad/sbtwc/

Rollin, B. (2006) *Science and Ethics*, Cambridge, Cambridge University Press

Sunshine Project (2004) *Mandate for Failure*, Austin, TX, Sunshine Project

UN (United Nations) (2003) *Annex Report of the Policy Working Group on the United Nations and Terrorism*, A/57/273-S/2002/875, Geneva, UN, 6 August

UN (2005) *Report of the Meeting of States Parties to the Convention on the Prohibition of the Development, Production and Stockpiling of Bacteriological (Biological) and Toxin Weapons and on their Destruction*, BWC/MSP/2005/3, 14 November, Geneva, UN, www.opbw.org

WHO (World Health Organization) (2006) *Biorisk Management: Laboratory Biosecurity Guidelines*, Geneva, WHO

World Medical Association (2002) *Declaration of Washington on Biological Weapons*, 17.400 WMA, Ferney-Voltaire, www.wma.net/e/policy/b1.htm

4

Dual Use: Can We Learn from the Physicists' Experience? A Personal View

John L. Finney

Now we're all sons of bitches.[1]

Not as literary as Oppenheimer's quote from the *Bhagavad Gita*. But this response to the Alamogordo plutonium bomb test from the scientist in charge of it, Kenneth Bainbridge, perhaps encapsulated the gut feelings of many of the scientists and engineers present. And in a way that now underlines the feeling that, with the development and subsequent use of two atomic bombs, the atomic physicists had 'known sin; and this is a knowledge they cannot lose'.[2] They had alerted the US president of the possibility of a bomb, and were directly responsible for the initiation of the Manhattan Project. However, for many working on the project, it 'was really the great time in their lives':[3] the problems were challenging, the colleagues stimulating, the funding essentially inexhaustible. It was fun – a creative high point in their lives. Once the bomb was known to work, some of them applied pressure to prevent its use. Others, including Oppenheimer, argued that it should be used against a civilian Japanese target, although he later felt the scientists had 'blood on [their] hands'.[4]

Immediately after the bomb

The consequent feeling of guilt may have driven many immediate post-war actions that aimed to prevent these weapons from ever being used again. A formal visit to the confessional would not have been enough to absolve the atomic scientists from the perceived sin. More positive and concrete actions were needed.

Back in Liverpool, Joseph Rotblat, who had resigned from the project as soon as it became clear that Germany was not building a bomb, formed the Atomic Scientists' Association. Its aims were to inform the public about the potential uses of atomic physics, to work towards international control of its results and to influence British government policy in related matters.[5] He even obtained government funding for a travelling exhibition – the Atom Train – which included positive aspects such as its application in medicine and the generation of energy, as well as facts about the bomb (Halliday, 2006). Several of the Manhattan scientists refused to work further on weapons-related research. Rotblat himself shifted the focus of his research to medical applications of nuclear physics and spent the rest of his life campaigning for the abolition of nuclear weapons.

Bethe and Oppenheimer proposed that an international body should have control of all nuclear developments. This was included in the 1946 Acheson–Lilienthal report that was presented to the UN – to be rejected by the USSR and receiving only a lukewarm response from the British. Bethe argued against the development of the hydrogen bomb and continued arguing against the development of more advanced nuclear weapons. In 1945, two former Manhattan Project scientists set up *The Bulletin of the Atomic Scientists*, a scientist-led journal 'dedicated to security, science and survival'. This journal is perhaps unique in being a direct result of the post-1945 bomb scientists' soul-searching that is still alive today.

There are other examples, some well known, others not. But related to the number of scientists that were involved in the genesis of the bomb, they are perhaps rather few in number. Most of the atomic scientists involved saw no need to apologize. It was a reasonable proposition for many that the use of the bomb had saved thousands of lives and brought the war to an end. And they saw no reason to query the deterrent argument that even Rotblat had accepted earlier (Rotblat, 1999). Couldn't the same theory keep the peace in the developing Cold War situation?

So, when the war ended, many returned to academic research, with their scientific confidence high, and in an environment in which the US and UK governments realized the potential power of science. After the flurry of concerned activity in the immediate post-1945 period, the world of research physics appeared to settle down in an environment that was well funded and well supported. Science was neutral. It could be used for good or evil, and for most, it seemed, it was not the physicist's job to decide on the use to which the science was put. Scientists, many felt, were responsible for doing research, not for how the results of their research might be used.[6]

The hydrogen bomb

This quiet period was broken during the early 1950s. The public announcement that the US would develop the hydrogen bomb galvanized strong responses from many scientists who realized both its possibility and its potential effects. It was a step too far for several of the Manhattan Project scientists – Hans Bethe campaigned actively against it, and James Chadwick, the discoverer of the neutron who had played a major role in the Manhattan Project and who never recanted the use of the bombs against Japan, saw a qualitative difference between the horrors wreaked by using a fission bomb and those threatened by the proposed new generation of 'super' weapons. The scientific community that voiced its concern was, however, broader, and included not only nuclear physicists – for example, both the chemist Linus Pauling and physicist and crystallographer Desmond Bernal are on record as opposing its development. Bernal called the hydrogen bomb 'criminal lunacy' (Bernal, 1950). A Science for Peace group was set up in the UK in 1950.

Perhaps the most important response came not from a scientist – nuclear or other – but from a mathematician and philosopher, Bertrand Russell. Deeply concerned about the prospects of the hydrogen bomb, he contacted a number of scientists, including Einstein, in an attempt to raise public concern. The resulting *Russell–Einstein Manifesto*, penned by Russell and signed by Einstein just before he died, was signed, in addition, by eight prominent scientists of the day.[7] Most were physicists who had worked on nuclear-related issues, although Rotblat was the only signatory who had been part of the Manhattan Project.

Included in the manifesto was a call to action. Following the release of the statement, a number of trends and discussions merged (Butcher, 2005) and the first Pugwash Conference on Science and World Affairs was held in Pugwash, Nova Scotia, Canada, in 1957. The 22 participants from 10 countries included 16 physicists, 2 chemists, 1 biologist, 2 physicians and a lawyer. Rotblat was one of two co-organizers and wrote the section of the report that dealt with the consequences of the use of nuclear weapons. In his own paper he stressed the importance of scientists not attempting to gain public attention by exaggerating the effects of nuclear weapons, and the necessity of separating scientific from political and ethical issues.

This was the start of the Pugwash movement. It was of special importance during the Cold War: scientists from both sides of the Iron Curtain were able to speak freely together and report back to their governments. Pugwash's high scientific standards and objectivity encouraged their governments to listen. During the Cold War, Pugwash was one of the few significant channels of communication between the East and West. Never abandoning its long-term aim of disarmament, it focused on arms control. Operating mainly behind the scenes, it was influential in making possible a number of international treaties. These concerned not only nuclear weapons (the 1963 Partial Test Ban Treaty and the 1972 Anti-Ballistic Missile Treaty, as well as laying the foundations of the 1968 Nuclear Non-Proliferation Treaty), but also the 1972 Biological Weapons Convention and the 1993 Chemical Weapons Convention. It established contact between the US and the North Vietnamese during the late 1960s and helped to resolve the Cuban Missile crisis.

Pugwash was not – and was not intended to be – a mass movement. It involved only a small number of concerned scientists. But their expertise was relevant to the particular issues being addressed.

The Campaign for Nuclear Disarmament was launched in 1958 at a time of high international tension and concern about nuclear weapons tests. Physicists were prominent in the organization, including some of the new generation scientists, in addition to those who had been active during the building of the bomb. However, it would be an exaggeration to claim that more than a small minority of physicists worked actively to counter nuclear weapons. A cartoon showed a group of science students doing a practical experiment in the lab. Outside there was a demonstration. 'It's alright for the social scientists', said one. 'They can count that as part of their practical.' Physics (and other science) students did have heavy work loads. But was that anything more than an excuse to not be involved?

During the 1960s, nuclear weapons issues faded from prominence. It was the Viet Nam War that reinvigorated concerns about the misuse of science in war. The British Society for Social Responsibility in Science had its inaugural meeting in 1969, with primary objectives of educating scientists about the control of science and its abuses. But it wasn't the nuclear weapons issue that led to its formation; rather, it was the use of chemical and biological agents in Viet Nam. These problems caught the attention of a wider scientific constituency than the physicists. Nevertheless, there were problems in involving working scientists generally. Students and post-docs, as well as established scientists, tended to see themselves as being small parts of the machine and not in a position to influence the way in which science was used.

This was a long way from the feelings of the concerned Manhattanites some 25 years earlier.

Where have the concerned physicists gone?

Physicists, however, still seem to have a good press, a reputation for being concerned about the use and abuse of science. The nuclear physics community is brought up as an example of one that is progressive in its thinking about the role of science generally, and with respect to weapons of mass destruction specifically. 'They have known sin', and are therefore sensitized to the possible catastrophic misuse of their science. It's 'because of Hiroshima and Nagasaki'. We might like to bask in this warm reflected glory; but the above potted history – and other more professional works (see, for example, Rose and Rose, 1972; Palevsky, 2000) – suggest that this might be an oversimplification. Developments since 1945 seem to catalogue a progressive withdrawal of physicists generally from concern about the ethical problems surrounding nuclear weapons. Yes, of course, there are still concerned physicists, often with high profiles who are well known outside their immediate specialities. But are there many of them? Has the concern of the original bomb scientists been passed down to the younger generations? Are later generations of physicists still concerned about how their work may be misused? Can the nuclear weapons experience inform current discussions on dual use in relation to biological and chemical weapons?

Physics and biology: Nuclear and biological weapons

Physics and biological science are both sciences. But it can be argued that they differ in a major respect. And this difference is relevant to the nature of the dual use issue as it relates to nuclear weapons on the one hand, and to biological weapons on the other.

Physicists study the nature and properties of matter and energy, and processes relating thereto. Physics research can, therefore, be argued to be fundamental, with discoveries at the basic level of matter and energy feeding into other sciences. As a physicist, therefore, I can argue that pretty well anything I uncover could be exploited further down the line for either good or ill. I am searching for fundamental knowledge, and it would be unreasonable to curtail an investigation because the fundamental understanding that may result could be used to 'do harm'. The responsibility for possible misuse lies elsewhere with society – of which, of course, I am a part. To paraphrase one of my current first-year classes: should someone who discovers a law of nature be responsible for the consequences of the application of that law?

This comfortable view of physics is, however, a simplified one. Not all practising research physicists work at that fundamental level. Many of us work on materials whose behaviour and properties may well be of potential use in areas that we might personally view as unacceptable. Here the dual use problem *is* relevant in physics. However, many of my colleagues will still argue that the potential uses of the research outcomes are too broad – and potentially positive – that it would be unreasonable to consider not doing a particular piece of research because of possible later misuse. Quantum computing promises great things in terms of future computational power, with much potential good. The fact that such computers can be used for military applications is a matter for society. Materials development and nanotechnology are similar cases. It *can* be argued that the positive uses of research outcomes in areas such as these are potentially massive. So it could even be regarded as irresponsible to close down research in such areas just because they *could* be used for ill.

The nature of nuclear weapons also bears on the physicist's position. The basic science relating to these weapons was sorted out during the 1940s. Once the initial discovery of nuclear fission had been made, it was a matter of measuring a number of properties to establish the feasibility of a weapon. From then on it was an engineering operation to build a bomb that would explode. Further scientific developments were needed in the early 1950s to develop the hydrogen bomb, and since then there have been speculations about other variants, such as the cobalt bomb and the neutron bomb. However, the basic science has been well established for decades. Refining weapons and delivery systems can make use of subsequent scientific developments, improved materials and advances in control systems; but these are not central to the science of the weapons themselves. It is highly unlikely that future physics research will lead to a new kind of nuclear weapon. In effect, the concept of 'dual use' in relation to nuclear weapons has been spiked by the fact that the physics of nuclear weapons has already been done. The more general use–abuse argument may remain in relation to other applications perceived to be negative, but it is not relevant to nuclear weapons themselves.

On the other hand, research in the biological science field looks significantly different from that in physics. It concerns processes relating to living systems, and works with relatively large molecular entities and assemblies that have particular functionalities, such as cells, organelles, ribosomes, genes, enzymes and DNA. For example, we want to know how enzymes work, how material gets into and out of cells, how the genome influences our response to disease or drugs, and how proteins fold or misfold. We want to understand how biologically relevant entities operate and interact, and how their operation can be tailored to work more or less effectively.

Consequently, the relationship of biological weapons to bioscience research looks different from that between nuclear weapons and physics research. There is not just one kind of possible biological weapon: a range of biological systems might be exploited as weapons. A discussion of these issues in Chapter 5 lists a range of areas of potential relevance to biological weapons development, including synthetic biology, post-genomic technologies, immunological research, drug discovery and delivery, agricultural and environmental biotechnology, and diagnosis and surveillance of infectious diseases. There is not just one toxin that might be used as a weapon, but many.

In contrast, there are only two kinds of physical processes relevant to nuclear weapons: nuclear fission and fusion. The fission process might occur with different nuclei (e.g. ^{238}U and ^{239}Pu), for which the 'weaponization' might be different; but the physical process is essentially the same in both cases and is well understood. The biological science situation is different. There are many possible biological processes and agents that might be weaponized. The basic understanding required to develop many of these possibilities is still in its initial stages; this understanding is essentially the same that is needed to enable a particular system or process to be used in a beneficial way – hence, the higher profile of the dual use issue in the biological weapons context.

A further difference between the nuclear weapons and biological weapons situations is a legal one. The Biological and Toxin Weapons Convention puts legal constraints on scientists not to work on biological weapons. The implementation of subsequent legal instruments works down to the bench as rules that the research biological scientist has to observe. The very existence of these rules raises awareness of possible biological weapons development and, hence, can sensitize the researcher to dual use issues more generally. In contrast, working on nuclear weapons is not illegal. They may be potentially more destructive than chemical or biological weapons; but, within the five nuclear weapons states as defined by the Nuclear Non-Proliferation Treaty, there is no international convention prohibiting working on them. A physicist is legally able to work on issues related to nuclear weapons, not only within the classified confines of Aldermaston, but also within a university environment. Such research need not be directly related to the nuclear processes themselves. We can work on aspects of laser physics to understand more about the fusion process or on computer modelling of a nuclear explosion itself in order to facilitate numerical testing of potential new weapons designs. These examples are both challenging areas of science. However, they are *directly* related to weapons development rather than dual use issues – the physicist concerned is in no doubt that his or her research has a weapons-directed aim. And even though they are directly related to weapons, the research is legal. In the biological weapons context, such work would not be.

Cross-fertilization of dual use consciousness?

The early part of the second half of the 20th century saw intensive efforts by part of the physics community to counter the harm that they saw was done by the development of the atomic bomb. This pressure came primarily from those who felt a responsibility for the bomb and from those close to them. Scientists in the Pugwash movement influenced the development and implementation of a number of arms control treaties; but, again, these developments involved only a minority of the research physics community, and probably again mainly those who were affected by being involved in the development of the bomb.

The younger generations of physicists do not seem to have been significantly involved in these initiatives. During my time as an undergraduate in the early 1960s, a physics student involved in wider 'political' issues was a rarity. In the following decades, few of my physicist research colleagues interested themselves with these wider concerns. The fading of nuclear weapons issues catalogued in the earlier part of this chapter is entirely consistent with my own experience from 'inside' physics. So, also, was a limited consciousness among my peers of the more general use–abuse issues. The predominant view was that it was a physicist's job to do the physics. It was society's job to make the decisions on the use to which that work was put. We would have the occasional argument in the pub; but the predominant attitude was one of lack of interest in the use–abuse problem. Working specifically on nuclear weapons may have been a minority taste; but the work we did was unlikely to be used directly in nuclear weapons development anyway – and if it did result in improved weapons indirectly, through producing improved materials or better computers, then that was something we could not control. Even if our work was applied to weapons development, this would be only a small part of the potential application portfolio. Most of the portfolio would more than likely contain positive potential applications that would far outweigh the few negative ones.

Why should the intense feelings of responsibility felt by many of the Manhattan scientists have apparently faded over time? Perhaps 'education, education, education' – or, rather, lack of it? Scientific responsibility issues were never raised formally during my physics education, even though that started barely a decade after the bomb was dropped and while the UK was building – and testing – its own Union Jack-decorated bomb. My undergraduate course was purely on physics and mathematics, with a bit of metallurgy and crystallography thrown in to widen my appreciation of condensed matter science. But there was no teaching to widen my appreciation of the science–society relation-ship. There was more encouragement to discuss wider issues of the possible misapplication of physics when I was still at school – we at least had a General Certificate of Education (GCE) general paper, whereas there was nothing at all like this once you entered the tertiary gateway. Perhaps this missing element in the physicist's education is one reason why the concern of the original nuclear physicists was not passed on to the following generations of physicists.

Things have hardly changed today. Name one single university that runs a compulsory course on the social responsibility of scientists for its biologists and chemists, let alone for its physicists. It is my experience that today's young physi-cists are not particularly aware of use–abuse issues in physics. Every year I ask a first-year undergraduate physics class for examples of scientific research with potential ethical implications. Invariably, one example that they give me is stem cells – biology. Example two is usually genetic engineering – biology again. Example three will then be animal testing – biology a third time. Only when I push for an example from physics does the bomb raise its head. It seems that the physicist's memory of the Manhattan Project and its implications is, indeed, fading. A worrying thought.

So, what can be learned about dual use in the biological weapons sphere from the physicists' experience? Depressingly, I suspect the answer is little. I have tried to argue that there are significant differences between research in physics and in biology, and between the nature of nuclear weapons and biological weapons, and that these differences affect the nature of the dual issue in the two communities and may also be relevant to the apparently low consciousness of use–abuse issue among physicists. The physics of the bomb was sorted decades ago; so physics research today is unlikely to have dual use implications with respect to the creation of new physics-based weapons of mass destruction (WMDs). Basic physics research today can, of course, be of potentially dual use with respect to improved weaponization and improved delivery of a nuclear weapon; but, deal-ing as it does with fundamental aspects of matter and energy, such research is more than likely to have many more potentially positive applications. As my first-year student said, should someone who discovered a law of nature be responsible for the consequences of the application of that law? In contrast, biological weapons could involve a range of biological agents and processes, as well as a host of possible toxins. The dual use problem here is clearer and easier to relate to the development of biological weapons.

Let's conclude by being more positive.

Working on biological weapons is illegal – something we can, perhaps, partly thank the early concerned physicists for, as some of them played a significant part in realizing the BWC. The consequent restrictions that this illegality places on biological research constitute a useful device for raising awareness of dual use issues, not only with respect to biological weapons specifically, but also, by extension, to more general use–abuse issues.

Were it illegal to work on nuclear weapons, a similar enhanced awareness of use–abuse issues in physics and engineering might be galvanized. But in the absence of that prohibition, perhaps the increased awareness of dual use issues induced by the legal constraints of the BWC could begin to diffuse into the physicists' territory? The traditional boundaries between the sciences are becoming increasingly permeable as interdisciplinary research becomes more widespread. So, why shouldn't concern over dual use problems also diffuse across these boundaries? As John Ziman (2000) has said in the context of ethical audit of research using human subjects:

> *Up to now, physicists have seldom had to face this sort of situation. But this will change as they become more entangled with other disciplines … [you] have to reopen the kit of human values that you were fitted up with in your childhood, and consult your heart and spirit as much as your lovely mind.*

Notes

1   Kenneth Bainbridge, quoted in Shapin (2000).
2   Robert Oppenheimer, quoted in Shapin (2000).
3   Hans Bethe, quoted in Shapin (2000).
4   'Never mind', responded President Truman, 'it'll all come out in the wash' (quoted in Shapin, 2000).
5   See p312 of Rowlands and Attwood (2006).
6   See, for example, the interviews with Manhattan Project scientists in Palevsky (2000).
7   Chemist Linus Pauling added his name later once he received word of the statement (see Butcher, 2005).

References

Bernal, J. D. (1950) 'Letter to L. Pauling', JDB papers, J.175, Cambridge University Library, cited in Brown, A. (2005) *J. D. Bernal: The Sage of Science*, Oxford, Oxford University Press, p523, note 54

Butcher, S. I. (2005) *The Origins of the Russell-Einstein Manifesto*, Pugwash Conferences on Science and World Affairs

Halliday, B. (2006) 'Professor Rotblat and the atom train', in Rowlands, P. and Attwood, V. (eds) *War and Peace: The Life and Work of Sir Joseph Rotblat*, Liverpool, University of Liverpool, pp139–144

Palevsky, M. (2000) *Atomic Fragments: A Daughter's Questions*, Berkeley, University of California Press

Rose, H. and Rose, S. (1972) 'The radicalisation of science', *The Socialist Register*, vol 9, pp105–132

Rotblat, J. (1999) 'My early years as a physicist in Poland', talk given to the History of Physics Group of the Institute of Physics, 8 March, reprinted in Rowlands, P. and Attwood, V. (eds) (2006) *War and Peace: The Life and Work of Sir Joseph Rotblat*, Liverpool, University of Liverpool, pp39–55

Rowlands, P. and Attwood, V. (eds) (2006) *War and Peace: The Life and Work of Sir Joseph Rotblat*, Liverpool, University of Liverpool

Royal Society (2006) *Report of the RS-IAP-ICSU International Workshop on Science and*

Technology Developments Relevant to the Biological and Toxin Weapons Convention, RS Policy Document 38(06), London

Shapin, S. (2000) 'Don't let that crybaby in here again', *London Review of Books*, vol 22, no 17, 7 September

Ziman, J. M. (2000) 'Technoscience and ethical questions in the new century', Max von Laue Lecture, Deutschen Physikalishen Gesellschaft, Munich

5

Science and Technology Developments Relevant to the Biological Weapons Convention

The Royal Society

This chapter conveys the main elements of a report of a workshop held at the Royal Society from 4 to 6 September 2006. The workshop brought together 84 leading international scientific and policy experts from 23 countries to discuss scientific and technological developments most relevant to the operation of the Biological Weapons (BWC) Convention in order to inform delegates at the Sixth Review Conference (held at the United Nations in Geneva from 20 November to 8 December 2006). Developments addressed at the workshop included synthetic biology, post-genomic technologies, immunological research, drug discovery and delivery, and agricultural and environmental biotechnology. Additional points were made about the importance of the diagnosis and surveillance of infectious diseases.

Assessing the direction of developments in science and their implications for the prohibition of biological weapons is a basic element required of any web of prevention. The scientific advances addressed in the workshop will undoubtedly bring positive benefits to humankind. The challenge facing the international scientific and political communities is to identify what measures can be taken to reduce the chance of misusing them without jeopardizing their enormous potential benefits – that is, to manage what is often called the 'dual use' risk (see the Introduction to this volume). Having outlined the dual use dilemma facing research in the life sciences, this chapter begins by summarizing the presentations made at the workshop on these developments, as well as discussions of their associated dual use risks. Key issues that emerged are then presented, followed by the workshop's conclusions. The presentations from the speakers are also available on the Royal Society website (www.royalsoc.ac.uk/policy) and are referred to in this chapter.

The BWC and dual use dilemmas

The workshop participants stressed that the BWC will only work properly if it evolves in directions that are scientifically sound and make sense in terms of politics, sociology, law and international relations in its military and diplomatic dimensions. Care must be taken to keep the right balance of incentives and disincentives favourable to compliance, and governments need to give it more continuous attention and demonstrate more visibly that they hold it in high esteem. However, this care and attention and high esteem cannot come from government alone, but must also continue to come from national academies of science, international scientific unions and the relevant professional organizations in the life sciences, as well as universities, research institutes and NGOs, and other civil society organizations.[1]

Participants also stressed that 'dual use' relates to the threat of misapplying information or technologies, rather than the carrying out of research itself. This highlights the extent of dual use dilemmas since many types of research may be dual use by implication. However, just because a piece of research is considered to be dual use, this does not mean that it should not be carried out. Rather, this classification serves to emphasize that special consideration may be warranted regarding how the research is carried out and how its results are communicated. This highlights the problem of defining dual use in the life sciences. One definition is provided by the US National Science Advisory Board for Biosecurity: 'biological research which may provide knowledge, products or technology that can be directly misapplied with sufficient scope so as to threaten public health or other aspects of national security, such as agriculture, plants, animals, the environment and materiel' (NSABB, 2006). Examples of dual use research include the 'experiments of concern' highlighted in the US National Research Council report *Biotechnology Research in an Age of Terrorism* (NRC, 2004). These are experiments that would:

- demonstrate how to render a vaccine ineffective;
- confer resistance to therapeutically useful antibiotics or antiviral agents;
- enhance the virulence of a pathogen or render a non-pathogen virulent;
- increase transmissibility of a pathogen;
- alter the host range of a pathogen;
- enable the evasion of diagnostic/detection modalities;
- enable the weaponization of a biological agent or toxin.

Participants stressed the importance of involving the wider international scientific community in formulating new rules and regulations. In light of these preliminary points, the following sections examine the dual use issues associated with the areas of development addressed at the workshop.

Synthetic biology

Unlike systems biology, which analyses large quantities of data on the simultaneous activity of many genes and proteins, synthetic biology reduces the same systems to their simplest components by modelling patterns of gene expression as genetic circuits. Pieces of DNA are treated as fundamental black box modules that can be spliced together to construct what are effectively biochemical logic boards. Circuits are introduced into bacteria and those that perform best are selected. In this way, biological circuits are empirically refined to arrive at the best computational solutions. Like electronic circuits, live bacterial circuits perform simple computations to function as sensors and input and output devices. For example, researchers have engineered bacteria to be sensitive to their external environment so that given certain environmental conditions, genes coding for fluorescent proteins are activated and the bacteria flash or glow. Synthetic biology, therefore, has many useful potential applications, such as designing bacteria to detect chemical and biological agents and to diagnose disease.[2] Synthetic biology and attempts to synthesize simple bacterial genomes are also driving the development of better ways to make larger pieces of DNA. Furthermore, synthetic biology has helped to catalyse progress across biological engineering disciplines since researchers no longer need the expertise to prepare DNA relevant to their research and thereby save time and money. This technique is available commercially worldwide; so it is now significantly easier to engineer more genes on increasingly larger scales, especially since genetic material can be ordered by mail and DNA synthesizers can even be bought over the internet.

Dual use risk

Synthetic biology promises to deliver extensive benefits to progress in the life sciences and humankind. However, participants felt that the potential dual use risk of synthetic biology is high. The ease with which genetic material can be synthesized deskills the process of biological engineering; therefore, 'backyard or garage biology' may simply be inevitable. The concern is that an eradicated or extinct biological agent may be reconstituted or a pathogenic agent or toxin could be generated outside of existing controlled and regulated frameworks. One way of reducing the risk of misuse of synthetic biology is through increased training and awareness-raising amongst scientists about dual use issues and relevant national and international laws and regulations. This applies equally to those working in academia, government and the private sector.

Post-genomic technologies

Genetic targeting and pharmacogenetics

The Human Genome Project has significantly expanded our knowledge of genetic polymorphisms (DNA sequences that vary between members of a species), some of which affect the susceptibility of individuals to some infections and therapeutic drugs. For example, genetic variation has a significant role in the development of AIDS. Genetic analyses have revealed genetic polymorphisms regulating HIV-1 cell entry and cytokine defences to HIV-1. Many other genes and the systems that they control are yet to be discovered.

Genetic polymorphisms not only exist at the level of the individual but also at the level of the group. Stable genetic differences and similarities exist between population groups of differing geographic origin, race and ethnicity. For example, homozygosity for a mutation in the *CCR5* gene is presently considered to be the most relevant genetic factor explaining resistance to the HIV-1 virus, but only Europeans appear to have it. Studies have also highlighted significant genetic polymorphisms across African, Asian and European populations for gene families that mediate the metabolism of certain clinically useful drugs and environmental toxins. Even subpopulations show genetic variations with significant differences between White Americans and African Americans, and between Portuguese and Black Brazilians.[3]

Pharmacogenetics, therefore, aims to target these differences and similarities in order to design more effective personalized diagnoses and vaccines. However, this sort of research has only been possible due to powerful computational techniques of bioinformatics, which can extract biological information that would have previously been lost as background cellular noise (Royal Society, 2005a). At the scientific level, previously difficult and intractable problems can now be tackled and solved in radically shorter times; clinically, these new information techniques have given rise to user-friendly diagnostic technologies that provide rapid genomic analyses of individuals.

Bioinformatics has also enabled the global management of biological information. There is a vast repository of public domain software for computational biology, and individual accounts for remote access and data processing can be opened at high-performance computer facilities and bioinformatics regional centres, including Fundação Oswaldo Cruz (FIOCRUZ) in Brazil, South African National Biodiversity Institute (SANBI) in South Africa, Centro Nacional de Calculo Cinetifico (CeCalCULA) in Venezuela and International Centre for Genetic Engineering and Biotechnology (ICGEB) in Italy and India. In this way, digital libraries of biological research results allow the global sharing of knowledge. Biological research can be distributed over multiple laboratories so that investigators can work collaboratively around the world. Bioinformatics also requires relatively modest hardware and technical support, which helps to explain, in part, the rapid rise of biotechnology in Africa. Linux operating systems, for example, permit the use of personal computers as powerful workstations, and information technology training for African scientists has been available online, although this has been constrained by limited internet connectivity.

Proteomics

The aim of proteomics is to understand the expression and modification of proteins and their involvement in metabolic pathways in real time in a single (or set of) cell(s). This has only been possible due to advances in the speed, automation and availability of basic techniques. For example, new array technologies and advances in mass spectrometry provide improved resolution of protein species, while fluorescent probes, coated nanoparticles and Raman and fluorescent optical spectroscopies can monitor intracellular signals more effectively. One valuable application of proteomics has been the manufacture of sensitive biosensors to diagnose certain illnesses in individuals.[4]

However, a major challenge has been that seemingly simple pathways are, in fact, embedded in extremely complex intra- and intercellular networks. Consequently, there is a growing awareness of the usefulness of systems biology and its powerful computational techniques to analyse and integrate the complex interactions of individual molecular elements of biological systems within manageable and predictive models. For example, it is now possible to look at the effect of a particular stimulus on many different signal transduction pathways that control cellular responses to infection, and this has helped to advance the understanding of pathogenesis, virus morphology and drug resistance in microorganisms, as well as mechanisms of disease and related cellular biochemistry in humans.

Transcriptomes and metagenomics

Whereas much of a cell's DNA does not code for proteins, a cell's transcriptome (which refers to all messenger RNA molecules or transcripts produced in that cell) reflects all the protein coding genes that are being actively expressed at any given time in a cell. Transcriptome analyses are therefore valuable contributions to understanding transcriptional regulation, and have been used to investigate how cancer cells progress and how stem cells maintain their unique properties.

One new post-genomic technique that has facilitated these analyses is paired end ditagging (often known as PET), which has significantly improved the efficiency of DNA sequencing. This technology has also been used in metagenome analysis, which identifies and studies genomes recovered from environmental samples rather than from clonal cultures. This area of research has received attention especially given recent public health concerns over severe acute respiratory syndrome (SARS) and avian flu. One aim has been to discover previously uncharacterized viruses that are relevant to human health. For example, one set of studies carried out in Singapore investigated microbial communities found in human-associated environments. Unexpectedly, many of the microbial communities taken from indoor air samples were of human origin, and certain genes were found to be enriched in some of the air microbes, including genes involved in resistance to desiccation and oxidative stress, and possible virulence factors.

Dual use risk from post-genomic technologies

Given the continued presence of ethnic tensions and conflicts in the world today, the fear is that genetic polymorphisms could be used to target specific populations for non-therapeutic purposes. Some participants felt that this fear was exaggerated because inter-ethnic, and thereby genetic, admixture is becoming common or increasing at a fast pace, and so it is rare that a given polymorphism is specific to one population. Moreover, although there are a large number of polymorphisms within the human genome, the proportion of them lying in functionally important areas is small and therefore reduces the risk of selective targeting. Others argued that targeting need not be hugely effective or completely selective. Public perception of the risk posed by bioterrorism feeds into the geopolitical response to incidents, and so even a moderate level of selectivity would be sufficient for seriously damaging societal structures. The social panic resulting from the attack would be enough to trigger effects far in excess of those from the initial attack itself. However, targeting need not involve individual polymorphisms. For example, certain cell surface antigens have distinctive distributions that vary with geographic origin. As a result, viruses could be used to target distinct ethnic groups with characteristic cell surface molecules without needing to identify population-specific genetic variations (IoM and NRC, 2005).

In addition, genomic medicine presupposes a sound understanding of the relationship between genetic differences and pathogens' mechanism of disease. For example, researchers have investigated how genes in the bacteria *Mycobacterium tuberculosis* and *Vibrio cholera* control the invasion of the bacteria into host environments. In doing so, potential drug targets have been identified, as well as novel virulence factors. The concern is that this knowledge could be misused to enhance the susceptibility of host populations to pathogen infection. Similarly, some participants felt that knowledge of the diagnostic applications of post-genomic technologies could be misused to enable biological agents or toxins to evade detection methodologies. Others also raised concerns that the problem-solving promise of systems biology could be misused to identify ways of deliberately manipulating biological systems with the intent to do harm.

Immunological research

Manipulating innate immunity

'Innate immunity' represents the first line of non-specific defence against pathogens and is essential for keeping an infection in check before longer-lasting, specific 'acquired immunity' can be induced. Cells of the innate immune system respond to pathogen-associated molecular patterns (PAMPs) on alien microbes and produce cytokines, which in moderate amounts contribute to defence processes, but when overproduced can lead to autoimmunity and even death. The severe reactions suffered by volunteers during clinical drug trials at Northwick Park Hospital in London in spring 2006 highlighted the disastrous clinical effects of agents that induce a cytokine storm. Several recent reports in the scientific literature describe the possibilities of targeting the innate immune system for therapeutic purposes, especially using PAMPs, whether in natural form or artificially designed. For example, synthetic imidazole quinolones target innate immune system receptors for the treatment of genital warts and other diseases caused by human papillomaviruses; and synthetic oligodeoxynu-cleotides can provide generic immunity in rodents against many different bacteria, viruses and parasites.

Manipulating acquired immunity

Short interfering RNA (siRNA) or silencing RNA refers to a class of small RNA molecules that can act upon and interrupt RNA-related pathways, most notably those controlling gene expression. For example, the introduction of siRNA complexes can silence gene expression in mammalian cells without triggering an innate immune response. This has been important for cancer treatments where immunity can be boosted by silencing immune-suppressive genes. Conversely, immune-responsive genes can be silenced to lower immunity, which is useful to treat allergic and autoimmune diseases, as well as graft rejection after trans-plants. In addition, siRNA methods are beneficial because they can inhibit specific genes that have been inaccessible to conventional drugs.

Dual use risk

The concern is that immunity or the effectiveness of immunization could be disrupted for non-therapeutic purposes. A worst case scenario would involve designing a tool to interfere with the signalling mechanisms within immune systems to manipulate either the innate or acquired immune systems. On the one hand, cytokine production could be overstimulated as a biological weapon. On the other hand, over-silencing immune suppressive genes too much could produce a hypo-immune response, leading to the development of cancer, while over-silencing immune responsive genes could trigger a hyper-immune response, leading to autoimmune disease. Manipulating the innate system is considered to be the more dangerous of the two because as a non-specific mech-anism it would have more widespread effects.

The immune system does not act in isolation, but interacts with other systems and bioregulators, such as the nervous and endocrine systems. Consequently, the dual use risk is raised to a whole new order of complexity. By affecting the functions of these other systems, even small manipulations to the immune system could be amplified to bring about devastating consequences.

On the whole, participants agreed that immunological research does pose a dual use risk; but they felt that this potential risk should not be exaggerated, especially since current delivery systems do not allow effective targeting of human or animal immune systems.

Drug delivery

Gene therapy and vectorology

Nucleic acids, such as DNA, can be delivered into cells, after which they are decoded and translated into therapeutically useful proteins. This allows cells to be targeted while avoiding some of the toxic side effects caused by conventional drugs. There has been considerable research into 'artificial viruses'– polymer-based complexes containing DNA with special molecular features to enhance the efficiency of DNA uptake into specific cells. This technique has been used in cancer treatment, for example, where DNA is released within cancer cells and translated into proteins that can kill tumour cells directly, block the cell cycle or stimulate anti-tumour immunity. In one study, local applications of synthetic double-stranded RNA on different tumours in mice led to the eradication of intracranial glioblastoma; and DNA coding for cytochrome P450 isoforms directed at tumour cells activated cyclophosphamide, which helps to boost acquired immunity against cancerous cells. The presentation made by Manfred Ogris at the workshop went into further detail on these issues.[5]

Dual use risk

This area of research is already generating benefits. However, participants felt that its potential dual use risk is high because the feasibility of delivery is central to the targeting of genes and biological systems (whether for therapeutic or non-therapeutic purposes). The concern is that vectorological research could be used to deliver harmful genes into host cells and increase the stability, transmissibility or ability to disseminate of harmful biological agents or toxins. While delivery is currently problematic, research is being carried out to improve delivery, exploiting nanotechnology to enhance absorption of aerosols and liposome and lipid nanoparticle formulations of chemically modified and stabilized siRNA complexes (Royal Society–Royal Academy of Engineering, 2004).

Agriculture and environmental biotechnology

Biopharming

The agricultural applications of biotechnology are varied and have helped farmers to grow crops with larger yields that are more robust in the face of disease and drought, as well as crops with improved nutritional content and greater photosynthetic efficiency. Crops have also been genetically modified to produce and deliver vaccines, and engineered plants can elicit an immune response in humans. For example, clinical trials on humans are currently under way to test vaccine produced in edible crops.

Pest control

One new application of biotechnology concerns non-chemical controls on insect pest infestations, which cause great losses, especially in developing countries with agriculturally dependent economies. In Tanzania, for example, maize is a staple food and a major cash crop. Tanzania has traditionally relied on the use of persistent non-specific chemical pesticides to combat pest outbreaks. However, this has led to great environmental damage, including contamination due to residual poisons, build-up of toxins in food chains and the killing of beneficial organisms. These have all been compounded by the spread of resistance in pest populations. Moreover, chemical pesticides in Africa are often very expensive, especially when these associated risks and social costs are included.

To combat these problems, Tanzania has tried to diversify its insect pest management, especially through biological controls, such as introducing naturally occurring pest-specific predators and parasites. Programmes of sterilizing males have also been tried, as well as pheromone use to control sexual behaviour. Researchers have also genetically engineered crops to be pest resistant and investigated the ecology of pests to look at ways of interrupting pest development and reproduction.[6]

Environmental biotechnology

Biotechnology applications also extend outside of the farm. In Pakistan, for example, the Centre for Molecular Genetics at the University of Karachi has isolated bacteria from indigenous sources and developed them for large-scale industrial and medical applications. Bacteria have been used to filter and digest toxic aromatics, such as pesticides and crude oil components, and certain oil-eating bacteria have even been successfully used to decontaminate beach sand after oil spills. Bacteria have also been used to produce bio-fertilizers and biodegradable plastics, which have been used in surgical equipment and baby and female hygiene products, allowing them to be safely broken down.[7]

Therapeutics and vaccines

One promising security application of biotechnology is creating strategic stockpiles of therapeutics and vaccines against biological agents. In 2004, Project Bioshield was launched in the US with a US$5.6 billion budget (to spend by 2014) on strategic reserves of therapeutics and vaccines against known biological agents to be stored as the Strategic National Stockpile (MacKenzie, 2006). However, strains can easily mutate and become resistant to stockpiled vaccines; long-term reserves of therapeutics tend to be unstable; and large-scale manufacturing of therapeutics takes one to three years using traditional techniques.

Alternative genetic engineering techniques are being explored to avoid these problems. One technique involves transient gene expression in plants where genes coding for relevant protein antigens are inserted into a plant virus, which is then introduced into plant hosts. Replication of the virus leads to the production of the protein antigens, which can then be harvested. Another method is to convert viral RNA into a DNA sequence, insert this into a delivery vector and then introduce the vector into a plant. With each replication the RNA expressed from the DNA leads to the production of the antigen. Similarly, research has been carried out to produce countermeasures against organophosphate nerve agents, such as sarin. Organophosphate toxicity occurs by inhibiting the neurotransmitter breakdown by acetyl cholinesterase (AChE), and so plants have been engineered to bio-manufacture human AChE that can be used as a molecular sponge to mop up nerve gas agents and, hence, decrease their toxicity.

The major appeal of this technology is that plant manufacturing facilities are cheap and can be easily and rapidly scaled up to produce large quantities of vaccines. US army research on producing plague vaccines from plants found that 100 plants could yield 1 gram of purified vaccine, the equivalent of 75,000 doses, and time from the initial infection (of the vector into the plants) until harvest took only 12 days (see the workshop presentation made by Charles Arntzen for further details[8]). The protein antigens produced were then purified for delivery by injection. This means that highly effective vaccines can be produced in a cost-effective manner for countries wishing to create, on demand, strategic stockpiles of threat reduction agents.

Dual use risk

Participants felt that the dual use risk of this area of biotechnology is low. However, it was noted that transgenic plants could be malevolently engineered to mass produce large quantities of non-therapeutic (toxic) proteins. Concerns were also raised that targeting crop production could have broader ramifications since by entering the human food chain biological agents and toxins could be easily delivered across large populations.

A note on diagnosis and surveillance of infectious diseases

Participants at the conference generally agreed that there is little difference between preparing for, and responding to, a bioterrorist attack and a natural outbreak of disease. Both cases will require the same sort of diagnostic and surveillance infrastructure. However, given their different socio-political consequences, it is vital that a bioterrorist attack is not misinterpreted as a natural outbreak of disease, and vice versa.

Determining whether a bioterrorist event has taken place will be difficult. Clinical signs may not appear for days or weeks, and initial symptoms may be non-specific. Likely indicators will include large numbers of causalities with unusual epidemiologies and/or multiple simultaneous outbreaks of multi-drug resistant pathogens. Guides, such as Category A, B and C lists from the US Centers for Disease Control and Prevention (CDC) website, are available to identify key diseases (CDC, 2006). One problem is that these do not include non-indigenous diseases. However, given the scale of today's international trade and travel, diseases have spread across the world, and so non-indigenous diseases should not be overlooked, especially in cases of unusual symptomology. It is also important that knowledge about diseases that are supposedly extinct, such as smallpox, is not lost as this would be vital for early diagnosis and response if the disease were to reappear.

The activities and responses of the health services and intelligence and law enforcement agencies must also be coordinated. Health and security services need to agree on what must be monitored and on the use of surveillance guidelines, including instructions on the detection of events and the collection of appropriate laboratory specimens for forensic evidence. There also has to be a suitable laboratory service with a hierarchy of competence to conduct various types of investigation depending upon the perceived level of biohazard.

Some participants felt that bioterrorism had generated considerable political interest, disproportionate to the importance of the events, and that natural outbreaks of diseases (such as SARS and avian flu) are much more likely to occur than bioterrorist attacks. Loss of life has been far greater from natural diseases than from bioterrorist attacks. For example, it has been suggested that the geopolitical impact from the US anthrax letters in autumn 2001, which resulted in 22 cases and 5 deaths, was of a similar scale to the 2002 to 2003 SARS outbreak, which caused an estimated 8098 cases and 774 deaths (Royal Society–Wellcome Trust, 2004). Other participants from developing countries stressed the enormous loss of life caused by naturally occurring diseases, such as AIDS, malaria and tuberculosis, and suggested that bioterrorist threats should be viewed in this context. Even so, establishing and maintaining national and global surveillance systems for human, animal and plant disease is a key element of the defence against the misuse of scientific and technological developments.

One major challenge is that effective medical surveillance infrastructures only exist in the most well-developed countries where diagnosis may take only a few hours, whereas in less developed countries it may take several weeks. This significantly decreases the efficiency of responding to an outbreak of deliberate or naturally occurring infectious disease. Given the increase in global travel, which has increased the spread of disease across the world, no country can afford to act in isolation. The acquisition of the necessary infrastructure, communications and skills for monitoring infectious diseases in less developed countries should therefore be of paramount concern for all countries. States Parties should cooperate with each other and international organizations – such as the World Health Organization (WHO), the World Organization for Animal Health and the United Nations Food and Agricultural Organization (FAO) – to further the development and application of scientific discoveries for the detection, prevention and countering of disease, under Article X of the BWC (Joint Science Academies, 2006).

Key issues

Strengthening scientific input into the BWC

Participants stressed the importance of the universal application of the BWC. The BWC unequivocally covers all naturally or artificially created or altered microbial or other biological agents or toxins, as well as their components, whatever their origin or method of production, that have no justification for prophylactic, protective or other peaceful purposes. Participants agreed that States Parties to the BWC should reaffirm that the misapplication of the scientific and technological developments discussed at the workshop is covered under BWC Article I. Participants also emphasized States Parties' obligations under BWC Article IV to 'prohibit and prevent' the development, production, stockpiling, acquisition or retention of biological toxins and weapons, and to translate their international obligations into national laws and regulations of enforcement. However, this raises three major challenges to ensure the following:

• National legislation and regulations of enforcement should encompass the full range of BWC prohibitions, while making scientific sense.
• Measures that go beyond the implementation of BWC obligations should not inhibit scientific progress.
• Implementation of BWC obligations into national legislation should be sensitive to the particular political and scientific context of individual countries.

The scientific community can assist in addressing these challenges by regularly contributing to the BWC regime. For example, this could be achieved through interim structures such as independent scientific advisory panels and regional scientific meetings. If they do not already do so, States Parties should also seek advice from their scientific community as part of their preparation for BWC meetings and should consider including scientists in their delegations. The pace of technological development is now so rapid that the implications need to be reviewed more frequently than allowed by the five-year cycle of BWC Review Conferences. Participants suggested that interim structures such as independent scientific advisory panels and regional meetings could also assist in keeping track of developments.

Scientific practices, infrastructure capacities and the political will to enact national BWC-related legislation and regulation vary between countries. Consequently, national academies of science, professional societies, universities and research institutes, NGOs and other civil society organizations can all play a role in their own countries by promoting the importance of the BWC to ensure that their governments fulfil their BWC obligations. This sort of national input is particularly important to promote scientific progress in developing countries since, as some participants noted, there is a perception that BWC related legislation and regulation could be used by the developed world to inhibit scientific progress in developing countries.

Concerns were also raised that the BWC binds and refers only to states, rather than individuals, and this might be undermined by the existence of terrorist groups. Although the BWC was not primarily intended as a counter-terrorism device, a closer reading of the text shows that states' obligations to prevent and prohibit misuse on their own territory makes them responsible in this respect. Moreover, this aspect of prevention and prohibition is reinforced by other international measures against both state actors, such as the Chemical Weapons Convention, and non-state actors at the national level, such as UN Security Council Resolution 1540 on the non-proliferation of weapons of mass destruction.

Improved risk management

It was widely agreed that dual use research in the life sciences poses a potential security risk. However, the complexity of biological systems continues to make it extremely challenging to understand fully or manipulate them. It is also difficult to predict the details and application of breakthroughs given the serendipitous nature of scientific research; and it is becoming increasingly difficult to know where technological breakthroughs will occur in the world as many countries have sophisticated research facilities. Furthermore, technological developments are now also bringing processes that could feasibly be used to make and deploy biological and toxin weapons within the capability of small groups below state level because of the reduction in costs and expertise required.

Participants agreed that although misuse can be minimized, it cannot be completely eliminated; however, the scope and immediacy of the risk of misuse must not be exaggerated. Sensible policies must be guided by critical and realistic risk assessments. Therefore, risk management processes that deal with dual use technologies need to be improved. Methods are needed for undertaking assessments across the full spectrum of biological threats, ranging from the deliberate weaponization of biological agents, through the inadvertent misuse of technologies, to emerging naturally occurring diseases, and there should also be further investigation of best practice in communicating the associated risks. Risk management processes would require close interaction with scientists working at the forefront of dual use technologies who are better equipped to predict and mitigate science-based security risks. In addition, research in the life sciences should not be considered in isolation from other scientific disciplines because the development and weaponization of biological agents can involve techniques from fields such as mathematics, engineering, physics and computer science.

A major challenge is how to factor the perception of risk into dual use risk analysis, particularly by the public. This is made more complicated since risk environments and risk perceptions differ around the world, and the likelihood of abuse in the life sciences and the harm to public health may vary according to the perception of the risks and individual countries' efforts to reduce them. Participants felt that a shared risk methodology and terminology would be particularly useful to understand how countries perceive biosecurity threats differently.

Openness and transparency

Throughout the workshop it was stressed how open communication has been intrinsic to the scientific tradition, providing a forum for validating, repudiating and building upon scientific ideas necessary for intellectual and technological progress. Some participants from developing countries were especially concerned about censorship since access to training, technology and the results of research carried out elsewhere in developed countries is necessary to further the development of scientific capacities in their countries (Joint Science Academies, 2005). Participants therefore stressed the importance of BWC

Article X, which promotes international cooperation in biology for the prevention of disease, including the free flow of information and scientists in both the developing and developed world.

Although a piece of research may be considered to be dual use, publication can still be possible. For example, the American Society for Microbiology (ASM) introduced formal procedures as part of the peer review process for its 11 journals for manuscripts dealing primarily, but not exclusively, with research conducted on select agents. In 2002, 313 select agents manuscripts received special screening from a total of 13,929 manuscripts submitted. Only two of the manuscripts receiving special screening were sent to the full ASM publications board for further screening. Between January and July 2003, of the 8557 manuscripts submitted, only 262 select agents manuscripts were screened and none was referred to the publications board for further review (Royal Society, 2005b).

Classifying research as dual use serves to emphasize that special consideration may be warranted regarding how its results are communicated. There are a set of communication options, ranging from full and immediate publication, to delayed and/or modified publication to restricted or no publication at all. These options could be used singly or in combination on a case-by-case basis. In very rare cases, consideration could be given to delaying publication of highly sensitive information or releasing only some of the information into the public domain. However, in these instances, there would need to be a very clear benefit in delaying publication.

Censoring research would not necessarily prevent misuse. Information is likely to be published elsewhere, such as in other journals, websites or conference proceedings, or communicated informally via email, telephone or face-to-face discussion. Publishing also makes others aware of unintended results. For example, the publication of the paper on the insertion of the interleukin-4 gene into mousepox made a large number of researchers aware of the discovery that the insertion of this gene enabled the virus to overcome both genetic resistance and immunization against the disease (Royal Society–Wellcome Trust, 2004). A common opinion at the workshop was that censoring the results of dual use research in order to prevent bioterrorist activity may, in fact, be counterproductive. Censorship would simply suffocate new research in the life sciences; yet, with greater scientific expertise, including knowledge of its harmful applications, it would be easier to prepare for and combat bioterrorism most effectively.

Participants also highlighted that dual use concerns are not limited to the scientific community and its academic journals, but are also relevant to the general public and media. Public confidence and trust in the scientific community cannot be ignored, and the media needs to be encouraged to report dual use aspects of science and technology responsibly. This is crucial since, as mentioned above, a major issue is the perception of biosecurity risks, which is determined by the level of public confidence and trust in science. The media therefore needs to be educated on these issues as much as scientists themselves.

Education and training

It is essential to continue to raise awareness of dual use issues within the scientific community, including scientists working in academia, government and the private sector, and thereby help responsible stewardship to be furthered in the life sciences. Academic and industrial researchers, as well as university students, should be educated on the matter, perhaps by undertaking courses in ethics and responsible research practice, and should be taught about relevant international law obligations of their governments, especially relating to the BWC. Bioethics curricula should build on local values and ethical norms. Some participants suggested post-14-year-olds should also be taught about these issues at school.

Many participants supported the use of codes of conduct as a valuable educational tool. However, codes of conduct are also useful tools to lower the risks associated with using or transferring sensitive knowledge. Many participants were particularly concerned about the possibility of 'backyard' or 'garage' biology by both state and non-state actors; and some felt that codes of conduct can play a key role in developing a strong scientific culture of responsible stewardship.

The presence and level of codes of conduct and safety regulation vary between countries. Accordingly, if an international scientific culture of responsible stewardship is to be furthered in the life sciences, there need to be international strategies to harmonize, and thereby raise, the standard of national regulation and to promote adherence to codes of conduct. One example is the statement on biosecurity released by the InterAcademy Panel, which was signed by 69 national academies of science (InterAcademy Panel on International Issues, 2005). The statement highlighted fundamental guiding principles for formulating codes of conduct in order to minimize the possibility of the misuse of scientific research.

Some participants felt that simply reaffirming codes of conduct does not provide any further illumination over important details of their scope and meaning. There still need to be more efforts to engage with scientists directly to educate them about dual use issues and the value of codes of conduct, and to encourage their participation in formulating these codes. In this way, misperceptions within the scientific community that codes of conduct are just another level of regulation to interfere with their research can be overcome. Work has been conducted in this area by sets of seminars and workshops (see Rappert et al, 2006, and Chapter 3 in this volume).

Conclusions

Strengthening scientific input into the BWC

The BWC unequivocally covers all naturally or artificially created or altered microbial or other biological agents or toxins, as well as their components, whatever their origin or method of production, that have no justification for prophylactic, protective or other peaceful purposes. Participants agreed that

States Parties to the BWC should reaffirm that the misapplication of the new scientific and technological developments discussed at the workshop are covered under BWC Article I.

BWC Article IV obliges States Parties to 'prohibit and prevent' the development, production, stockpiling, acquisition or retention of biological toxins and weapons, and to translate their international obligations into national laws and regulations of enforcement. However, national legislation and regulations of enforcement must encompass the full range of BWC prohibitions while making scientific sense, and measures that go beyond the implementation of BWC obligations must not inhibit scientific progress.

The scientific community can assist in addressing these challenges. Processes need to be explored through which the scientific community can regularly contribute to the BWC regime – for example, through interim structures, such as independent scientific advisory panels and regional scientific meetings. If they do not already do so, States Parties should also seek advice from their scientific community as part of their preparation for BWC meetings and consider including scientists in their delegations.

The pace of technological developments is now so rapid that their implications need to be reviewed more frequently than allowed by the five-year cycle of BWC Review Conferences.

Improved risk management

The risk of misuse of dual use technologies can be minimized, though not completely eliminated, through national controls and regulations and through increased awareness of the prohibitions of the BWC.

Risk management processes that deal with the misuse of dual use technologies need to be improved. Methods are also required for undertaking assessments across the full spectrum of biological threats, ranging from the deliberate weaponization of biological agents through the inadvertent misuse of dual use technologies to naturally occurring diseases. There should also be further investigation of best practices in communicating the associated risks.

Technological developments outside the classical life sciences are equally relevant to the BWC, especially those involved with the delivery of agents for hostile purposes. These technologies will converge with traditional and current biotechnologies and should be closely monitored.

Openness and transparency

Restricting the flow of information about new scientific and technical advances is highly unlikely to prevent potential misuse and might even encourage misuse. Freedom of communication and movement of scientists is fundamental to scientific progress and, therefore, to achieving the potential benefits for human, animal and plant health. Governments may take steps to protect their own security by occasionally restricting some information. However, they should also promote transparency and confidence-building.

BWC Article X must be respected. Legislation and regulations of enforcement must encourage the flow of information and the participation of scientists amongst the international community in both the developing and developed world.

States Parties should also cooperate with each other and international organizations (such as the WHO, the World Organization for Animal Health and the FAO) to further the development and application of scientific discoveries for the detection, prevention and countering of disease.

Education and awareness-raising

National and international scientific organizations and industry should encourage and engage with those involved in scientific endeavours, including scientists working in academia, government and the private sector, to increase awareness of the BWC and dual use issues, especially through codes of conduct.

University students should also be educated on dual use issues, perhaps by undertaking ethics and responsible research practice courses, and should be taught about the relevant international legal obligations of their governments, especially relating to the BWC.

These measures would promote in-depth implementation of the BWC and help to further responsible stewardship in the life sciences and ensure vigilance when work with dual use potential is undertaken.

Notes

1   For further details, see the presentation made by Nicholas Sims at www.royalsoc.ac.uk/downloaddoc.asp?id=3445.
2   See Drew Endy's presentation at www.royalsoc.ac.uk/downloaddoc.asp?id=3450.
3   See Guilherme Suarez-Kurtz's presentation at www.royalsoc.ac.uk/downloaddoc.asp?id=3464.
4   Additional information is given in Andrew Pitt's presentation at www.royalsoc.ac.uk/downloaddoc.asp?id=3449.
5   Available at www.royalsoc.ac.uk/downloaddoc.asp?id=3465.
6   See the presentation made by Costancia Rugumamu at www.royalsoc.ac.uk/downloaddoc.asp?id=3460.
7   For further details, see Nuzhat Ahmad's workshop presentation at www.royalsoc.ac.uk/downloaddoc.asp?id=3459.
8   Available at www.royalsoc.ac.uk/downloaddoc.asp?id=3463.

References

CDC (Centers for Disease Control and Prevention) (2006) *Bioterrorism Agents/Diseases*, Atlanta, GA, CDC, www.bt.cdc.gov/agent/agentlist-category.asp
IAP (InterAcademy Panel on International Issues) (2005) *IAP Statement on Biosecurity*, Trieste, IAP, www.interacademies.net/Object.File/Master/5/399/Biosecurity%20St.pdf

IOM (US Institute of Medicine) and NRC (National Research Council) (2005) *Globalization, Biosecurity and the Future of the Life Sciences*, Washington, DC, National Academies Press

Joint Science Academies (2005) *Joint Science Academies' Statement: Science and Technology for African Development*, London, Royal Society, www.royalsoc.ac.uk/displaypagedoc.asp?id=13609

Joint Science Academies (2006) *Joint Science Academies' Statement: Avian Influenza and Infectious Diseases*, London, Royal Society, www.royalsoc.ac.uk/displaypagedoc.asp?id=20740

MacKenzie, D. (2006) 'Biodefence: Fortress America?', *New Scientist*, 17 October, pp18–21

NRC (US National Research Council) (2004) *Biotechnology Research in an Age of Terrorism*, Washington, DC, National Academies Press

NSABB (National Science Advisory Board for Biosecurity) (2006) *NSABB Draft Guidance Documents*, Bethesda, MA, National Institutes of Health, www.biosecurityboard.gov/pdf/NSABB%20Draft%20Guidance%20Documents.pdf

Rappert, B., Chevrier, M. and Dando, M. (2006) *The Life Sciences: Biosecurity and Dual Use Research*, www.projects.ex.ac.uk/codesofconduct/BiosecuritySeminar/Education/index.htm

Royal Society (2005a) *Personalised Medicines: Hopes and Realities*, London, Royal Society

Royal Society (2005b) *The Roles of Codes of Conduct in Preventing the Misuse of Scientific Research*, London, Royal Society

Royal Society–Royal Academy of Engineering (2004) *Nanoscience and Nanotechnologies: Opportunities and Uncertainties*, London, Royal Society, www.nanotec.org.uk

Royal Society–Wellcome Trust (2004) *Do No Harm: Reducing the Potential for the Misuse of Life Science Research*, London, Royal Society

6

Options for a Scientific Advisory Panel for the Biological Weapons Convention

Catherine Rhodes and Malcolm Dando

In April 2002, in the aftermath of the failure of the 2001 Review Conference of the Biological Weapons Convention to agree a Final Declaration, the UK Foreign Office produced a Green Paper (Secretary of State, 2002) setting out a range of options that might be taken up in order to strengthen the convention. One such suggestion was for a Scientific Advisory Panel (SAP). As the report noted in its executive summary:

> ... *in view of the dramatic pace of technical change in the life sciences as described here, an open ended body of government and non-government scientists should meet every one or two years to review the rate of change and assess their implications for the convention and measures being taken to strengthen it.*

The body of the paper supported this argument by pointing out that the 'accelerating pace of scientific developments now makes it quite unsafe only to have five-yearly technology reviews by the States Parties to support the five-yearly Review Conferences'.

In its response to the Green Paper, the UK Royal Society concentrated on just two topics: scientific responsibility and ethics in research, and the question of a Scientific Advisory Panel. In regard to the SAP, it argued that (Royal Society, 2002):

> *Successful Scientific Advisory Panels have in common a number of key features that should be taken into account in the creation of a body to improve the efficacy of the BTWC. These include highly respected membership directed by bodies set up as the result of international political agreement.*

The Royal Society has maintained its support for an SAP, arguing in 2005 in the run-up to the 2005 BWC Meeting of Experts that (Royal Society, 2004):

> *The Society strongly advocates the formation of a properly resourced international scientific advisory panel supporting the BTWC ... There would be many benefits to forming such a panel, including promoting the proper use of scientific advances.*

While the form of an SAP or scientific input, more generally, was not exactly specified, the view that something was needed to help strengthen the convention was of longstanding interest at the Royal Society.

The Royal Society–InterAcademy Panel–International Council of Scientific Unions workshop in autumn 2006, discussed in Chapter 5, was intended as a scientific input to the BWC Sixth Review Conference in November–December of that year. The conclusion of this international meeting was again clear cut (Royal Society, 2006):

> *It is essential that processes are explored by which the scientific community can regularly input into the BTWC regime, such as independent scientific advisory panels and regional scientific meetings.*

Again, it was argued that the pace of scientific and technical change was such that more frequent review was needed and that, if necessary, interim structures should be used to keep track of developments.

Although the need for more regular scientific and technical reviews of developments relevant to the convention was raised at the Sixth Review Conference (e.g. by the European Union), no agreement was reached on this topic in the final declaration (UN, 2006a). Thus, there is no prospect of any official SAP being set up under the auspices of the BWC until the next review in 2011, although international scientific organizations may decide to take some independent action in the meantime.

This chapter examines options for scientific advice to help strengthen the convention and thus further a web of prevention more generally. In doing so it seeks to contextualize the findings reported in the previous chapter against a wider set of questions about expertise, arms control and international decision-making. It begins by briefly reviewing how scientific advice has been used or identified within the convention's framework to date, and then takes a broad view of the use of scientific advice in biotechnology-related international agreements and organizations. This leads on to the construction of a tentative typology of possibilities and then to suggestions with regard to improving scientific and technical input to the BWC. In the long term, scientific advice needs to be made a formal part of the BWC regime based on consensus because advice from outside organizations may be dismissed as politically motivated by some states.

The Biological Weapons Convention regime and science

In his study of *The Evolution of Biological Disarmament*, Sims (2001) points out that scientific expertise cannot easily be incorporated within the BWC treaty regime. This is not, of course, to say that scientific input has not been used to develop the treaty regime in relation to issues of a technical nature. In 1986, at the Second Review Conference of the BWC, States Parties agreed to implement measures (Dando, 1994):

> ... *in order to prevent or reduce the occurrence of ambiguities, doubts and suspicions, and in order to improve international cooperation in the field of peaceful bacteriological (biological) activities.*

This Review Conference also decided that a special group of scientific and technical experts should meet during the following year to work out precisely what was required in those annual submissions of confidence-building measures (CBMs). Scientific and technical input would also have been required at the Third Review Conference in 1991 when the CBMs were upgraded.

At the Third Review Conference, States Parties also agreed to set up a VEREX (Ad Hoc Group of Government Experts to Identify and Examine Potential Verification Measures from a Scientific and Technical Standpoint) series of meetings to identify measures that could determine:

> *Whether a State Party is developing, producing, stockpiling, acquiring or retaining microbial or other biological agents or toxins, of types and in quantities that have no justification for prophylactic, protective or peaceful purposes; and*

> *Whether a State Party is developing, producing, stockpiling, acquiring or retaining weapons, equipment or means of delivery designed to use such agents or toxins for hostile purposes or in armed conflict. (UN, 1991)*

Significantly, the identification and examination of the potential verification measures was to be carried out 'from a scientific and technical standpoint'. The report of the VEREX meetings led on to the special conference that mandated the ad hoc group chaired by Ambassador Tibor Toth, which attempted to negotiate a protocol to the convention and in which, of course, many issues required scientific and technical analysis.

Less well known, but also requiring scientific and technical analysis, was the process initiated under Article V of the BWC in 1997 when Cuba accused the US of using the pest *Thrips palmi* against its agriculture (Pearson, 1998). Although it was not possible for the consultative meeting to reach a definitive conclusion on the subject, numerous States Parties submitted analyses of the issue to the meeting, and these were necessarily of a scientific and technical character.

Yet it seems clear that the UK Foreign Office Green Paper and the Royal Society documents did not have such technical analysis in mind. They appeared to be much more concerned with the implications of the ongoing rapid scientific and technological developments in the life sciences. This topic, which forms the basis of this chapter, has had a long history within discussions under the BWC.

Scientific and technological developments and the BWC

Under BWC Article XII, it is stated that the Review Conference to be held five years after entry into force 'shall take into account any new scientific and technological developments relevant to the convention'. It has become the regular practice for States Parties to be invited to contribute their views on such issues at each Review Conference and for the conference secretariat to issue a background paper, including the submitted contributions. While a relatively small number of States Parties make contributions, and a smaller number have made regular contributions, the background papers for the successive Review Conferences do give a picture of the developing understanding of advances in the life sciences since 1980.

At the successive Review Conferences, these contributions to the background paper on relevant scientific and technical advances have undoubtedly influenced what was subsequently agreed in the final declarations under Article I. Thus, for example, in the Final Declaration of the Fourth Review Conference in 1996, it was stated that (UN, 1996):

> 5   *The Conference also reaffirms that the Convention unequivocally covers all microbial or other biological agents or toxins, naturally or artificially created or altered, as well as their components, whatever their origin or method of production, of types and in quantities that have no justification for prophylactic, protective or other peaceful purposes.*

This would appear to unequivocally mean that any synthetic agent or organism is covered by the prohibition embodied in the convention, and this statement was clearly made well before the current rising concern about synthetic biology.

The statement also noted apprehensions, as well as reaffirmations. Thus, the following paragraph noted that:

> 6   *The Conference, conscious of apprehensions arising from relevant scientific and technological developments, inter alia, in the fields of microbiology, biotechnology, molecular biology, genetic engineering, and any application resulting from genome studies, and the possibilities of their use for purposes inconsistent with the objectives and the provisions of the Convention, reaffirms that the undertaking given by the States Parties in Article I applies to all such developments.*

Here, again, we see the States Parties noting that 'any application resulting from genome studies' was covered by the prohibition well before the completion of the sequencing of the human genome.

Yet, by 2001 during the Fifth Review Conference, even the UK – a regular and substantial contributor to these background papers – was to declare the mechanism inadequate. Its major contribution to the background paper stated blankly (UN, 2001):

> *Given the accelerating pace in science and technology, the UK wonders whether it is prudent to maintain a five year gap between such assessments under the BTWC.*

It then went on to state:

> *The UK suggests that the upcoming Review Conference consider establishing a mechanism for States Parties to work together on a more frequent basis to conduct such scientific and technical reviews and to consider any implications at the necessary level of expertise.*

That idea, however, was lost along with much else in the failure to agree during 2001. It is, perhaps, partly because of frustration with the continuation of five-yearly reviews of science and technology that States Parties at the Sixth Review Conference in 2006 merely maintained in regard to the issue under Article I that (UN, 2006b):

> 2   *The Conference reaffirms that Article I applies to all scientific and technological developments in the life sciences and in other fields of science relevant to the Convention.*

This is despite the fact that there are a number of documents produced by States Parties (although these were not as widely available as in previous Review Conferences), a summary of the contributions made by the secretariat (UN, 2006c), and the report issued by the Royal Society, the InterAcademy Panel and the International Council of Scientific Unions.

As a related stream of developments, when the 2001 Review Conference resumed in 2002, it agreed upon an inter-sessional process that included as a topic for the 2005 meetings the content, promulgation and adoption of codes of conduct for scientists.

And the detailed discussion of this issue necessarily considered the ongoing scope and pace of change in the related fields of science and technology, but only indirectly. The Sixth Review Conference also agreed upon on an inter-sessional series of meetings and included as a topic for 2008 (UN, 2006b):

> *Oversight, education, awareness-raising, and adoption and/or development of codes of conduct with the aim to prevent misuse in the context of advances in bio-science and biotechnology research with the potential for use for purposes prohibited by the convention.*

It might be argued that this topic is much more closely related to (or at least necessitates) a proper review of ongoing science and technology, and might be a step towards a more regular in-depth review of science and technology advances relevant to the convention. However, this is by no means an assured outcome; thus, the future of such reviews under the BWC remains uncertain.

This section has outlined previous concern about scientific and technological developments within the BWC. Yet the exact organization of that advice has so far not been addressed. In order to discuss what might be best now and in the future for the BWC, we first review some current models that could be considered relevant.

Models of scientific input

A range of processes for scientific input into regulatory regimes can be found in other international organizations and agreements related to the areas of development associated with the BWC. Seven of these, which illustrate the range of mechanisms, are outlined here:

1   Organization for the Prohibition of Chemical Weapons (OPCW) Scientific Advisory Board;
2   Office International des Epizooties (OIE) Specialist Commissions;
3   Convention on Biological Diversity (CBD) Subsidiary Body on Scientific, Technical and Technological Advice;
4   World Health Organization (WHO) Chemical and Biological Weapons Science Advisory Board;
5   WHO International Health Regulations Emergency and Review Committees;
6   Joint United Nations Food and Agriculture Organization (FAO)/WHO Expert Consultations on Safety and Nutritional Aspects of Genetically Modified Foods; and
7   United Nations Educational, Scientific and Cultural Organization (UNESCO's) International Bioethics Committee and Intergovernmental Bioethics Committee.

This will be followed by a discussion of the options that are most appropriate for enhancing scientific input within the BWC regime.

Organization for the Prohibition of Chemical Weapons Scientific Advisory Board

This is an interesting case to examine because it is part of another major arms control treaty and would be expected to deal with similar issues as an advisory panel for the BWC would.

Article VIII.21 (h) of the Chemical Weapons Convention instructed the Director-General of the OPCW to (OPCW, 1993):

> ... *establish a Scientific Advisory Board to enable him, in the performance of his functions, to render specialized advice to the conference, the council or States Parties in the areas of science and technology relevant to the convention.*

The Scientific Advisory Board has 20 members who serve for three-year terms, which are renewable once. They are appointed by the Director-General in consultation with States Parties. Members must be citizens of States Parties; but they serve in their personal capacity. Members are selected 'on the basis of their expertise in particular scientific fields relating to the implementation of the convention', and consideration is given to their qualifications and experience (OPCW, undated). It is preferred that they 'are knowledgeable about the relevant scientific and technological developments' and 'familiar with the implementation of the convention'. There will always be a balance of members from different regions. The terms of reference for the SAB can be found in Decision 10 of the Second Session of the Conference of the Parties (OPCW, 1997).

Meetings of the SAB are usually held once or twice a year. For the consideration of particular scientific and technical issues or questions, the Director-General appoints temporary working groups from the SAB. Issues covered by temporary working groups include sampling and analysis, education and outreach, and biomedical samples. The groups report on their findings to the SAB Chair and to the Director-General. The SAB reviews their findings and may make recommendations to the Director-General, who informs states of proposed action. The proposed actions are then considered by the Executive Council and the Conference of the Parties. For the Chemical Weapons Convention's (CWC's) First Review Conference, the SAB published a special report on developments in science and technology and how they affected the implementation of the convention.

Interestingly, the input of scientific advice was increased in two ways for the CWC's First Review Conference in 2003. The International Union of Pure and Applied Chemistry (IUPAC) was asked to prepare a report (IUPAC, 2002), and at the conference itself a special NGO session for the delegations was held (OPCW, Media and Public Affairs Branch, 2003).

Office International des Epizooties Specialist Commissions

The Office International des Epizooties has four specialist commissions that provide scientific advice and input into the development and updating of OIE standards and guidelines. They are the:

1   Terrestrial Animal Health Standards Commission;
2   Scientific Commission for Animal Diseases;
3   Biological Standards Commission; and
4   Aquatic Animal Health Standards Commission.

The four commissions cover different areas of expertise and advice, but share some procedures, particularly in terms of selection of members and reporting.

Terrestrial Animal Health Standards Commission

The Terrestrial Animal Health Standards Commission (TAHSC) is also known as the Code Commission. It provides scientific advice and input into the development and revision of the OIE's Terrestrial Animal Health Code. It has responsibility for two permanent working groups on animal welfare and animal production food safety, and is permitted to establish ad hoc groups to consider particular issues in depth.

The TAHSC meets several times a year, with one of these meetings held jointly with the Scientific Commission on Animal Diseases and the Aquatic Animal Health Standards Commission. Each meeting provides a report to the OIE Director-General on its work. The President of the Commission also reports to the OIE's International Committee (its governing body). Texts produced by the TAHSC for adoption in the Terrestrial Code are submitted to the General Session of the International Committee for approval, and are then published in the next edition of the code. The general sessions are held annually in May.

The TAHSC has six members, including a bureau with a president, vice-president and secretary-general. Members are elected by the International Committee for three-year terms, which are renewable. Members are required to be (OIE, undated a):

> *Veterinarians with a broad knowledge of the major diseases of animals …*
> *[and to have] experience and expertise in the animal health aspects of the*
> *international trade in animals and animal products, and an understand-*
> *ing and practical experience of the relevant international trading rules.*

The OIE Director-General can invite other specialists to attend parts of the TAHSC meetings, where appropriate, to assist their work.

Scientific Commission for Animal Diseases

The Scientific Commission for Animal Diseases (SCAD) provides advice to the OIE on 'identifying the most appropriate strategies and measures for disease prevention and control' (OIE, undated b). More specifically, its functions include examining applications for disease-free status; exchanging information on terrestrial animal diseases; assessing developments in disease control and eradication; providing up-to-date scientific information to the Director-General and other specialist commissions; and advising the Director-General on any problems relating to the diseases. The up-to-date scientific information provided by the commission feeds into revisions of the OIE's standards and guidelines.

The Scientific Commission generally meets once or twice each year. It is also required to hold a specialist conference at least once every three years. It oversees the Working Group on Wildlife Diseases and can establish *ad hoc* groups to give in-depth consideration to particular issues. The reporting procedures are very similar to the TAHSC – commission meetings present reports on their work to the Director-General and the President of SCAD also reports to the International Committee. Any texts produced by SCAD are put forward to the International Committee's general session for consideration.

The Scientific Commission has five members, including a bureau with a president, vice-president and secretary-general. Members are elected by the International Committee for three-year terms that are renewable. As with the TAHSC, the Director-General can appoint specialists to attend parts of the commission's meetings, as appropriate. Members of the Scientific Commission have to be (OIE, undated c):

> ... *veterinarians with post-graduate training in a field relevant to the control of infectious diseases of animals ... [and to have] a curriculum vitae and scientific publication record appropriate to an international specialist in a field or fields relevant to the control of infectious diseases of animals ... [and] appropriate experience in animal disease control.*

Biological Standards Commission

The Biological Standards Commission (BSC) is also known as the Laboratories Commission. It is mandated to (OIE, undated d):

> ... *keep the Director-General and the International Committee informed of advances in scientific knowledge that could have implications for the diagnosis and prevention of terrestrial animal diseases.*

The BSC is also responsible for the development and revision of the OIE's *Manual of Diagnostic Tests and Vaccines for Terrestrial Animals* and 'for establishing or approving methods for diagnosing diseases ... and for recommending the most effective biological products such as vaccines' (OIE, undated e). It also advises the Director-General on OIE's list of experts, referencing laboratories and collaborating centres.

The BSC is required to meet at least annually. It can establish ad hoc groups for the in-depth consideration of particular issues, but does not oversee any permanent working groups. Reports from BSC meetings are presented to the Director-General, and the President of the BSC reports annually to the International Committee. Texts produced by the BSC, including updates to the terrestrial manual, are presented to the International Committee's general session for discussion and approval. They may subsequently be published in a revised version of the manual.

The BSC has five members, including a bureau with a president, vice-president and secretary-general. The members are elected by the International Committee for three-year terms that are renewable. Members should be (OIE, undated f):

> *... recognised specialists in the field of infectious terrestrial animal disease diagnosis and/or prevention, particularly in laboratory methods and operations ... [and have] international experience ... in the area of laboratory diagnosis and/or immunological prevention of infectious animal disease.*

Again, the Director-General can appoint specialists to attend parts of BSC meetings.

Aquatic Animal Health Standards Commission

The fourth specialist commission of the OIE is the Aquatic Animal Health Standards Commission (AAHSC), also referred to as the Aquatic Animals Commission. It provides scientific information and advice to the OIE on the prevention and control of aquatic animal diseases and is responsible for the development and revision of the Aquatic Animal Health Code and the *Manual of Diagnostic Tests for Aquatic Animals.*

The AAHSC is also required to meet at least once a year. It can establish ad hoc groups for the consideration of particular issues, but does not oversee any permanent working groups. Reports from its meetings are provided to the Director-General and the AAHSC president reports once a year to the International Committee. Texts produced by the AAHSC, which include new or revised chapters for the *Aquatic Code and Aquatic Manual,* are presented to the International Committee's general session for approval.

The AAHSC also has five members, including a bureau with a president, vice-president and secretary-general. Its members are elected by the International Committee for three-year terms that are renewable. Members should be (OIE, undated g):

> *... internationally recognised specialists in the field of methods for surveil-lance, diagnosis and prevention of infectious aquatic animal disease ... [and have] extensive international experience ... of aquatic animal infectious disease surveillance, diagnosis, control and disease prevention methods.*

The Director-General can invite specialists to attend parts of AAHSC meetings.

The Convention on Biological Diversity's Subsidiary Body on Scientific, Technical and Technological Advice

The Convention on Biological Diversity's (CBD's) Subsidiary Body on Scientific, Technical and Technological Advice (SBSTTA) is subsidiary to the CBD's Conference of the Parties (COP). Unlike the other scientific advisory bodies considered here, however, it is not made up of independent scientific experts, but of government representatives 'competent in the relevant field of expertise' (CBD Secretariat, 1992).

The SBSTTA was established by Article 25 of the CBD 'to provide ... timely advice relating to the implementation of the convention', particularly assessments of the status of biodiversity and of implementation measures. It is also expected to:

> *identify innovative, efficient and state-of-the-art technologies and know-how relating to the conservation and sustainable use of biological diversity ... [and] provide advice on scientific progress and international cooperation in research and development [in this area]. (CBD, Article 25.2)*

The SBSTTA is open to participation by all States Parties. It has a bureau, including a Chair, who are elected by the Conference of the Parties for two-year terms, which are staggered to provide continuity. Candidates for the chair 'should be recognized experts, qualified in the field of biological diversity and experienced in the process of the convention and the Subsidiary Body on Scientific, Technical and Technological Advice' (CBD, Conference of the Parties, 1998).

To obtain further scientific input for particular issues, a roster of experts upon which the SBSTTA can draw to establish ad hoc technical expert groups has been compiled. These groups have 15 members selected from the roster.

Under the SBSTTA's rules of procedure (COP Decision IV/16 Annex I, as amended by Decision V/20), it should meet annually. The COP sets themes for the meetings. Documentation for the meetings, including draft technical reports and proposed recommendations, is circulated three months prior to the meeting. When preparing this documentation, the SBSTTA bureau may set up liaison groups with other international and regional organizations. The SBSTTA reports to the COP after each meeting. There have been 12 meetings of SBSTTA so far; the most recent was held during 2 to 6 July 2007, and 129 recommendations for the COP have been produced. The COP can endorse these recommendations in full, in part or in modified form; they then become Conference of the Parties decisions.

World Health Organization's Chemical and Biological Weapons Scientific Advisory Board

The World Health Organization's Chemical and Biological Weapons Scientific Advisory Group (CBW/SAG) was set up following a request for continued provision of 'international guidance and technical information on recommended measures to deal with the deliberate use of biological and chemical agents to cause harm' from the 2002 World Health Assembly – the WHO's governing body (WHO, 2002).

It is different from the other science advisory boards outlined so far because it does not provide input to a particular regulation. Instead, it provides general guidance to the international organization, its Director-General and the secretariat, on CBW issues of relevance to public health. It is requested to:

> *Provide strategic advice on scientific and technical issues related to the*

public health implications of CBW preparedness and response ... Provide independent evaluation at a strategic level of WHO's activities ... including priority setting of the programme on CBW preparedness and response... Identify and advise on new scientific opportunities, international initiatives, and collaboration. (WHO, 2002)

Members of the CBW/SAG are scientists and technical experts external of the WHO. Twelve to fourteen members are selected to be representative of 'the range of public health disciplines relevant' for two-year terms that are renewable and staggered for continuity.

WHO International Health Regulations' Emergency and Review Committees

The International Health Regulations (IHR) are a core treaty of the WHO, designed to limit the international spread of infectious diseases and assist states in dealing with any serious outbreaks. They were substantially revised and a new version of the regulations was adopted in 2005. In this version, two mechanisms for expert advice were created – the Emergency Committee and the Review Committee.

Under the 2005 IHR, states are instructed to report any public health emergency of international concern. Part IX, Chapter II, of the IHR (WHO, 2005a) enables the WHO Director-General to establish an Emergency Committee when needed to provide an opinion on 'whether an event constitutes a public health emergency of international concern', when this status can be terminated, and 'the proposed issuance, modification, extension or termination of temporary recommendations'.

As such, an Emergency Committee is established when the need arises, and for a duration determined by the event. To enable the committee to be rapidly formed, its members are selected from the IHR Roster of Experts, based on the expertise and experience needed to deal with the event. At least one member will be selected from the country in which the event is taking place. The Roster of Experts was established under Chapter I of Part IX of the 2005 IHR. Members are appointed to it by the Director-General, including one as requested by each State Party. It is designed to include 'experts in all relevant fields of expertise' (WHO, 2005b).

Meetings of the Emergency Committee are convened by the Director-General who sets their agenda. The Director-General provides information on the event and presents proposed recommendations to the committee. The committee produces a summary report of the meeting and presents its views to the Director-General. The Director-General makes decisions on action and communicates these to member states and to the public. The Director-General can approve temporary recommendations to deal with public health emergencies independently of the World Health Assembly.

The IHR Review Committee also draws its members from the IHR Roster of Experts. It was established under Part IX, Chapter III, of the 2005 IHR to provide technical advice and recommendations to the WHO's Director-General on the IHR. The Director-General decides on the number of members and selects them from the roster. The Director-General also sets the duration of the committee. In selecting members, consideration is given to geographic representation; gender balance; balance between developed and developing country members; interdisciplinary balance; and diversity of scientific opinion.

The Review Committee reaches decisions by majority. Each meeting provides an advisory report to the Director-General. The Director-General communicates this advice to the World Health Assembly and the WHO's executive board.

Joint Food and Agriculture Organization/WHO Expert Consultations on Safety and Nutritional Aspects of Genetically Modified Foods

These consultations take place as the need arises and there are no regular meetings for providing scientific advice in this area. While the consultations do provide information and advice to FAO/WHO member states, they are primarily designed to assist in the development of standards and guidelines within the Codex Alimentarius Commission (CAC), an international body concerned with food safety, which is jointly overseen by the FAO and WHO.

The FAO/WHO expert consultations provide advice to the FAO, WHO, CAC and their member states on safety and nutritional aspects of genetically modified (GM) foods, aiming to provide a scientific basis for policy-making in this area. This includes a review of assessment practices and recommendation of priority areas for research.

Members are selected for meetings from a roster of experts. Inclusion in the roster is based on the approval of an assessment panel. Members are expected to have an advanced university degree in a relevant area; professional experience in the field and in a multidisciplinary or international environment; and experience in presenting scientific opinions.

The need for consultation on a particular issue will be identified by the FAO, WHO or CAC. So far, there have been five expert consultations on:

1 Biotechnology and Food Safety (1996);
2 Safety Aspects of Genetically Modified Foods of Plant Origin (2000);
3 Evaluation of Allergenicity of GM Foods (2001); and
4 Safety Assessment of Foods Derived from GM Animals, Including Fish (2003).
5 Safety Assessment of Food Derived from Biotechnology (2007).

The advice provided by the consultation is considered by the CAC's Ad Hoc Intergovernmental Task Force on Foods Derived from Biotechnology, which develops standards, guidelines and recommendations for adoption by the CAC.

United Nations Educational, Scientific and Cultural Organization's International Bioethics Committee and Intergovernmental Bioethics Committee

The procedure for providing scientific advice for the United Nations Educational, Scientific and Cultural Organization's (UNESCO's) bioethics programme is noteworthy because it involves input from both independent experts and government representatives. The International Bioethics Committee (IBC) and Intergovernmental Bioethics Committee (IGBC) have played important roles in the development of three UNESCO declarations: the Universal Declaration on the Human Genome and Human Rights; the International Declaration on Human Genetic Data; and the Universal Declaration on Bioethics and Human Rights.

The IBC 'follows progress in the life sciences and its applications in order to ensure respect for human dignity and freedom', and it provides advice and recommendations to UNESCO and its member states (UNESCO, undated a). The IGBC examines the 'advice and recommendations of the IBC' (UNESCO, undated b).

The IBC has 36 members who are independent experts. Its members are appointed by UNESCO's Director-General for four-year terms. They are expected to be 'qualified specialists in the life sciences and in the social and human sciences ... with the necessary competence and authority to perform the IBC's duties' (IBC Statutes, Article 3.2) (UNESCO, undated c). Consideration is given to cultural diversity and geographic representation. The IGBC also has 36 members; these are representatives of UNESCO member states and they are elected by its general conference for terms of approximately four years.

The IBC meets at least once a year. Its advice and recommendations are adopted by consensus and are 'submitted to the Director-General for transmission to the member states, the executive board and the general conference' (UNESCO, undated a). The IGBC meets biennially and produces opinions on IBC's work, which are submitted to the IBC and the Director-General for dissemination.

A typology of options for scientific advice

From this examination it is clear that there are a variety of options for providing formal science advice within the BWC regime. Some of the options will be outlined here before a typology is presented. First, the point should be made that it is difficult to evaluate the relative effectiveness of the different mechanisms. The report *Knowledge and Diplomacy: Science Advice in the United Nations System* (NRC, 2002) involved a thorough examination of scientific advice mechanisms relating to sustainable development within the UN system; but even this study noted the difficulty in evaluating the processes and the lack of information available on their impact. The same is true of the mechanisms outlined here.

However, the report also noted that 'there are an impressive number of important cases in which solid scientific inputs have made critical contributions to policy' (NRC, 2002, p20). Where scientific advisory bodies have transparent reporting mechanisms, it should be possible to track where their advice has been taken up.

Scientific advice can be provided by permanent standing bodies or bodies that are set up as the need arises. Generally, the latter type will have an established list or roster from which experts can be rapidly selected. Advisory bodies can meet on a regular basis, or again only as the need arises. Those which meet on a regular basis may meet several times a year, or just once every one or two years. Frequently, there will be a smaller group from the advisory body which meets more regularly, and this group will often take on a preparatory role for the larger meetings (e.g. the bureaus from the OIE specialist commissions).

The size of the group can vary from just a few members (OIE specialist commissions), to slightly larger groups (OPCW advisory board), and even bodies that allow all member states to be represented (SBSTTA). Where there is a large advisory group, it is generally possible for smaller, more focused, groups to be established in order to consider particular matters (on an ad hoc or longer-term basis). Where there is a small advisory group there will generally be a mechanism to draw in further specialist advice.

Members will have expertise in a relevant area. They may be serving independently or as government representatives. There is the possibility of creating a dual mechanism that has both independent and government advice, as the IBC and IGBC do. Most of the mechanisms here have independent experts. Although they may specify that the expert must be from a State Party, they will still be expected to serve in a personal capacity. The reason for choosing independent experts is to provide some separation between science advice and national positions on the issues under consideration. Achieving such a break in treaty regimes can be very difficult; but if scientific advice is to be trusted, particularly by the public, experts should try to maintain a degree of independence.

All the advisory bodies considered here have specific qualification requirements for their members. This is obviously important in order to ensure that quality information is provided. Most bodies specified that other factors should be taken into consideration in the selection of members, including geographic representation and representation of a range of scientific disciplines and approaches. The IBC took this further than the other bodies, specifying that legal and human sciences should also be represented. The need for a range of scientific disciplines to be represented will obviously vary according to the subject area under consideration.

Most of the advisory bodies had specific lengths of term for members, usually between two and four years. Where the bodies have few members, this can assist in providing a range of expertise, as well as geographic representation. In most cases, the terms were renewable; in some cases, they were staggered. Both of these factors help to provide continuity. Members may be appointed (often by the Director-General of the parent organization), elected (often by the governing body) or selected from a pre-established list or roster (again, usually by the Director-General).

In the cases considered, similarities were evident in the reporting procedures. Each meeting of the advisory body provides a report on its work – generally to the Director-General of the parent organization. Where the body is responsible for providing draft texts or recommendations, these are usually passed to the organization's governing body (often via the Director-General) for approval. Both the advisory body and the governing body will have a system for adoption of reports/recommendations that is either based on consensus or majority decision-making. The latter may minimize political interference and make decision-making more efficient. Reports and recommendations are often published by the parent organization. This helps to make the process transparent, improving public trust.

In the mechanisms shown here, policy-relevant decisions were generally made by intergovernmental bodies, which considered the recommendations given by the advisory body. This is always likely to be the case, particularly with legally binding treaties, and cannot be avoided when implementation of these decisions rests with states. However, there was an exception in the work of the IHR Emergency Committee, where the Director-General has the authority to act directly on its advice; this could, at times, be appropriate for other bodies, when urgent action is required, but is only likely to be acceptable if the actions are temporary and of a set duration.

Appropriate options for a BWC Scientific Advisory Board

The report *Knowledge and Diplomacy: Science Advice in the United Nations System* (NRC, 2002) makes several arguments about the importance of scientific advice within any treaty regime that has inherently technical aspects. Not only do processes for science advice assist decision-makers – for example, through identification of policy issues requiring advice, formulation of questions, and the collection and provision of advice (NRC, 2002, p4), but they also provide an important link between policy-makers and the scientific community (NRC, 2002, p14).

There is a clear need for both of these roles to be fulfilled within the BWC regime. Policy-makers need assistance in reviewing scientific and technological developments and understanding their implications for the operation of the convention, as well as advice on the content of any implementation measures that will affect the scientific community (e.g. codes of conduct). In addition to this, there is the need for clear communication with the scientific community to ensure that they are aware of, and respect, the BWC and related implementation measures. This communication should assist policy-makers in achieving an appropriate balance between safeguards to prevent misuse and the facilitation of peaceful scientific research. As the Royal Society (2006, p12) points out: 'scientists working at the forefront of dual use technologies … are better equipped to predict and mitigate science-based risks', and so communication with them will help to maintain the relevance of the BWC regime.

In light of these possibilities, what form of scientific advice would make sense for the BWC? First, it will be appropriate to have a permanent body because the need for scientific advice in this area is continual. Having a small membership (e.g. six to ten members) will reduce costs. In this case, the creation of a roster from which additional expertise can be sought when necessary would be appropriate. This will help to provide a full range of relevant expertise. The body should be able to establish ad hoc groups to consider particular issues in depth. The roster would also provide the basis of membership for these groups.

The body should meet at least once a year in a regular session because progress in scientific and technological developments is so rapid. There should also be the possibility of interim meetings for when particular issues arise that need urgent attention. This might take the form of something like the IHR Emergency Committee.

Clearly, some members of the scientific advisory board would need to have expertise in bio-defence; but in view of the rate of advances in the life sciences, it would also be important that key scientists from a range of relevant disciplines were also involved.

The members of the body should be independent experts. Independence will be important for creating trust in advice and for providing a degree of separation from the political context. Other factors to be taken into consideration when selecting members are geographic representation and the inclusion of a range of scientific disciplines. These disciplines may be reflected more in the roster than in the core group.

If members were to be elected at the Review Conferences, this would mean five-year terms, which could not be staggered. This is longer than any of the examples considered and suggests that another mechanism for selection of members should be found. A term of three years – renewable once – would be suitable and would match the conditions used for the OPCW Scientific Advisory Board. Terms should be staggered for continuity.

It will be desirable for each meeting to produce a report on its work, which would be made publicly available (at least in part). Recommendations and reports on particular issues would need to be disseminated to States Parties. Again, if recommendations can only be considered at the Review Conferences, this could leave too long a gap before appropriate action is taken. Therefore, consideration should be given to alternatives – for example, a process for the body to make temporary recommendations that States Parties could adopt voluntarily. There should be the option, within the advisory board, of taking decisions by majority, if necessary.

In comparison with the other mechanisms examined, one important aspect is missing from this model. Because the BWC has no oversight organization, it has no Director-General. The other mechanisms made extensive use of the Director-General, who would often be responsible for selecting experts, setting agendas and providing a link between the advisory body and the governing body.

It may be necessary to find an alternative way of fulfilling these roles. One possibility may be to provide a body such as the IGBC, which is made up of a small number of governmental representatives and can provide opinions on reports and recommendations, although the final decisions would be left to the Conference of the Parties.

While the creation of formal advice mechanisms within the BWC should be the ultimate goal, it should be remembered that in the shorter term, it is the international scientific community that is likely to be the prime agent for contributing scientific advice to the BWC. Since the IUPAC has been requested to again supply a scientific report for the Second Review Conference of the CWC in 2008 (IUPAC, 2006), major scientific organizations in the life sciences might consider supplying such reviews to the BWC meetings in 2008 and 2010, where scientific input would be particularly appropriate. This would build on the experience of supplying scientific input to the 2005 and 2006 meetings and perhaps lead to an invitation to provide an input similar to that of the IUPAC's for the 2011 Seventh Review Conference of the BWC.

References

CBD (Convention on Biological Diversity) Conference of the Parties (1998) *Decision IV/16 Annex 1: Modus Operandi of the Subsidiary Body on Scientific, Technical and Technological Advice*, www.cbd.int/decisions/default.asp?m=cop-04&d=16#ann1

CBD Secretariat (1992) *Convention on Biodiversity*, Article 25: Subsidiary Body on Scientific, Technical and Technological Advice, CBD Secretariat, www.cbd.int/convention/articles.shtml?a=cbd-25

Dando, M. R. (1994) *Biological Warfare in the 21st Century: Biotechnology and the Proliferation of Biological Weapons*, London, Brassey's

IUPAC (International Union of Pure and Applied Chemistry) (2002) *Pure and Applied Chemistry*, Special Issue, vol 74, no 12, pp2229–2352

IUPAC (2006) *Current Project No 2006-036-1-020: The Impact of Advances in Science and Technology on the Chemical Weapons Convention*, www.iupac.org/projects/2006/2006-036-1-020.html

NRC (National Research Council) (2002) *Knowledge and Diplomacy: Science Advice in the United Nations System*, www.nap.edu/catalog/10577.html

OIE (Office International des Epizooties) (undated a) 'Qualifications of members', in *Terrestrial Animal Health Standards Commission Terms of Reference*, www.oie.int/tahsc/eng/en_tahsc.htm

OIE (undated b) *Specialist Commissions*, www.oie.int/eng/OIE/organisation/en_CS.htm

OIE (undated c) 'Qualifications of members', in *Scientific Commission for Animal Diseases Terms of Reference*, www.oie.int/scad/eng/en_scad.htm

OIE (undated d) *Biological Standards Commission Terms of Reference*, www.oie.int/bsc/eng/en_bsc.html

OIE (undated e) *Biological Standards Commission Terms of Reference*, www.oie.int/bsc/eng/en_bsc.html

OIE (undated f) 'Qualifications of members', in *Biological Standards Commission Terms of Reference*, www.oie.int/bsc/eng/en_bsc.html

OIE (undated g) 'Qualifications of members', in *Aquatic Animal Health Standards*

Commission, www.oie.int/aac/eng/commission/en_overview.htm

OPCW (Organization for the Prohibition of Chemical Weapons) (1993) *Convention on the Prohibition of the Development, Production, Stockpiling and Use of Chemical Weapons and on Their Destruction*, www.opcw.org

OPCW (1997) Conference of the States Parties, Second Session, *Decision 10: Scientific Advisory Board*

OPCW (undated) *Scientific Advisory Board*, www.opcw.org

OPCW, Media and Public Affairs Branch (2003) *Open Forum on the Chemical Weapons Convention: Challenges to the Chemical Weapons Ban*, OPCW, www.opcw.org/cdq/html/cdq2/cdq2_art6_prt.html1 May

Pearson, G. S. (1998) *Cuban Allegation of BW Attack: The Final Report*, ASA Newsletter, no 98-2, 30 April, p28

Royal Society (2002) *Royal Society Submission to the Foreign and Commonwealth Office Green Paper on Strengthening the Biological and Toxin Weapons Convention*, Policy Document 25/02, London, Royal Society, September

Royal Society (2004) *Issues for Discussion at the 2005 Meeting of Experts of the Biological and Toxin Weapons Convention*, Policy Document 04/05, London, Royal Society, June

Royal Society (2006) *Report of the RS-IAP-ICSU International Workshop on Science and Technology Developments Relevant to the Biological and Toxin Weapons Convention*, Policy Document 38(06), London, Royal Society, October

Secretary of State (2002) *Strengthening the Biological and Toxin Weapons Convention: Countering the Threat from Biological Weapons*, Cm5484, London, HMSO, April

Sims, N. A. (2001) *The Evolution of Biological Disarmament*, Oxford, Oxford University Press for SIPRI

UN (United Nations) (1991) *Final Declaration: Third Review Conference of the Parties to the Convention on the Prohibition of the Development, Production and Stockpiling of Bacteriological (Biological) and Toxin Weapons and on their Destruction*, BWC/CONF. III/23, Geneva, UN

UN (UN) (1996) *Final Declaration: Fourth Review Conference of the Parties to the Convention on the Prohibition of the Development, Production and Stockpiling of Bacteriological (Biological) and Toxin Weapons and on Their Destruction*, BWC/CONF.IV/9, Geneva, UN

UN (2001) *Background Paper on New Scientific and Technological Developments Relevant to the Convention on the Prohibition of the Development, Production and Stockpiling of Bacteriological (Biological) and Toxin Weapons and on Their Destruction*, BWC/CONF.V/4/Add.1, Geneva, UN, 26 October

UN (2006a) *Sixth Review Conference of the States Parties to the Convention on the Prohibition of the Development, Production and Stockpiling of Bacteriological (Biological) and Toxin Weapons and on Their Destruction*, BWC/CONF.VI/CRP.4, Geneva, UN, 8 December

UN (2006b) *Draft Final Document: Sixth Review Conference of the States Parties to the Convention on the Prohibition of the Development, Production and Stockpiling of Bacteriological (Biological) and Toxin Weapons and on Their Destruction*, BWC/CONF.VI/CRP.4, Geneva, UN, 8 December

UN (2006c) *Sixth Review Conference of the States Parties to the Convention on the Prohibition of the Development, Production and Stockpiling of Bacteriological (Biological) and Toxin Weapons and on Their Destruction: Background Information Document on New Scientific and Technological Developments Relevant to the Convention*, BWC/CONF.VI/INF.4, Geneva, UN, 28 September

UNESCO (United Nations Educational, Scientific and Cultural Organization) (undated

a)   *International Bioethics Committee*, http://portal.unesco.org/shs/en/ev.php-URL_ID=1879&URL_DO=DO_TOPIC&URL_SECTION=201.html

UNESCO (undated b) *Intergovernmental Bioethics Committee*, http://portal.unesco.org/shs/en/ev.php-URL_ID=1878&URL_DO= DO_TOPIC&URL_SECTION=201.html

UNESCO (undated c) *Statutes of the International Bioethics Committee*, http://portal.unesco.org/shs/en/ev.php-URL_ID=2026&URL_DO=DO_TOPIC&URL_SECTION= 201.html

WHO (World Health Organization) (2002) *CBW Scientific Advisory Group*, www.who.int/csr/delibepidemics/sac/en/

WHO (2005a) *International Health Regulations 2005, Article 48*, WHO, www.who.int/csr/ihr/IHRWHA58_3-en.pdf

WHO (2005b) *International Health Regulations 2005, Article 47*, WHO, www.who.int/csr/ihr/IHRWHA58_3-en.pdf

7

Dual Use Biotechnology Research: The Case for Protective Oversight

Elisa D. Harris

During recent years, there has been growing concern in the US and in other countries about dual use research.[1] Much of this has focused on the risk that advances in biotechnology could lead, either inadvertently or deliberately, to the creation of new pathogens more destructive than those that currently exist. This is not a future threat. Research with potentially destructive consequences is already being carried out in university, private sector, and government laboratories around the world.

Perhaps the most famous example of such research, and the one that first alerted some scientists and policy-makers to the potential risks from biotechnology research, was the mousepox experiment in Australia. In this work, published in February 2001, researchers trying to develop a means of controlling rodent populations inserted an interleukin-4 gene into the mousepox virus and in so doing created a pathogen that was lethal even to some mice that had been vaccinated against the disease (Jackson et al, 2001). US scientist Mark Buller later built upon this work, producing a mousepox virus so lethal that it killed all of the mice that had been infected, even those that had been both vaccinated and treated with antiviral drugs (MacKenzie, 2003). These projects and others that followed have led to concerns that the introduction of IL-4 into other orthopox viruses (such as smallpox) could have similarly lethal effects.

In another study funded by the US Department of Defense and published in July 2002, researchers from the State University of New York at Stony Brook created an infectious poliovirus 'from scratch', using genomic information available on the internet and custom-made DNA material purchased through the mail (Cello et al, 2002). Eighteen months later under a US Department of Energy grant, US Nobel laureate Hamilton Smith and colleagues reported that they had built a simple artificial virus in a record two weeks' time using commercially available DNA (Smith et al, 2003). These projects have raised concerns about the de novo synthesis of other, far more dangerous, pathogens.

Controversy also has surrounded research done by US army scientists and others with the 1918 influenza virus, which killed an estimated 20–40 million people in a single year. In 1997, researchers at the Armed Forces Institute of Pathology recovered fragments of the 1918 virus from preserved tissue samples. The genome was then sequenced. Since that time, researchers have used reverse genetics to reconstruct the 1918 virus and have done re-assortment studies with segments of the 1918 virus and the H5N1 avian virus (see, for example, Taubenberger et al, 1997; Taubenberger et al, 2005; Tumpey et al, 2005; Kash et al, 2006). Although the stated purpose of such research is to facilitate our understanding of, and preparations for, a future human influenza pandemic, the unintended release of the 1918 virus, or of a new hybrid containing segments of it, or the deliberate misuse of the associated research results could have catastrophic consequences.

This chapter considers how formalized oversight procedures might contribute to efforts to prevent the misuse of biotechnology research, focusing particularly on the US, where some of the most extensive discussion of oversight measures has taken place. It begins by examining the response of key US scientists and the US government to the growing concerns about advances in biotechnology. The chapter then outlines an alternative approach for managing the risks posed by this highly promising field of scientific endeavour. It concludes with a discussion of incremental measures that could help to lay the foundation for this more effective approach.

Confronting the dual use problem?

Spurred on, at least in part, by the mousepox experiment, the US National Academy of Sciences decided in the summer of 2001 to explore the possibility of creating an ad hoc committee to examine the adequacy of US oversight arrangements for dual use biotechnology research. Following the September 2001 terrorist attacks and anthrax mailings, the need for such a committee became even more apparent. In April 2002, the Committee on Research Standards and Practices to Prevent the Destructive Application of Biotechnology, chaired by Massachusetts Institute of Technology Professor Gerald Fink, was established. In October 2003, the Fink Committee, as it became known, issued its report – Biotechnology Research in an Age of Terrorism (NRC, 2003).

The Fink Committee report made two significant contributions to the US debate on dual use research. First, it clearly articulated the threat, stating unequivocally that biotechnology research is dual use and has the capacity 'to cause disruption or harm, potentially on a catastrophic scale' (NRC, 2003, p1). Coming from the pre-eminent scientific advisory body in the US, this was a judgement that could not be taken lightly.

In addition, the Fink Committee report acknowledged a serious gap in the existing domestic US and international oversight arrangements for dual use research. As the report made clear, current regulation of biotechnology research is concerned primarily with protecting laboratory workers and the environment from dangerous pathogens, or with preventing unauthorized access to such pathogens. Only very limited efforts have been made thus far to ensure that legitimate research does not lead to destructive consequences.

To help fill this gap, the Fink Committee made three recommendations. The first was to add seven types of 'experiments of concern' to the National Institutes of Health Guidelines for Research Involving Recombinant DNA Molecules (NIH Guidelines) – the oversight process that has been in place in the US since the 1970s to ensure the safety of recombinant DNA research. Specifically, the Fink Committee called for prior review of any experiment that would:

- demonstrate how to render a vaccine ineffective;
- confer resistance to antibiotics or antiviral agents;
- enhance the virulence of a pathogen or render a non-pathogen virulent;
- increase the transmissibility of a pathogen;
- alter the host range of a pathogen;
- enable evasion of diagnosis or detection methods; or
- enable the weaponization of a biological agent or toxin (NRC, 2003, pp4–6).

The purpose of this review is to consider whether the risks associated with the proposed research and its potential for misuse outweigh the potential scientific or medical benefits.

The committee also recommended the creation of an International Forum on Biosecurity to develop and promote harmonized national, regional and international measures for addressing the dual use issue, including systems for reviewing and overseeing relevant research. As the committee's report explained: 'Any serious attempt to reduce the risks associated with biotechnology ultimately must be international in scope because the technologies that could be misused are available and being developed throughout the globe' (NRC, 2003, p10).

Finally, the Fink Committee called for the establishment of a National Science Advisory Board for Biodefense to provide advice on the new domestic US and international oversight efforts, as well as on education and training programmes for scientists and other self-governance mechanisms (NRC, 2003, pp7–8).[2]

In March 2004, the Bush administration responded to the Fink Committee report, announcing the creation of a new body to advise US government agencies on how to reduce the risk that legitimate biological research will be misused for hostile purposes (US Department of Health and Human Services, 2004). The charter establishing this new body, known as the National Science Advisory Board for Biosecurity (NSABB), made clear that its advice is to apply to US government-conducted or supported dual use biological research only (Secretary of Health and Human Services, 2004). Classified research is also outside its purview.[3]

Notwithstanding the 2004 announcement, it took more than a year for the Bush administration to select the members of the NSABB and for the board to hold its first meeting. At this event in June 2005, the NSABB agreed to establish working groups in five initial areas: criteria for dual use research; communication of research results; codes of conduct; international collaboration; and synthetic genomics. A sixth working group, on oversight of dual use research, was finally added a year later at the board's July 2006 meeting.[4]

At first glance, both the Fink Committee's recommendations and the efforts being undertaken by the NSABB seem to be an effective response to the challenges posed by advances in biotechnology. But on closer examination, both fall short in a number of important respects. First, both fail to include key segments of the biotechnology research community in their oversight arrangements. The Fink Committee has recommended adding experiments of concern to the NIH Guidelines. But only institutions that receive funding from the National Institutes of Health (NIH) for recombinant DNA research are required to adhere to the guidelines. This means that research at most US government and private labs would be outside the scope of any dual use oversight requirement under the Fink Committee's approach. The NSABB's oversight arrangements would go somewhat further in that dual use life sciences research at US government labs, or which is funded by the US government at private labs, would be covered. In a draft report in April 2007, the NSABB oversight working group recommended extending oversight still further to include all research at US government labs doing dual use research and at private labs receiving US government funding for dual use research (NSABB, 2007, p11). But even if this recommendation is adopted, this would still leave dual use research at private labs not receiving US government funding for such research, as well as classified research at both US government and private labs, outside the scope of the NSABB's proposed oversight plan.

Second, neither the Fink Committee approach nor that of the NSABB is legally binding. As the name implies, the NIH Guidelines, which are central to the Fink Committee's research oversight proposal, are exactly that: guidelines for researchers to follow when conducting certain types of recombinant DNA research. They have no legal effect. NIH can suspend, limit or deny funding for recombinant DNA research to any institution that fails to comply with the guidelines, or can require the institution to obtain NIH approval for other recombinant DNA research. But it is not clear whether this ever has been done. The NSABB, likewise, is developing guidelines for oversight of dual use research; nothing in the materials prepared either by the board or by its working groups thus far suggests that its proposed oversight arrangements will be legally based. Instead, in its April 2007 draft, the NSABB oversight working group appeared to draw from the NIH Guidelines enforcement procedures, proposing that compliance with guidelines for dual use research might be made a term and condition of funding. The working group also held out the hope that institutions not covered by the dual use guidelines would comply voluntarily (NSABB, 2007, p11).

Whether oversight arrangements that do not have the force of law will be adhered to is open to doubt. In a study published in October 2004, the Sunshine Project revealed numerous instances of non-compliance by US institutions with a cornerstone of the NIH Guidelines – the requirement to establish and operate a local body, known as an Institutional Biosafety Committee (IBC), to review recombinant DNA research projects. According to this study, scores of US biotechnology companies (including some three dozen companies conducting bio-defence research for the US government) had no IBC registered with NIH, and many of the US university and other IBCs that were registered either did not meet or issued blanket approvals, rather than review each specific research project (Sunshine Project, 2004).

Third, both the Fink Committee and the NSABB have limited their oversight proposals to the US. Although the Fink Committee called for the creation of an international biosecurity forum to help harmonize oversight arrangements nationally, regionally and internationally, its actual oversight proposal has a distinctly national focus. The NSABB has given even less attention to the international dimension of the dual use issue, setting its sights, at least thus far, on 'awareness-building' and 'information-sharing' at the international level (NSABB, 2007, pp29–30). Perhaps this should not be surprising considering the mandate given to each group; but as the mousepox experiment showed, the relevant research community is globally distributed. Of the nearly 14,000 manuscripts submitted to the American Society for Microbiology's 11 peer-reviewed journals in 2002, about 60 per cent included non-US authors from at least 100 different countries.[5] The adoption of a dual use oversight system in the US alone risks putting US researchers at a competitive disadvantage vis-à-vis their counterparts in other countries. It will also, in the words of the Fink Committee report, 'afford little protection if it is not adopted internationally' (NRC, 2003, p86).

An alternative approach

Even before the emergence of the Fink Committee report and the establishment of the NSABB, the Center for International and Security Studies at Maryland (CISSM) was pursuing a different approach to the problem of dual use biotechnology research. In a study first published in September 2003, CISSM outlined a prototype protective oversight system that applies comprehensively to all institutions conducting relevant research, whether government, private sector or academic, is legally binding and is international in scope.[6]

This prototype, known as the Biological Research Security System, includes two key elements. The first is national licensing of relevant personnel and research facilities. The personnel licensing requirement would extend to all scientists, students and technical staff proposing to conduct research covered by the oversight system. The purpose of the licensing would be to ensure that the affected individuals are technically qualified, have undertaken biosecurity training (and thus have been sensitized to the dual use potential of their work and educated about both national and international oversight rules) and have nothing in their background (such as a past biosafety violation) that would make it inappropriate for them to conduct consequential research. Receipt of a personnel license would be viewed as an acknowledgment of the individual's special status within his or her broader professional community. The facility licensing requirement would extend to all facilities where relevant research takes place, and would be designed to ensure that such facilities meet existing safety and security standards.[7]

Similar processes are already being used in advanced biology to ensure that certain individuals and facilities meet specified security and safety requirements. For example, under bioterrorism legislation and regulations adopted in the US, background checks are required on any individual having access to certain dangerous pathogens and toxins (designated as 'select agents'), and relevant facilities must be registered.[8] Various regulations in the US and other countries also require licensing of facilities that produce drugs and other products derived from biotechnology to ensure their safety and efficacy. Outside of biology, there are other examples of licensing requirements for individuals and facilities engaged in activities that could affect substantial numbers of people – such as doctors, or laboratories that work with radioactive materials.

The second element is independent peer review of relevant projects prior to their initiation. Any individual interested in conducting research covered by the oversight system would be required to provide information about their proposed project to an independent oversight body for review and approval.[9] This is consistent with the Fink Committee approach, which recommended using local IBCs for the initial review of experiments of concern. Unfortunately, the NSABB oversight working group appears to be disregarding this advice and is instead proposing, at least for now, to rely upon individual researchers to evaluate the dual use potential of their own research (NSABB, 2007, p10). In addition to having a self-interest in seeing their research proceed, such individuals are also unlikely to have the security and other expertise necessary to recognize the possible dual use risks of their work.

As with national licensing, precedents for independent peer review of consequential research can also be found. Within the US, review bodies already exist at the local level for research involving recombinant DNA techniques, human subjects and animals. Nationally, the Recombinant DNA Advisory Committee (RAC) exercises oversight over two particular categories of recombinant DNA research. Internationally, a special committee of the World Health Organization has been given responsibility for reviewing and approving smallpox research at the two designated repositories for the smallpox virus in the US and Russia.

Extensive research and consultations with scientists both in the US and in other countries were carried out by CISSM to develop illustrative categories of research activities for dual use oversight purposes.[10] A key consideration in developing these categories was the extent to which the research in question has the potential to expose very large numbers of people to lethal or otherwise debilitating effects. That is not to say that research that could affect smaller numbers of people is not important. But if the oversight system captures too broad a swath of research, the process will be unwieldy and research with the greatest destructive potential may not be reviewed promptly or effectively.

The resulting categorization developed by CISSM has a number of important features. First, it is narrowly focused in that only the most consequential types of dual use research are included. Most biomedical and agricultural research would be outside the oversight requirements. Second, it can be readily implemented in that the types of research that must be peer reviewed are clearly defined and presented. Researchers would be able to determine easily whether and, if so, where their proposed work falls within the oversight system and therefore what steps they must take to meet their peer review obligations. This is critical for any oversight system that is legally binding. Third, it is responsive to the threat in that it covers not just specific pathogens, but also the research techniques applied to those pathogens. In so doing, CISSM's proposal combines the best of the agent-based controls enacted by the US in 2002 and of the activity-based approach reflected in the Fink Committee's proposed experiments of concern. Finally, it is based on a tiered design in that the level of risk determines the level of oversight. As discussed below, most research would be reviewed locally at the institutional level, with a smaller subset of research considered at a higher level. This categorization is reflected in Table 7.1.

At the top of the CISSM oversight system there would be a global standard-setting and review body or International Pathogens Research Authority.[11] This new body would be responsible for overseeing and approving activities of extreme concern – research with the most dangerous pathogens or that could result in pathogens significantly more dangerous than those which currently exist. This would include work with an eradicated agent such as smallpox or the construction of an antibiotic- or vaccine-resistant controlled agent, as was done during the Soviet offensive biological weapons programme.

Table 7.1 *Illustrative categories of research activities*

Activities of extreme concern (AECs)
• Work with eradicated agent*
• Work with agent assigned as BSL-4/ABSL-4
• De novo synthesis of above
• Expanding host range of agent to new host (in humans, other animals and plants) or changing the tissue range of a listed agent**
• Construction of antibiotic- or vaccine-resistant listed agent

Activities of moderate concern (AMCs)
• Increasing virulence of listed agent or related agent
• Insertion of host genes into listed agent or related agent
• Increasing transmissibility or environmental stability of listed agent or related agent
• Powder or aerosol production of listed agent or related agent
• Powder or aerosol dispersal of listed agent or related agent
• De novo synthesis of listed agent or related agent
• Construction of antibiotic- or vaccine-resistant related agent
• Genome transfer, genome replacement or cellular reconstitution of listed agent or related agent

Table 7.1 *continued*

Activities of potential concern (APCs)

- Work with listed agent – or exempt avirulent, attenuated or vaccine strain of a listed agent – not covered by AECs and AMCs
- Increasing virulence of non-listed agent
- Increasing transmissibility or environmental stability of non-listed agent
- Powder or aerosol production of non-listed agent
- Powder or aerosol dispersal of non-listed agent
- De novo synthesis of non-listed agent
- Genome transfer, genome replacement or cellular reconstitution of non-listed agent

---

Notes: * This would include, for example, activities with the 1918 influenza virus and chimeric influenza viruses with at least one gene from the 1918 influenza virus.

** This would include, for example, activities with chimeric influenza viruses with at least one gene from a human influenza virus and at least one gene from an avian influenza virus.

Table key:

Agent: fungus, protozoan, bacterium or archaeon, virus, viroid or prion; or genetic element, recombinant nucleic acid or recombinant organism.

Listed agent: select agents or toxins regulated by the Centers for Disease Control and Prevention (CDC) and Animal and Plant Health Inspection Service (APHIS).

Related agent: for fungi, protozoans, or bacteria or archaea, an agent that currently is, or during the last two years was, assigned to the same genus as a listed agent; for viruses, viroids or prions, an agent that currently is, or during the last two years was, assigned to the same family as a listed agent; for genetic elements, recombinant nucleic acids or recombinant organisms, an agent orthologous to a listed agent (this category includes any avirulent, attenuated or vaccine strain of a listed agent, if said strain is exempt under the CDC or APHIS regulations.

Non-listed agent: agent other than a listed agent or related agent.

Eradicated agent: agent previously in circulation in nature, but not within the last decade, as determined by human, animal or plant cases, or by isolation from humans, animals or plants, or by detection of antibodies to the agent from individuals younger than the time span elapsed since the last recorded isolation.

De novo synthesis: construction of agent using synthetic genomic nucleic acid (non-prion agents) or synthetic protein (prions), irrespective of whether said construction requires additional reagents, extracts, cells or 'helper' entities. For the purposes of this definition, 'synthetic genomic nucleic acid' refers to nucleic acid that corresponds to an agent genome and that is prepared using, in any step or set of steps, chemically synthesized oligonucleotides corresponding to at least 5 per cent of said agent genome.

Antibiotic: antibiotic of therapeutic utility against listed agent.

Vaccine: vaccine of therapeutic utility against listed agent.

Powder: powder other than lyophilized reference specimen (<10 milligrams).

Source: Center for International and Security Studies at Maryland

In addition to overseeing research activities of extreme concern, the global body would also be responsible for defining the research activities subject to oversight under the different categories and establishing standards for review and reporting. It would also develop rules to protect against the misuse of information reported as part of the oversight process. The global body would also help national governments and local review bodies to meet their oversight obligations by, for example, providing software and technical support for a secure data management system and by assisting in achieving international standards for good laboratory practices. This will be particularly important for developing countries, many of which have neither the biosafety rules nor the institutional mechanisms that could provide the basis for dual use oversight efforts. No existing organization currently fulfils all of these functions. The closest model is WHO, which not only oversees one specific type of highly consequential research, but also has developed international guidelines for laboratory biosafety and biosecurity.

At the next level there would be a national review body or National Pathogens Research Authority. This body is analogous to the RAC in the US. It would be responsible for overseeing activities of moderate concern – research that involves pathogens or toxins already identified as public health threats, especially research that increases the weaponization potential of such agents. This would include research that increases the transmissibility or environmental stability of a controlled agent or that involves production of such an agent in powder or aerosol form, which are the most common means of disseminating biological warfare agents. The national body would also be responsible for overseeing the work of local review bodies, including licensing qualified researchers and facilities, and for interacting with the global body.

At the foundation of the oversight system there would be a local review body or Local Pathogens Research Committee. This committee is analogous to the review bodies at universities and elsewhere in the US that currently oversee recombinant DNA, human and animal research. It would be responsible for overseeing activities of potential concern – research that increases the potential for otherwise benign pathogens to be used as a weapon or that demonstrates techniques that could have destructive applications. This would include research that increases the virulence of a pathogen or that involves the de novo synthesis of a pathogen, as was done in the poliovirus experiment. Under the CISSM approach, the vast majority of microbiological research would either fall into this category or not be covered at all.

To ensure equitable treatment of all proposed research projects both within and between the different oversight levels, common criteria would be needed by the relevant review bodies for use in assessing the potential benefits of the work, as well as the possible risks.[12] A comparable risk–benefit assessment process currently is used in the US for reviewing human subject research. As in the review process for human subject research, the risk–benefit assessment of dual use biological research would apply to all relevant research, irrespective of whether it is carried out in a government, private sector or academic lab. In addition, the relevant review body would be required to consider certain issues as part of its deliberations and to document the discussion of those issues, as well as its overall risk–benefit assessment in its meeting minutes.

Based on a peer review simulation exercise of five hypothetical research projects,[13] CISSM developed dual use risk–benefit assessment criteria analogous to those used for human subject research. The first two issue areas, which focus on biosafety and the details of the proposed research plan, concern the conduct of the work. The remaining four issue areas relate to the justification for the work and cover public health, bio-defence, current necessity and potential impact. Similar issues and questions have been suggested by the British Royal Society for assessing dual use research (Royal Society, 2005). CISSM's proposed risk-benefit assessment criteria are listed in Table 7.2.

As these criteria show, meaningful peer review would require the disclosure of detailed information to the relevant review body to use in assessing the potential benefits and risks of the proposed experiment. In rare cases, the review body might decide to approve a proposed project but to restrict the dissemination of information about the project or its results. This would require agreed guidelines for determining whether and under what circumstances information might have to be restricted or even possibly classified. It would also require an agreed process for determining who could be given access to controlled information.[14]

Table 7.2 Notional risk–benefit assessment criteria

Biosafety issues

I   Does the proposed research plan contain appropriate protections to minimize risk to the public or environment?
   • Proposals receiving a 'no' answer would have a low biosafety rating.

Evaluation of research plan

I   Are the proposed research plan and the stated rationale for the work consistent with one another?
2   Are the risks posed by the agent (either from a public health perspective or bioterrorism perspective) and the stated rationale for the work consistent with one another?
3   Is the proposed research plan logically sequenced?
4   Are there scientific reasons why the same outcome cannot be pursued through alternative means – for example, by using alternative methods (e.g. in vitro versus in vivo) or alternative materials (e.g. non-pathogenic versus pathogenic strains)?
   • Proposals receiving two or more 'no' answers would have a low research plan evaluation rating.

Public health considerations

I   Do agents to be constructed, or equivalent agents, currently exist in nature?
2   If not, are said agents expected to be generated by natural processes?
3   Will the research advance our understanding of the disease-causing properties of currently existing agents?
   • Proposals receiving 'no' answers either to questions I and 2 or to question 3 would have low public health rationale.

Table 7.2 *continued*

Bio-defence considerations

1 Do agents to be constructed, or equivalent agents, currently exist in other facilities?
2 If not, is the work being done in response to a 'validated threat' (i.e. one for which there is credible information) or 'theoretical' threat (i.e. one that is possible but for which there is no credible information)?
3 Will the countermeasures that are expected to result from the work significantly reduce the threat posed by the agent?
   • Proposals receiving two or more 'no' answers would have a low bio-defence rationale.

Current necessity

1 Are countermeasures against agents to be constructed, or equivalent agents, currently unavailable?
2 Are there scientific reasons why countermeasures cannot be developed without access to such agents?
   • Proposals receiving one or more 'no' answers would be of limited current necessity.

Potential impact

1 Will the proposed research contribute to new knowledge (e.g. by furthering our understanding of basic life processes or of pathogenesis) rather than primarily confirm work already done?
2 Are the research results likely to be definitive enough to inform policy decisions (e.g. on vaccination strategy)?
3 Are there significant obstacles to using the research results to develop a more dangerous pathogen or to overcome current countermeasures?
   • Proposals with two or more 'no' answers would have a limited positive impact.

Source: Center for International and Security Studies at Maryland

To address this issue, CISSM proposed building upon the ideas outlined in an earlier report from a US National Academy of Sciences panel on scientific communication and national security chaired by former Cornell University President Dale Corson. The Corson Report, as it is known, concluded that US welfare, including US national security, is best served by allowing the free flow of all scientific and technical information 'not directly and significantly connected with technology critical to national security'. Accordingly, the report recommended that most fundamental research at universities should be unclassified; that a limited amount might require classification; and that a small grey area could require limited restrictions short of classification. It also suggested criteria for making classification decisions (NAS, 1982).[15]

Drawing on the criteria in the Corson Report, CISSM proposed that no restrictions should be placed on basic or applied biotechnology research or research results at university, private sector or government labs unless all of the following criteria are met:

- The technology is developing rapidly and the time from basic science to application is short.
- The technology has identifiable direct military applications, or it is dual use and involves process- or production-related technologies.
- The transfer of technology would give a biological weapons proliferator (e.g. national or sub-national level) a significant near-term capability.
- There are no other sources of information about the technology, or all of those that could also be the source have effective systems for securing the information.
- The duration and nature of the proposed restrictions would not seriously compromise the work of those directly responsible for public health.

The requirement to take account of the public health implications of any proposed restrictions was not part of the original Corson panel approach. But because legitimate applications of biotechnology research could have a profound impact on public health, considering only the security implications of such research would be insufficient. For similar reasons, in situations where certain research results might need to be restricted, individuals with a legitimate need to know for research or public health purposes would have access to the relevant information.

To help protect against the unauthorized release of information, as well as to facilitate the peer review process, CISSM proposed the use of advanced information technology at each level of the oversight system. To illustrate how this might be done, a prototype data management system was built using open-source software and financial-grade security standards. The system has a tree-like structure in which each oversight node (i.e. local institutions, national authorities and the international body) would operate its own secure server for storing information under its jurisdiction. In a fully developed data management system, information required for licensing and peer review would be collected using questionnaires that meet dual use reporting requirements as well as other reporting requirements, such as those required for human subject or animal research.[16]

Next steps

A key issue both in the Fink Committee report and in the deliberations of the NSABB is the potential impact of new oversight requirements on the conduct of dual use biotechnology research in the US. To help address this issue, particularly the possible impact of its proposed oversight system, CISSM commissioned a survey of scientific journal articles published in the US between

2000 and mid 2005 (Kuhn, 2005).[17] The survey indicated that less than 1 per cent of US publications concerning bacteria, viruses or prions involved research that would have been subject to oversight had CISSM's proposed system been in effect. Overall, based on their publications, some 310 US facilities and 2574 US scientists engaged in research activities that fell within CISSM's system. Among those that would have been affected, only 12 of the facilities and 185 of the individuals would have been subject to international oversight – a tiny fraction of the American biotechnology research community. Fourteen facilities and 133 individuals would have been subject to national oversight; and 231 facilities involving 2119 individuals would have been subject to local oversight. Fifty-three facilities and 137 individuals would have encountered multiple oversight levels. Those numbers suggest that the development of local and national oversight arrangements could begin to cover much of the research that would fall within CISSM's more comprehensive, legally binding and globally harmonized system and could help to lay the foundation for the eventual adoption of such a system. Other measures could do the same, some of which are already being undertaken.[18]

For example, individual scientists and professional scientific organizations have been discussing applicable scientific codes (Rappert, 2004; Royal Society, 2005; see also Chapter 1 in this volume). Much of this discussion is focused on ethical codes, which describe personal and professional standards, or codes of conduct, which provide guidelines on appropriate behaviour. Virtually no attention is being given to codes of practice, which outline enforceable procedures and rules. In November 2005, the InterAcademy Panel on International Issues released a set of general principles to guide the development of codes of conduct by individual scientists and local scientific communities (IAP, 2005). In its initial work, the NSABB has outlined various considerations that professional societies and others could draw upon in developing a code of conduct for scientists and laboratory workers.

But it is not enough to simply have scientific codes, whatever the type. Both students and established scientists must be educated about the details of such codes and the potential for misuse of their work. They must also be informed about relevant laws and regulations governing the conduct of dual use research and be provided with training to enable them to meet the oversight requirements that are in place (see Chapter 3 in this volume).

These initiatives could be significantly reinforced if scientific funding agencies and journals required all of those with whom they interact on a professional basis to explicitly consider the dual use implications of their work, and if all research institutions made this a condition of employment. In September 2005, the UK's three leading bioresearch funding agencies, the Medical Research Council (2005), the Wellcome Trust and the Biotechnology and Biological Sciences Research Council, announced that they would now require grant applicants, reviewers and funding agency board members to consider whether the proposed research could be misused for harmful purposes.[19]

In addition to these measures, other interim steps could be taken by national governments that could more directly strengthen oversight of dual use research.

As suggested above, the US and other countries that follow the NIH Guidelines or similar oversight processes for recombinant DNA research could include specified dual use research activities in their national regulations and require mandatory adherence by all facilities undertaking such work. These national standards and regulations could then be harmonized among like-minded countries, perhaps beginning with the 30 nations that comprise the Organisation for Economic Co-operation and Development (OECD). This would be consistent with the OECD's efforts since 2001 to develop a harmonized approach to the management and security of culture collections and other biological resources, as well as its more recent interest in promoting responsible stewardship in the biological sciences and preventing the abuse of research (OECD, 2007). The OECD could develop a uniform list of dual use research activities to be subject to oversight, as well as standardized criteria for assessing the risks and benefits of such research. It could also establish a process for periodic reporting on national implementation of these measures by OECD member states.

Efforts such as this by the OECD or other like-minded countries could be facilitated by the WHO, which has a long history of providing technical information, guidance and assistance to the public, healthcare professionals and policy-makers on the control of dangerous pathogens.[20] In mid 2004, the WHO initiated an exploratory project on the governance of life sciences research and its implications for public health (WHO, 2005). Many of the issues that were highlighted in this exploratory work are now being considered in a new WHO project aimed at examining the implications of life sciences research for global health security (see Chapter 13 in this volume). In addition to raising awareness about the opportunities and risks of life sciences research, this project could also lay the foundation for the development by the WHO and other stakeholders of technical guidelines for overseeing dual use research.[21]

There are thus a variety of incremental steps that can be pursued by scientists, national governments and international organizations to help prevent biotechnology research from leading either inadvertently or deliberately to the creation of new, more destructive, pathogens. None is sufficient; but all of them can help to lay the foundation for the type of comprehensive, legally binding, global system outlined by CISSM.

Notes

1   Portions of this chapter are drawn from Steinbruner and Harris (2003) and Steinbruner et al (2007).
2   The Fink Committee's other recommendations called for educating scientists about the dual use issue and their responsibility to mitigate its risks; reviewing publications for potential national security risks; ensuring adequate controls over access to dangerous pathogens and supervision of personnel working with such materials; and enhancing communication between the life sciences community and the national security and law enforcement communities.
3   Interestingly, this point appears to have been removed from the NSABB website, despite having been included in the original 'Frequently Asked Questions' section of

the website when it was accessed in March 2004.

4. Information on the NSABB's meetings is available on its website, www.biosecurity-board.gov/meetings.asp, accessed in April 2007.

5 Personal communication with Ron Atlas, president of the American Society for Microbiology, February 2003.

6 Successive versions of the study have been posted on the CISSM website since 2003. This chapter is based on the March 2007 version, which is available at www.cissm.umd.edu/papers/files/pathogens_project_monograph.pdf, accessed in April 2007.

7 The licensing process and requirements are discussed in more detail in Steinbruner et al (2007, pp27–28, 37, 67–70).

8 Select agents refer to specific human, plant and animal pathogens whose possession and transfer is regulated by the US government because they can be used for destructive purposes. The laws establishing this requirement and associated regulations are Public Law 107–188, 12 June 2002, 42 Code of Federal Regulations 73, 7 Code of Federal Regulations 331, and 9 Code of Federal Regulations 121.

9 The peer review process is discussed in more detail in Steinbruner et al (2007, pp28–30, 38–43, 71–78).

10 CISSM recognizes, as the Fink Committee did with its proposed experiments of concern, that its categorization is a starting point and that it will need to evolve to keep pace with emerging biological threats. The US select agent list, for example, is used for illustrative purposes only; an internationally agreed list would ultimately need to be developed and maintained.

11 The different research categories and corresponding oversight process are discussed in more detail in Steinbruner et al (2007, pp25, 37–43).

12 The risk-benefit assessment process is discussed in more detail in Steinbruner et al (2007, pp28–30).

13 The projects that were peer reviewed are Cloning of MHC I Immunomodulators into Vaccinia Virus; Enhancement of Virulence and Transmissibility of Influenza Virus; Immunosuppression and Immuno-transition in Plague-mouse Model; Manipulation of Temperate Sensitivity in Pospiviroidae; and Exploring New Non-lethal Incapacitation Options.

14 The issue of information disclosure is discussed in more detail in Steinbruner et al (2007, pp29, 31–32).

15 The rationale for using the Corson Report criteria is discussed in more detail in Steinbruner et al (2007, pp43–45).

16 The data management system is discussed in more detail in Steinbruner et al (2007, pp82–88).

17 As the working paper makes clear, these are rough estimates only: the author did not screen for all of the categories of research involving non-listed agents because of the overall number of papers and the absence of a suitable search strategy. The figures also do not reflect the broader definition of de novo synthesis used in the more recent version of CISSM's research categories table. At the same time, the author almost certainly included some scientists and facilities that were part of research projects outside of the US simply because they were American or affiliated with an American research facility. Although it is difficult to estimate, these factors could well increase the number of projects subject to local oversight, in particular, by 100 or more (see Kuhn, 2005).

18 For a more detailed discussion of these incremental measures, see Steinbruner et al (2007, pp45–48).

19 The Medical Research Council (MRC) appears to be using the Fink Committee's seven experiments of concern to define the types of research that should be reviewed for dual use risks; but it is unclear whether the other UK funding agencies are taking a similar approach. The MRC statement is at www.mrc.ac.uk/doc-bioterrorism_biomedical_research.doc, accessed in April 2007.
20 For information on the WHO's activities on the health aspects of biological weapons, see www.who.int/csr/delibepidemics/en/, accessed in April 2007.
21 This also was one of the priority areas identified by a scientific working group convened by the WHO in October 2006 (see WHO, 2007).

References

Cello, J., Paul, A.V., and Wimmer, E. (2002) 'Chemical synthesis of poliovirus cDNA: Generation of infectious virus in the absence of natural template,' *Sciencexpress*, 11 July, pp1016–1018

IAP (InterAcademy Panel on International Issues) (2005) IAP Statement on Biosecurity, 7 November, www.interacademies.net/Object.File/Master/5/399/ Biosecurity%20St.. pdf, accessed in April 2007

Jackson, R. J., Ramsay, A. J., Christensen, C. D., Beaton, S., Hall, D. F. and Ramshaw, I. A. (2001) 'Expression of mouse interleukin-4 by a recombinant Ectromelia virus suppresses Cytolytic lymphocyte responses and overcomes genetic resistance to mousepox,' *Journal of Virology*, February, pp1205–1210

Kash, J. C., Tumpey, T. M., Proll, S. C., Carter, V., Perwitasari, O., Thomas, M. J., Basler, C. F., Palese, P., Taubenberger, J. K., Garcia-Sastre, A., Swayne, D. E., Katze, M. G. (2006) 'Genomic analysis of increased host immune and cell death responses induced by 1918 influenza virus,' *Nature*, vol 443, 5 October, pp578–81

Kuhn, J. H. (2005) 'Qualitative and Quantitative Assessment of the "Dangerous Activities" Categories Defined by the CISSM Controlling Dangerous Pathogens Project', CISSM Working Paper, December, Maryland, CISSM

MacKenzie, D. (2003) 'US develops lethal new viruses', *New Scientist*, 29 October, pp6–7

MRC (Medical Research Council) (2005) Organizations Address Biomedical Research Misuse Threat, Media Release, 8 September, www.mrc.ac.uk/prn/public-press_08_sept_2005, accessed in April 2007

NAS (National Academies of Science) (1982) *Scientific Communication and National Security*, Washington, DC, NAS, www.nap.edu/books/0309033322/html/, accessed in April 2007

NRC (National Research Council) (2003) *Biotechnology Research in an Age of Terrorism*, Washington, DC, NRC

NSABB (National Science Advisory Board for Biosecurity) (2007) 'Draft Report of the NSABB Working Group on Oversight Framework Development', 11 April, www.biosecurityboard.gov/NSABB%20Draft%20DUR%20Ov%20Framewk8%20fo r%20public%20posting%20041907%20mtg2.pdf, accessed in April 2007

OECD (Organisation for Economic Co-operation and Development) (2007) *OECD Best Practice Guidelines for Biological Resource Centres*, DSTI/STP/BIO (2007)9FINAL, 5 April, Paris, OECD

Rappert, B. (2004) 'Towards a Life Sciences Code: Countering the Threat from Biological Weapons', Bradford Briefing Paper, 2nd series, no 13

Royal Society (2005) 'The Roles of Codes of Conduct in Preventing the Misuse of

Scientific Research', Royal Society Policy Document 03/05, June, www.royalsoc. ac.uk/displaypagedoc.asp?id=13648, accessed in April 2007

Secretary of Health and Human Services (2004) 'Charter: National Science Advisory Board for Biosecurity', 4 March, www.biosecurityboard.gov/ SIGNED%20NSABB %20Charter.pdf, accessed in April 2007

Smith, H. O., Hutchison, C. A., Pfannkoch, C. and Venter, J. C. (2003) 'Generating a synthetic genome by whole genome assembly: {phi}X174 bacteriophage from synthetic oglionucleotides', Proceedings of the National Academy of Sciences, 23 December, pp15440–15445

Steinbruner, J. D. and Harris, E. D. (2003) 'Controlling dangerous pathogens,' *Issues in Science and Technology*, spring, pp47–54

Steinbruner, J. D, Harris, E. D., Gallagher, N. and Okutani, S. (2007) 'Controlling Dangerous Pathogens: A Prototype Protective Oversight System', March, www.cissm.umd.edu/papers/files/pathogens_project_monograph.pdf, accessed in April 2007

Sunshine Project (2004) 'Mandate for Failure: The State of Institutional Biosafety Committees in an Age of Biological Weapons Research', October, www.sunshine-project.org/biodefense/tspibc.pdf, accessed in April 2007

Taubenberger, J., Reid, A. H., Krafft, A. E., Bijwaard, K. E. and Fanning, T. G. (1997) 'Initial genetic characterization of the 1918 "Spanish" influenza virus', *Science*, vol 275, 21 March, pp1793–1796

Taubenberger, J., Reid, A. H., Lourens, R. M., Wang, R. and Fanning, T. G. (2005) 'Characterization of the 1918 influenza virus polymerase gene', *Nature*, vol 437, 6 October, pp889–893

Tumpey, T. M., Basler, C. F., Aguilar, P. V., Zeng, H., Solorzano, A., Swayne, D. E., Cox, N. J., Katz, J. M., Taubenberger, J. K., Palese, P. and Garcia-Sastre, A. (2005) 'Characterization of the reconstructed 1918 Spanish influenza pandemic virus', *Science*, vol 310, 7 October, pp77–80

US Department of Health and Human Services (2004) 'HHS Will Lead Government-wide Effort to Enhance Biosecurity in "Dual-use" Research', Press release, 4 March, www.biosecurityboard.gov/NSABB_press_release.pdf, accessed in April 2007

WHO (World Health Organization) (2005) *Life Sciences Research: Opportunities and Risks for Public Health*, WHO/CDS/CSR/LYO/2005.20

WHO (2007) *Scientific Working Group on Life Science Research and Global Health Security, Report of the First Meeting*, WHO/CDS/EPR/2007.4

8

Reflections on the Role of Research Oversight in a Web of Prevention

Thomas V. Holohan

In her contribution in Chapter 7, Elisa Harris of the Center for International and Security Studies at Maryland (CISSM) proposed a system of tiered oversight of research involving dangerous pathogens. Four major components comprise this model: the evaluation is mandatory; there are processes for national and local review of research proposals; studies judged to be of the highest risk are referred for international review; and licensing or registration of researchers and facilities is required.

This is a novel and reasonable proposal directed towards preventing the harmful use of biological organisms, whether intentional or inadvertent, and is analogous to the precedent international cooperative agreement of the Biological Weapons Convention that is focused upon deliberate misuse of organisms and agents. It may be argued that sovereign states would perceive international oversight as having the potential to adversely affect their national interest; but a more basic question is whether all societies would be better served by the presence or absence of such agreed upon procedures, however imperfect or uncomfortable they might be.

Harris provides a concise and accurate view of the current state of international and national oversight, emphasizing the US domestic processes and procedures. In the latter, the focus has been on possession, transfer and biosafety of specific agents, as opposed to particular categories of research procedures. She would reserve review of research by an international body to those studies of 'extreme concern'. Such studies could focus upon agents such as those previously eradicated, newly created organisms or agents with engineered resistance to preventive or therapeutic interventions; but all would possess the potential for rapidly causing injury or death to very large numbers of people. Other research that could be misused for harmful purposes but would result in lesser degrees of damage are defined as of moderate or of potential concern, and are subject to national or local review, respectively. Harris identifies research activities of moderate concern and, thus, subject to national review as including listed controlled agents (e.g. the *Select Agent List* of the US and the *Pathogen Control List* of the UK). In this model, the research oversight associated with the several levels of concern is directly related to specific characteristics of the particular organisms under study, either natural or induced. These are further modified by the nature of the research procedures employed (e.g. production of vaccine- or antibiotic-resistant organisms) and by an assessment of the degree of overall risk.

This paradigm offers the potential to address some of the limitations of the BWC regarding what is compatible with developing, producing, stockpiling or otherwise acquiring agents and toxins 'for prophylactic, protective or other peaceful purposes', as well as the lack of application of the BWC to 'research' itself (as opposed to development). The model can do this by applying a review process to research proposals irrespective of the stated or presumed purpose. The work covered under the BWC is based upon the intention of the investigators, rather than upon the danger of the technology itself. Rules of evidence allowing a presumption of intent have a long history in law; but in a research plan, intent is nearly always opaque to a reviewing body (assuming there is one).

There are certain points in the Maryland proposal that may benefit from additional development and clarification, including the specific categorization of organisms as appropriate for assignment to the several levels of review. The major differentiation between national versus international review of research seems to be work involving organisms designated as 'identified public health threats' as opposed to those of 'extreme concern'. The descriptors of identified public health threats are listed or select agents. However, some believe that the current listings of controlled agents (e.g. the *Select Agent List* of the US and the *Pathogen Control Lists* of the UK) are insufficiently discriminative with respect to the degree of harm that might result from dissemination or malicious use of the various listed agents. For instance, Relman (2006) noted that the policy of ascribing threats to only a few agents is misleading, predates the current state of knowledge in molecular biology, and that the use of 'threat lists' is imprudent. Consequently, a means of distinction beyond public health threats or select agent listing could be necessary.

Another point at issue is that limiting international oversight to circumstances meeting the definition of extreme concern appears to exclude agents that are not transmissible. While the proposed international review process is arguably inclusive of the most dangerous agents with the intrinsic capacity to effect catastrophic harm, lesser but still quite profound effects may result from malicious employment of biologicals with lower threat potential. This is particularly true with respect to terrorist actions that have often been characterized by levels of harm disproportionately greater than the actual morbidity or mortality inflicted upon a target population, where severe collateral destructive consequences may be generated in economic, political, social and psychological spheres. A recent report of the Weapons of Mass Destruction Commission concluded that approaches to countering bioterrorism have been inadequate and complicated by political or parochial concerns. It recommended that bioterrorism should be addressed on a comprehensive basis, including the appreciation that such behaviour seeks to achieve a wider variety of outcomes than mass casualties (Ackerman and Moran, 2004). These considerations seem to place a great responsibility on the proposed national review process.

The prescribed assessment of risks and benefits of proposed research is reasonable, and having participated in the cited CISSM simulation exercise of hypothetical research projects, I believe it to have been an intriguing and informative process. However, the proposed risk assessment process is focused upon responses to questions that require value judgements of the investigators who may not be in the best position to act dispassionately. This approach differs from the formal methodological approaches of many conventionally recommended risk assessment procedures (*vide infra*). However, the complexities of traditional risk assessment or risk–benefit analyses add a significant level of intricacy and may make this difficult for local review bodies. More importantly, without a formal system of monitoring local review, its application may be problematic. As Harris noted in Chapter 7, the process of review of recombinant DNA research by Institutional Biosafety Committees (IBCs) in the US has been challenging. Some observers have alleged significant failures of IBC effectiveness, transparency and oversight (Sunshine Project, 2004). Whether or not this is an accurate evaluation of IBC performance, the process of assigning review responsibilities – including risk assessment or risk–benefit analyses – to local committees whose judgements could determine referral to an international body will benefit from formally established oversight of their work. Monitoring should include integrated mechanisms for independent evaluation of effectiveness, timeliness and defensibility of their recommendations.

The Maryland group proposed to accomplish a review at the national level through a National Pathogens Research Authority (NPRA). The composition of the authority was not specified. In the US, one could speculate its establishment as a group analogous to a committee of the National Academy of Sciences; but to exercise the degree of oversight and monitoring required, some formal association with a government body with regulatory authority seems likely as Harris believes the oversight should have the force of law. However, the effectiveness of the latter approach may be limited, particularly in the event that there are differences between the views of expert life science members or the professional community that they represent, and the policy preferences or intentions of the executive branch or the agency with which the NPRA interacts. At the very least, divergence of opinion, perspective or intention can result in delay and inefficiency of the process.

For example, Harris correctly identified a series of problems in the function of the US National Science Advisory Board for Biosecurity (NSABB). The NSABB was established as a federal advisory committee to provide recommendations to the Department of Health and Human Services (DHHS) regarding oversight and monitoring of life sciences research with the potential for harmful misuse, and to recommend mechanisms for international cooperation in implementing those recommendations. The NSABB charter was signed in March of 2004; but the board's appointment and first meeting was not accomplished by the DHHS until 15 months later, in June 2005. By the summer of 2006, the

NSABB began to submit draft definitions and criteria for identifying dual use research (*vide infra*); these were quite similar to those originally proposed by the National Research Council (NRC, 2003) in their report *Biotechnology Research in An Age of Terrorism*, published two years earlier. Three years after the NSABB charter, no formal recommendations have been forwarded and accepted for implementation by the DHHS. This protracted process has been cited by, for example, Leitenberg (2005) as evidence that the responsibilities of the NSABB were not viewed as a significant priority by the administration. In contrast, the NRC committee was established in April 2002, and a pre-publication copy of its complete report was released and made available in October 2003 (NRC, 2003).

Moreover, the DHHS utilization of the NSABB to review an article on the reconstruction of the 1918 Spanish influenza virus prior to publication in *Science* occasioned an editorial critique (Kennedy, 2005) that questioned government authority to prevent publication of non-classified research and the proper role of this board. Other examples of the tension between the views of government policy-makers and panels of scientific experts include the recent controversy over the White House Office of Management and Budget draft bulletin on technical standards for federal risk assessments. The National Research Council described the document as fundamentally flawed and recommended that it be withdrawn (NRC, 2007).

National licensing of individual researchers will be a very complex process, at least in the US. Harris correctly noted that there is precedent in such matters, including the federal approval of individual researchers for work with 'select agents', the licensing of certain occupations and certification of permission to prescribe controlled narcotic drugs. Likewise, federal oversight is established for institutional activities, such as manufacture of pharmaceuticals and possession and use of radioactive materials. However, the analogy to licensing of physicians fails because in the US, licensing of all health professionals remains solely the authority of the individual states. Establishing federal licensing authority over researchers, technicians and students will require congressional action; likely prerequisites for legislation could include specific definition of those specific professions subject to licensing, precise characterization of the parameters of research subject to the statute, and legally supportable specification of the degree and type of oversight and approval. Researchers in the life sciences may make the case that they should not be uniquely subject to such licensing, but that the process should be extended to the physical sciences as well, and this could add an additional level of collateral complexity to the CISSM proposal.

Harris appropriately presumed the inclusion of life science investigations that are classified and those that are sponsored by industry in this review process. Such work may have a significant impact upon the implementation of international sanction of research involving dangerous organisms; but it may be difficult to impose that control. The US, for example, has a large portfolio of funded bio-defence research that has grown dramatically from 2001 to 2006 (Harris and Steinbruner, 2005; Center for Arms Control and Non-Proliferation, 2006). In 2006, the Department of Homeland Security director of research and development claimed that all such research was defensive in nature and a former assistant secretary of the department was quoted as having said: 'How can I go to the people of this country and say: "I can't do this important research because some arms-control advocate told me I can't"' (Warwick, 2006).

Nevertheless, there remain very different viewpoints on the level of risk for pernicious use of biological material or research findings by terrorist groups or rogue states. The Wellcome Trust (2004) concluded that further investigations on harmful pathogens and toxins were crucial, and that a tangible cause for concern existed in only a small proportion of research. Others have expressed a less sanguine view of the potential risk, and have noted that biological weapons are attractive to terrorists because their manufacture is often simple due to the rapid increase of available information, laboratory facilities and trained personnel (Morenkov, 2002).

In considering the broad application of Harris's proposal, it is helpful to place it within the context of various characterizations of biological investigations that offer the potential for both good and evil, often referred to as 'dual use' research (see Chapter 12 in this volume). This term has been employed in several circumstances. One common usage refers to the application of a technology in both civilian and military settings. Dual use services or processes have been defined in US regulations as those that are capable of meeting requirements for both military and non-military applications (Title 10 United States Code 2500). The European Union controls export of dual use technologies, which are defined as those that can be used for both civil and military purposes (Council Regulation (EC) No 1334/2000). The NRC report recognized the military versus civilian use components of the phrase, but went on to observe that life sciences research has intrinsic potential for good or for malicious purpose (NRC, 2003). By contrast, the BWC exemption of prohibited agents or toxins when they are used for peaceful purposes makes the distinction upon the basis of the intent of the user rather than upon the technology itself.

The NRC noted that there was a need for review incorporating expert scientific judgement of both the risks and the benefits of proposed research believed to have dual use potential, and proposed a reliance on self-regulation by the scientific community supported by a formal system of review similar to that of the Recombinant DNA Advisory Committee in the US. However, the *National Institutes of Health Guidelines* for recombinant DNA research are predicated upon an assumption of beneficent intent and directed towards safeguarding the public and research subjects from accidental or unintentional misadventures, not malevolent use (NIH, 2002). In addition, their oversight is limited to federally funded research and their enforcement to recommendations related to that funding. The NRC also identified seven categories of 'experiments of concern' believed to require review by informed members of the scientific and medical community before they are undertaken or published in full detail. The categories are broadly defined, plausible and capture scientifically defensible attributes of harm. Although they can be considered as prototypical of research that clearly provides the potential for harm to public health or national security, they are also consistent with a sound bio-defence research portfolio providing for protection of public health and national security.

The medical and scientific literature demonstrates that a number of interpretations of dual use biomedical research exist. The most inclusive perspective proposes that virtually all materials, technology and interventions used in biomedical research are indistinguishable with respect to the potential for intentional harm, and thus all biomedical investigation is inherently dual use research (Fischer, 2004). While theoretically defensible, such broad, inclusive classification provides little guidance for determining the appropriateness and level of oversight, monitoring or review of any research.

Other definitions of potentially dangerous research have focused specifically upon characteristics of organisms or agents. This has been the most prevalent approach employed to establish the boundaries of dual use research. Some have systematized assessments of danger through estimates of transmissibility, infectivity and lethality on the premise that no technology or research procedure per se seems to match the danger posed by an infectious pathogen possessing the ability to propagate with serious effect (Harris, 2001; Steinbruner et al, 2003). Other investigators have proposed additional paradigms for evaluating the risk of harm or the probability of effective malevolent use of biomedical research (Casadevall and Pirofski, 2004). Their models assess the risk of research based upon such factors as the intrinsic virulence of the organism; the size of inoculum causing symptomatic infection; the time to demonstrated effect; communicability of the infection; and factors that influence weaponization potential. Some have suggested stratification such that extreme risk would include only agents such as *Variola major*, and moderate risk organisms would include most select agents (Gaudioso and Salerno, 2004). Proposed measures for low- and moderate-risk categories would largely rely on existing safety and security evaluations, in part because the risk of misuse by lone individuals and well-developed states was judged as low, and by 'rogue' states and by non-state actors the risk was low to moderate (Salerno et al, 2004). These perspectives therefore emphasize oversight based more upon the characteristics of the organism or agent of interest than on the research manipulation or intervention employed.

Information has itself also been viewed as providing opportunity for intentional misuse, and in the life sciences much information that could conceivably provide an opportunity for misuse is in the public domain. For example, the field of synthetic genomics has demonstrated the ability to generate harmful organisms or products (Curtis et al, 2001; Cello et al, 2002), and the majority of genome data are openly available (NRC, 2004). Such open access has the potential for mischief, but also permits timely progress among biomedical researchers and clinicians in countering biological threats to public health (e.g. the rapid progress in response to the 2003 SARS outbreak; see Yang et al, 2004). A cogent argument against the restriction of data is that the information and research most likely to be restricted is that most relevant to the development of countermeasures and treatments for bioweapons. Additionally, the spectrum of what specific types of data could be related to definable risks of misuse remains unclear. These considerations led the UK House of Commons Science and Technology Committee (2002 to 2003, among many others) to conclude that restrictions imposed upon research data would likely hamper the necessary scientific response to terrorism.

In Chapter 7, Harris notes that a process of formally assessing risks of research proposals holds promise as a technique for permitting distinctions of potential danger, and in fact there is a large information base addressing life sciences risk assessment/risk management. A 1983 NRC report on risk assessment for the US government established assessment principles now frequently employed by various agencies (NRC, 1983). The report identified four processes fundamental to assessing risk: hazard identification; dose-response assessment; exposure assessment; and risk characterization. A subsequent Presidential and Congressional Commission (1997) on risk assessment published a comprehensive report 14 years later. It suggested more qualitative descriptions of uncertainty, remarking that among the difficulties in attempting to impose precision on the process was a lack of consensus on the definition of a weight of evidence sufficient to drive conclusions. Some experts in risk analysis and threat assessment have proposed a similar model for bioterrorism risk assessment that begins with hazard and risk characterization (Zilinskas et al, 2004). However, while qualitative risk assessments offer the appeal of relative simplicity in application, it must be recognized that they can have significant limitations, among which are imprecision in discriminating between quantitatively small and quantitatively large risks (Cox et al, 2005).

The literature on risk assessment and risk–benefit analysis indicates that such studies, while effective, are often complex and resource intensive. This can make it difficult for local peer reviewers, IBCs or other analysts to provide timely, detailed assessments of risk for the wide variety and great volume of life sciences research with the potential for designation as dual use. However, it is possible that the key principles of risk assessment could be developed into a paradigm for application at several levels of review, with monitoring of the process as appropriate. Some believe that at the grant application stage, it is exceedingly difficult to accurately assess the risk of misuse; for this reason, in part, the process of risk assessment should be viewed not as static, but as dynamic (Wellcome Trust, 2004). The results of research may be unexpected, as in the case of the effect of viral vector-induced mouse IL-4 expression on resistance to mousepox (Jackson et al, 2001).

Thus, the majority of the various standards that have been proposed for evaluating dual use research in the life sciences are based upon estimates of potential harm inherent to specific characteristics of the individual organisms and their products. In these approaches, the experimental manipulations, equipment and knowledge acquired are often viewed as significant only in the manner in which they may affect virulence, pathogenicity, transmissibility, disease prevention or diagnosis, therapy, stability and transport/dispersal. However, other informed opinion has emphasized the importance of advances in molecular biology, genomics and experimental technology as more critical than the attributes of specific organisms or agents (NRC, 2004; Relman, 2006). The application of the tools and methodology of formal risk assessment or risk–benefit analyses offers an approach that can bridge the gaps between strategies that focus upon organisms, information or experimental procedures and technologies.

Viewed in this context, the paradigm proposed by CISSM for research oversight is consistent with the approach directed more towards organisms than information, specific procedures, processes or technologies. The review by an international body may be most appropriately limited to highly dangerous organisms such as *Variola* or BSL-4 level organisms, though the magnitude and spectrum of potential harm from research on less hazardous biologicals mandate careful attention to the quality and reliability of national and local reviews. Formal mechanisms for oversight of those bodies should be established; but assignment of national review primarily to a government agency with the scientific community acting only in an advisory capacity may be problematic. Moreover, established, reliable and defensible methods of risk assessment that are endorsed by experts in the field should be explicitly stipulated for implementation at the local, national and international levels of research review. Finally, it is certainly possible that the greatest risks for both biosafety and international security may derive from classified and proprietary research that are currently subject to no publicly accountable oversight processes. Enfolding that research into a combined national and international mandatory review process will be challenging.

References

Ackerman G. A. and Moran, K. S. (2004) *Bioterrorism and Threat Assessment,* Weapons of Mass Destruction Commission Study No 22, Stockholm, Sweden, WMD Commission

Casadevall, A. and Pirofski, L. (2004) 'The weapon potential of a microbe', *Trends in Microbiology,* vol 12, no 6, pp259–263

Cello, J., Paul, A. V. and Wimmer, E. (2002) 'Chemical synthesis of poliovirus cDNA: Generation of infectious virus in the absence of natural template', *Science,* vol 297, no 5583, pp1016–1018

Center for Arms Control and Non-Proliferation (2006) *Federal Funding for Biological Weapons Prevention and Defense,* Washington, DC, Center for Arms Control and Non-Proliferation, www.armscontrolcenter.org, accessed in June, 2006

Cox, L. A., Babayev, D. and Huber, W. (2005) 'Some limitations of qualitative risk rating systems', *Risk Analysis,* vol 25, no 3, pp651–662

Curtis, K. M., Yount, B. and Baric, R. S. (2001) 'A simple strategy to assemble infectious RNA and DNA clones', *Advances in Experimental Medicine and Biology,* vol 494, pp475–481

Fischer, J. E. (2004) *Speaking Data to Power: Science, Technology, and Health Expertise in the National Biological Security Process,* Washington, DC, Henry L. Stimson Center

Gaudioso, J. and Salerno, R. M. (2004) 'Biosecurity and research: Minimizing adverse impacts', *Science,* vol 304, p687

Harris, E. D. (2001) Statement before the House of Representatives International Relations Committee, 5 December

Harris, E. and Steinbruner, J. D. (2005) 'Scientific openness and national security after 9-11', *CBW Conventions Bulletin,* vol 67, pp1–6

House of Commons Science and Technology Committee (2002–2003) *The Scientific Response to Terrorism,* Eighth Report of Session 2002–2003, vol 1, London, HMSO

Jackson, R. J., Ramsay, A. T., Christensen, C. D., Beaton, S., Hall, D. F. and Ranshaw, I. A. (2001) 'Expression of mouse interleukin-4 by a recombinant *Ectromelia* virus suppresses *Cytolytic lymphocyte* responses and overcomes genetic resistance to mousepox', *Journal of Virology*, vol 75, no 3, pp1205–1210

Kennedy, D. (2005) 'Better never than late', *Science*, vol 310, no 5746, p195

Leitenberg, M. (2005) *Assessing the Biological Weapons and Bioterrorism Threat*, Strategic Studies Institute Monograph, Carlisle, PA, US Army War College

Morenkov, O. S. (2002) 'Bioterrorism', in *High-Impact Terrorism: Proceedings of a Russian-American Workshop*, Washington, DC, National Academies Press

NIH (National Institutes of Health) (2002) *NIH Guidelines for Research Involving Recombinant DNA Molecules*, 66 FR 57970, Federal Register, vol 66, no 223, pp5790–5797, Bethesda, MD, NIH

NRC (National Research Council) (1983) *Risk Assessment in the Federal Government: Managing the Process*, Washington, DC, National Academic Press

NRC (2003) *Biotechnology Research in an Age of Terrorism*, Washington, DC, National Academies Press

NRC (2004) *Seeking Security: Pathogens, Open Access, and Genome Databases*, Washington, DC, National Academies Press

NRC (2007) *Scientific Review of the Proposed Risk Assessment Bulletin from the Office of Management and Budget*, Board on Environmental and Toxicological Studies, Washington, DC, National Academies Press

Presidential/Congressional Commission on Risk Assessment and Risk Management (1997) 'Framework for environmental health risk assessment', www.riskworld.com

Relman, D. (2006) 'Bioterrorism – preparing to fight the next war', *New England Journal of Medicine*, vol 354, no 2, pp113–115

Salerno, R. M., Gaudioso, J. and Frerichs, E. D. (2004) 'A BW risk assessment', *Nonproliferation Review*, vol 11, no 3, pp25–55

Steinbruner J., Harris, E. D., Gallagher, N. and Okutani, S. M. (2003) *Controlling Dangerous Pathogens: A Prototype Protective Oversight System*, Center for International and Security Studies at Maryland (CISSM), www.puaf.umd.edu/cissm/projects/amcs/amcs.html/, accessed March 2005

Sunshine Project (2004) *Mandate for Failure: The State of Institutional Biosafety Committees in an Age of Biological Weapons Research*, October, Austin, TX, Sunshine Project, www.sunshine-project.org/, accessed September 2006

Warrick, J. (2006) 'The secretive fight against bioterror', *The Washington Post*, 30 July, pA1

Wellcome Trust (2004) *Position Statement on Bioterrorism and Biomedical Research*, www.wellcome.ac.uk/, accessed September 2005

Yang Z. Y., Kong, W. P., Huang, Y., Roberts, A., Murphy, B. R., Subbarao, K. and Nabel, G. J. (2004) 'A DNA vaccine induces SARS coronavirus neutralization and protective immunity in mice', *Nature*, vol 428, pp561–564

Zilinskas, R. A., Hope, B., North, D. W. (2004) 'A discussion of findings and their possible implications from a workshop on bioterrorism threat assessment and risk management', *Risk Analysis*, vol 24, no 4, pp901–908

9

Export Control and the Non-proliferation of Materials: National Boundaries in International Science?

Jez Littlewood

The idea of controlling the export of certain materials, equipment and goods has a long history. During the negotiation of the 1925 Geneva Protocol, which prohibited the use in war of chemical and biological weapons, the US proposed 'to control the traffic in poisonous gases by prohibition of exportation of all asphyxiating, toxic or deleterious gases and all analogous liquids, materials and devices manufactured and intended for use in warfare' (Goldblat, 1971, p60). Because, however, 'it was practically impossible to discriminate between chemical products used for industrial, pharmaceutical or other purposes and those which might be used in chemical warfare', the US proposal was considered unworkable (Goldblat, 1971, p64).

This early attempt at international control of dual use goods and materials illustrates two important issues when considering the web of prevention and the governance of research. First, export controls are not a new phenomenon. Second, many of the contemporary difficulties of ensuring the weapons, materials or equipment necessary for the development, production or use of chemical or biological weapons are not a result of the recent emergence of 'dual use' items or from globalization during the last 20 years. As the UK noted in 1968 during the negotiations of the Biological Weapons Convention, 'most of the microbiological agents that could be used in hostilities are also needed for peaceful purposes' (Goldblat, 1971, p256).

Contemporary international bases for export controls related to nuclear, chemical and biological weapons stem from the obligations contained in each of the different conventions and treaties related to these weapons – namely, the 1968 Nuclear Non-Proliferation Treaty (NPT), the 1972 Biological Weapons Convention (BWC) and the 1993 Chemical Weapons Convention (CWC). All three agreements contain non-proliferation obligations. The dominant paradigm of the state-to-state nature of export controls changed, however, in 2004 when export controls for non-state actors were mandated under United Nations Security Council Resolution (UNSCR) 1540 (2004). This resolution affected perceptions and practice of export controls in two ways. First, it internationalized export controls by requiring all states to adopt and enforce them with respect to nuclear, chemical and biological weapons, and their means of delivery to prevent terrorist acquisition of such weapons. Second, implementing the resolution requires effective internalized licensing and control of many of the materials and equipment subjected to export controls within states, as well as for their export. As a result, UNSCR 1540 (2004) provides increased legitimacy to previously diverse national and like-minded state export-control arrangements. It also provides an opportunity for greater coherence for international export-control policies in the future.

This chapter examines the role and function of export controls in managing the threat posed by biological weapons. Section one provides an overview of export-control issues and non-proliferation. The second section focuses on the UK and the evolution of its export-control policy and practice related to biological weapons. In the third section the role of regional, like-minded and international efforts in the export-control arena are examined. Finally, in the fourth section, consideration is given to the key question of whether or not export controls represent a boundary to international science.

Export controls: A primer

States license (control) certain materials, goods, technology and knowledge for a variety of reasons. Explanations for the existence and application of export controls can be found in at least four theoretical approaches, including realism, institutionalism, domestic politics and liberalism (Grillot, 1998). The principal rationale for such controls is national security. As a result, states that are concerned with external threats to their security may use export controls to prevent an enemy from acquiring critical military equipment, supplies and knowledge (Croft, 1996, p136).

States do cooperate in the international system, as few threats can be truly managed by a state acting on its own. For example, during the Cold War, Western states implemented export controls under the Coordinating Committee on Multilateral Export Controls (CoCOM). Obligations contained in treaties and agreements, such as the BWC, offer additional explanations as to why states may apply controls to certain materials. Indeed, behaving responsibly internationally has given rise to adherence to international norms or expectations of behaviour and the idea of there being a community of states that act together for their own and (as they perceive it) each others' benefit in certain issue areas.

Taking the UK as an example, the UK mainland has long been known to be vulnerable to attacks using biological weapons (Balmer, 2006, p49). It is not in the strategic interests of the UK for other states or actors to have in their arsenals biological weapons that might be used against UK forces or to attack the UK homeland. If this provides a realist-led rationale for export controls, of equal significance is that the UK is a member of all the major arms control agreements and non-proliferation arrangements from the NPT, BWC and CWC, through to the Nuclear Suppliers Group (NSG), Australia Group, Waessenaar Arrangement and Missile Technology Control Regime (MTCR), as well as the Proliferation Security Initiative (PSI). These agreements contain non-proliferation commitments and impose obligations on the UK with which it must comply.

Domestic political pressures are also evident in the UK. Were the UK to supply another state with an offensive biological weapons capability, directly or indirectly, wittingly or unwittingly, it would be a breach of UK law and would highly likely cause public outrage: not least because the UK went to war in 2003 ostensibly to prevent a state (Iraq) from building up such a capability. Finally, and linked to much of the above, the place of the UK in the world is, in part, built on its liberal democratic identity. Over the last 50 years, the liberal democracies have developed export controls and non-proliferation commitments as part of their own identity. Put simply, the UK acts in its own strategic interest by preventing proliferation; acts in conformity with others because of the international rules concerning proliferation; acts nationally to achieve these objectives because it is required to and because there is an expectation among the public and parliamentarians that it will do so; and acts in a manner by which it would like to be perceived as a state that does not proliferate and one that abides by the obligations that it has undertaken.

Export-control realities for biological weapons

Export controls in the 21st century must contend with a number of competing pressures. On the one hand, the Geneva Protocol has only 133 parties, leaving over 60 states not bound by the prohibition of use on biological (and chemical) weapons. The BWC has only 156 States Parties, leaving close to 40 states that refuse to commit to biological disarmament. Of equal note, not all State Parties to the BWC are believed to be in compliance with their disarmament obligations (Rood, 2006) and there are increasing concerns about the interest of non-state actors, such as terrorists, in biological weapons (Wenger and Wollenmann, 2007). These factors point to the necessity of maintaining export controls on dual use materials and equipment relevant to biological weapons.

On the other hand, biological weapons have rarely been used in conflict or warfare and no State Party to the BWC has formally been found to be in non-compliance with its obligations, although Russia admitted that the Soviet Union violated the convention and Iraq was in contravention of its obligations for a number of years. These factors point to reduced salience for biological weapons and, insomuch that no state is using biological weapons or has been found to be in non-compliance with the BWC, it might be argued that export controls are not necessary. Linked to the above, the dual use materials, knowledge, equipment and agents relevant to biological weapons are spreading internationally as a result of legitimate economic growth and scientific and technological development. This factor puts increased pressure on the effectiveness of export controls applied by states, or groups of states, in isolation from other potential suppliers or sources of materials for offensive biological weapons programmes. Finally, the acceptability of export controls is still under question, with a number of states maintaining that export controls applied by the few harm the legitimate techno-logical development and peaceful economic interests of other states (Moaiyeri, 2006).

These developments present three different types of pressures on export controls. First, it is essential for the core group of Western suppliers to maintain and enhance their own export controls in the face of new threats such as terror-ism, determined proliferators using sophisticated techniques to circumvent and overcome export controls, and in the face of globalization. Second, the effec-tiveness of export controls internationally depends upon the adoption and implementation of export controls by an ever increasing number of states because of the impact of globalization and the emergence of second- and third-tier suppliers of dual use material and technologies. Third, there is a continuing perception of export controls hampering scientific endeavour, trade and inter-national development. This is particularly true in the new terrorist-led security environment where licensing and control is as much facing inward – that is to say, national controls on access to and transfers of particular dual use items – as well as outward in terms of traditional export controls. So far, in the UK the newer provisions do not appear to have had an adverse effect on UK science (McLeish and Nightingale, 2004).

What these developments mean for the future of export controls is far from certain. It is unlikely that the controls will be abandoned; but their effectiveness depends upon their acceptance and application by an ever increasing number of states.

Effectiveness of export controls

Since the end of the Cold War, questions have been raised about the durability and effectiveness of the existing export-control regimes and many proposals have been made to strengthen them (Bertsch and Gower, 1992; Karp, 1993; Müller, 1993; Kellman, 1994; Alves and Hoffman, 1997; Smithson, 1997; Roberts, 1998; Feakes, 2001; Sokolski, 2001). Further changes have been pursued with vigour since 11 September 2001 (Beck et al, 2002; Gahlaut et al, 2004; Joyner, 2004; Lipson, 2005). To an extent, all these call for a reform of the export-control regimes, with many favouring a realignment of the NSG, Australia Group, MTCR and, occasionally the Waessenaar Arrangement, to cope with current challenges. Underlying all of the proposals is a recognition that export controls can no longer be maintained solely by a group of Western states and remain effec-tive because of the globalization of science and technology.

Globalization and science and technology

The 2006 publication of *Globalization, Biosecurity and the Future of the Life Sciences* (NRC, 2006) indicated that developments in the life sciences and biotechnology, as well as in other scientific disciplines, could have a profound impact on the norm against biological weapons. The warnings have been replete over the last few years in the academic literature (Meselson, 2000; Hoyt and Brooks, 2003; Koblentz, 2003; Chyba and Greninger, 2004; Pearson, 2006). The dual use nature of many of the advancements in the life sciences, as well as other relevant scientific and technological disciplines, means that at the same time as offering great social and economic benefit, there are potentially great risks. While experts and commentators have long sounded warnings and issued notes of caution, there has been, and remains, little consensual international agreement on what to do about the security dilemmas that these developments pose.

The new security environment
Compounding the above is greater concern about the new multilateral security environment. A greater understanding of proliferation dynamics, past failures and the limits of export controls in preventing proliferation – albeit mainly of nuclear weapons – has indicated the necessity for national and like-minded action, as well as multilateral activity (Gould and Folb, 2000; Braun and Chyba, 2004; Albright and Hinderstein, 2005; Corera, 2006; Dunn, 2006). In addition to these predominant state-level concerns, there are also fears about terrorist acquisition of biological weapons, which gave rise, *inter alia*, to UNSCR 1540 (2004).

What these conflicting trends mean has yet to fully emerge; but, from the point of view of a web of prevention, transparency and accountability in export controls have increasing resonance. Through actions that make the application of export controls more transparent and accountable, states will not only counter the claims that export controls harm economic development, but will disseminate standards and benchmarks for application to other states in order to cast the net of export controls wider and enhance their effectiveness at the international level.

Transparency and standards

Over the last decade and a half, biological weapons-related export controls have shifted from relative secrecy in government application to relative transparency. Prior to the mid 1990s, export controls were mired in an opacity that made it difficult to assess their real policy intentions and/or their effectiveness. Now, internet sites across the globe, particularly in the US, UK and Australia,[1] and the official sites of the principal export-control bodies, can be accessed, and it is also possible to read the submissions of many states to the United Nations 1540 Committee on export controls.

Separate to the emergence of transparency has been the shattering of political difficulties regarding the legitimacy of export-control arrangements. During the 1990s, export-control debates became ossified between their staunch supporters (mainly Western states) and their opponents (mainly vocal developing states). Such political problems had a major impact threatening the existence, maintenance and strengthening of key arms control agreements

(Moodie, 1995; Feakes, 2001; Littlewood, 2005, pp140–157). Following the adoption of UNSCR 1540 (2004), the debate over the legitimacy of export controls was, in effect, closed. The United Nations Security Council had, during the Iran–Iraq war, endorsed export controls in the chemical weapons area under UNSCR 620 (1988); but this application of export controls was viewed as a special case. However, the operative paragraphs of the resolution remain extant and equally applicable to any future use of chemical weapons by parties to a conflict.

The internationalization and internalization of export controls and licensing procedures under the NPT, CWC, BWC and UNSCR 1540 (2004) have also seen the emergence of benchmarks for what constitutes 'effectiveness'. This is neither a uniform nor linear process; but in a report prepared for the US Bureau of Nonproliferation (US Department of State, 2004), nine criteria were identified in order for an export-control system to be considered effective. They included legislative purpose or intent; jurisdiction of territory, transactions and people; jurisdiction over items; authority to implement export-control processes; assurances of transparency; responsibilities of the parties; requirements for documentation; confidentiality and procedures for information sharing; and authority to enforce the law and penalties for violations. Running parallel to this development, *de facto* standards for export-control implementation have been established by the core states and original members within the NSG, Australia Group, MTCR and Waasenaar Arrangement. The separate membership of these arrangements has increased over the last decade to encompass the likes of Russia, China, Brazil, Argentina, Ukraine and South Africa. Not all are members of each arrangement; but the former Warsaw Pact states have been embraced in most of the arrangements and important developing states have joined in recent years.

The evolving politics of export controls

In the BWC context, export controls were an extremely divisive subject during the 1990s. By 2006, however, at the Sixth Review Conference of the BWC (20 November–8 December 2006), the debate on export controls was muted, and in contrast to the discussions held by the same States Parties during the 1990s, a mature and useful exploration of the issues relating to export controls was achieved in 2003. Of greater import, there was consistency in the identification of the principal elements of effective implementation of actual measures under the BWC, including export controls: inter-agency cooperation; regular reviews of both scientific and technological developments and the monitoring system in place; lists of controlled items; catch-all clauses; and both domestic and international licensing or monitoring of certain materials and equipment (Guthrie et al, 2004, p663).

The existence of the Australia Group remains, however, a bone of contention for some states, albeit a decreasing number. In simple terms, states such as Iran believe that as State Parties to the BWC – as well as the CWC and the NPT – they have provided the international community with adequate assurance that they do not develop, produce, stockpile, acquire or retain biological weapons.

Their word (or in this case their signature and ratification of an international treaty) is their bond. The idea that signature or ratification equals compliance is a powerful sentiment. Certainly, in the lead-up to entry into force of the CWC, some industry personnel believed the Australia Group had outlived its usefulness and that the provisions of the CWC would be the basis for 'the abolition of the obsolete export-control regime' and its replacement by the CWC provisions (Wyszomirski, 1995, p2). Such a view is wholly out of line with the lessons from proliferation over the last 30 years. First, it has become clear that a large number of States Parties to the BWC, as well as the CWC, do not have in place the necessary national implementation mechanisms to ensure that they prohibit and prevent the development, production, stockpiling, acquisition, retention or use of biological weapons (Dunworth et al, 2006, p94). Without such provisions, and implementation of them, there is no assurance to other states that dual use materials will not be diverted to malicious ends. Second, there have been a sufficient number of states which are party to international agreements but have still violated them or conducted activities that are not in compliance with their obligations to warrant continued caution at the national and international level, and to underline ratification does not equal compliance. The Soviet Union and the BWC, Iraq and the Democratic People's Republic of Korea (DPRK) and the NPT, and Iran and its International Atomic Energy Agency (IAEA) Safeguards serve as recent examples of the need for caution. As a result, the closely guarded right of each state to determine its national export licensing remains and the views of key Western states that 'no multilateral organization can ever address, consider, decide upon, review or overturn any decision taken by a State Party that a potential transfer is inconsistent with the non-proliferation obligations undertaken by that State Party' (UN, 2001, p2) are still pertinent.

Those states and entities seeking to circumvent export controls have long employed sophisticated measures to overcome the controls, as is clear from the Iraqi case during the 1980s and 1990s (Miller, 1996, pp141–150) and from the more recent use of sophisticated front companies in Iranian nuclear procurement activities (Lincy and Milhollin, 2007). Countering proliferators has always been a cat-and-mouse game of action and reaction, counter-action and innovation (Dunn, 2006, pp485–486). This means that 'given the increasingly global reach of determined proliferators, the success of export control measures depends on the combined commitment of as large a number of countries as possible' (Cruise, 2003, p2).

Counterbalancing this is the gradual acceptance of export controls among a wide variety of states: membership of, or adherence to, export-control arrangements as a symbol of good standing within the international community. Hence, casting the net of export controls to an ever wider number of states is not simply a public relations exercise to blunt criticism that export-control arrangements discriminate against non-members (Bevan, 2003, p2) even though this has been one (semi-deliberate) effect of the policy, but is essential in maintaining effective non-proliferation efforts in place. This led to efforts by the Australia Group to establish benchmarks and standards for national export licensing and the 2003 decision to support non-member adoption or enhancement of export controls compatible with the Australia Group controls (Australia Group, 2003).

These developments signal greater acceptance of export controls; but, as UK Foreign Secretary Margaret Beckett noted: 'it is one thing to put something into legislation and it is another thing for it to be effective' (House of Commons, 2007).

UK approaches to biological weapons-related export controls

The first of the UK's ten international priorities is 'making the world safer from global terrorism and weapons of mass destruction' (Foreign and Commonwealth Office, 2006, p28). Export controls are central to UK efforts at preventing the supply of such weapons to both states and terrorists. Until 2002, UK export controls on all goods were rooted in the 1939 Import, Export and Customs Powers Act. This act permitted the UK to control any goods or services being exported from the UK. However, concerns about the ability of the act to withstand legal challenges after the end of the Cold War led to the 1990 Import and Export Control Act. Developments in and related to Iraq are critical to UK export-control evolution from this date, not because of the importance of Iraq per se to UK security or non-proliferation policy, but because of investigations into exports to Iraq. The Scott Inquiry into export of defence equipment and other dual use goods to Iraq during the 1980s, for example, raised serious doubts about the efficacy of UK export controls. The Scott Report, (HMSO, 1996) *inter alia*, stated that the existing structure of export controls in the UK provided the government with 'unfettered power to impose whatever export controls it wishes and to use those controls for any purpose it thinks fit' and, as a result, should 'be replaced as soon as practicable' (House of Commons, 2003b, p4). This had far-reaching consequences culminating in the passage of the 2002 Export Control Act and secondary legislation in 2003 to support it (House of Commons, 2003b, pp4–5; Miller, 1996; Davis, 2002).

The 2002 Export Control Act, the 2003 Export of Goods, Transfer of Technology and Provision of Technical Assistance (Control) Order and the 2003 Trade in Goods (Control) Order, which followed, provide the substance of what items, both tangible and intangible, are subject to licensing for export in the UK. These items are controlled as a result of UK legislation and require-ments under other agreements, such as EU Council Regulation 1334/2000, which establishes a common regime for the export of dual use items and tech-nology within the EU. This regulation is amended, usually at least annually, to take into account changes in practice and new proliferation risks related to certain technology and materials.

Prior to the passage of the act in 2002, there was a shift in the UK in terms of transparency of export licensing following the publication by the government of the *Annual Report on Strategic Export Controls* in March 1999 and the formation of a new joint Committee of the House of Commons, which brought together the committees on foreign affairs, defence, trade and industry, and international development as the Quadripartite Committee (House of Commons, 1999). Greater transparency also resulted in the publication of *The Consolidated European Union and National Arms Export Licensing Criteria* in October 2000. While the Foreign and Commonwealth Office had previously provided memoranda to the House of Commons that indicated some of the criteria upon which export licence decisions were based (Davis, 2002, p131), the publication of the criteria in their entirety was a significant change in practice. A reading of the partial information provided by the Foreign and Commonwealth Office (FCO), Department of Trade and Industry (DTI) and others indicates that there is a strong element of continuity in the criteria themselves, although periodic changes in the interpretation of the criteria did have significant impacts, in the past, on specific countries such as Iraq (Miller, 1996, p91).

Today, the principal criterion relevant to biological weapons and the related dual use materials is contained within 'criterion one' of the eight criteria under UK licensing regulations and guidelines (FCO, 2000). The chapeau to the criteria states that:

> *An export licence will not be issued if the arguments for doing so are outweighed by the need to comply with the UK's international obligations and commitments, by concern that the goods might be used for internal repression or international aggression, by the risks to regional stability or by other considerations as described in these criteria.*

It then goes on to identify the criteria, and criterion one states, *inter alia*:

> *Respect for the UK's international commitments, in particular sanctions decreed by the UN Security Council and those decreed by the European Community, agreements on non-proliferation and other subjects, as well as other international obligations.*

The government will not issue an export licence if approval would be inconsistent with, *inter alia*:

- the UK's international obligations and its commitments to enforce UN, OSCE [Organization for Security and Co-operation in Europe] and EU arms embargoes, as well as national embargoes observed by the UK and other commitments regarding the application of the strategic export controls;
- the UK's international obligations under the Nuclear Non-Proliferation Treaty, the Biological and Toxin Weapons Convention and the Chemical Weapons Convention;
- the UK's commitments in the frameworks of the Australia Group, the Missile Technology Control Regime, the Nuclear Suppliers Group and the Wassenaar Arrangement.

How are UK export controls devised and implemented?

Export licensing in the UK is a multi-departmental function of government. The Export Control Organization (ECO) within the DTI coordinates and leads on these issues because any licences 'to export arms and other goods controlled for strategic reasons are issued by the Secretary of State for Trade and Industry (DTI) acting through the Export Control Organization (ECO)'. As the ECO website goes on to note (DTI, 2007):

> *ECO's chief task is to process applications for licences to export strategic goods from the UK. Licences are approved on the advice of the Foreign and Commonwealth Office, the Ministry of Defence and, where sustainable development issues are involved, the Department for International Development.*

The involvement of specific departments of government, the DTI, the FCO, Ministry of Defence (MoD) and the Department for International Development (DFID) also covers inputs from other agencies and departments, including Her Majesty's Revenue and Customs (HMRC), the Defence Science and Technology Laboratory (DSTL) and the intelligence agencies. In July 2002 the Counter-Proliferation Committee (CPC) was formed as the principal mechanism to coordinate the UK strategic counter-proliferation policy, and the strategy is put into effect by the cross-departmental Counter-Proliferation Implementation Committee (CPIC) (UN, 2004, pp2–3). It is the latter which coordinates technical and tactical issues, as well as providing guidance to individual government departments. A further cross-departmental body, the Restricted Enforcement Unit (REU), reports to CPIC and acts on intelligence concerning attempted and suspected breaches of UK export controls (UN, 2004, pp2–3). In practice, the DTI receives the export licence requests and these are shared with the MOD, FCO and DFID, among others, to determine whether or not an export licence should be granted.

Licensing is not a simple or purely mechanistic matter. The government has repeatedly stated that export-control decisions are taken on a case-by-case basis. This implies that there is no automatic blanket ban on exports to certain states. It is also clear that controlling biological-related dual use materials and equipment in the UK is not based solely on export-control legislation. In the biological sphere it involves legislation such as the 1974 Biological Weapons Act, the 1996 Chemical Weapons Act and the 2001 Anti-terrorism, Crime and Security Act. Indeed, legislation stretching as far back as 1861, such as the Accessories and Abettors Act, has been interpreted and appropriated to mean that aiding and abetting others to contravene the 1974 Biological Weapons Act is an offence (UN, 2005, p3).

Legislation in the form of Acts of Parliament is supplemented by various control orders and regulations, such as the 1980 Import of Animal Pathogens Order; the 1993 Plant Health (Great Britain) Order; the 1996 Carriage of Dangerous Goods by Road Regulations; the 1998 Specified Animal Pathogens

Order; and the European Commission Directive on Biological Agents (2000/54/EC), implemented in the UK under the Control on Substances Hazardous to Health (COSHH) regulations. Thus, the Health and Safety Executive (HSE) in the UK has a Biological Agents Unit, which assesses the information supplied under EC/54 relating to specified biological agents and maintains the information on the employer, place of storage, identity of the agent, the risk assessment of the work to be undertaken, and preventive and protective measures in place at the location (UN, 2004, p8). Physical protection of facilities and materials where biological dual use materials or sensitivities exist is overseen by the National Counter Terrorism and Security Office (NaCTSO), and transport issues are covered by the 2004 Carriage of Dangerous Goods and Use of Transportable Pressure Equipment Regulations, as amended and entered into force on 22 July 2005.

In simple terms, a panoply of measures are in place. Some are clearly focused on the control of biological weapons directly; others are health and safety measures that now have an additional security rationale. The dynamic nature of security threats involving pathogens and toxins necessarily requires continued oversight and evolution of export-control mechanisms. This reflects the cat-and-mouse nature of proliferation and counter-proliferation. For example, in January 2007, changes to Schedule 5 of the 2001 Anti-terrorism, Crime and Security Act (ATCSA) – which under Part 7 provides for the security and control of specified dangerous pathogens and toxins that could be used in an act of terrorism, endanger life or cause serious harm – reflected increasing concern over the biological threat from terrorists (Clout, 2007).

This development is illustrative of the evolution of export licensing in the post-11 September 2001 era. The system of controls, checks and licences has now encompassed national territory and become internalized. Returning to the 2001 ATCSA, Part 6 of the Act amended the 1974 Biological Weapons Act to prohibit transfers both for export and domestically of pathogens and toxins of types, and in quantities, that cannot be justified for peaceful purposes. The contemporary system not only focuses outwards on what is leaving the country, but faces inwards in terms of what is entering the UK and how materials, equipment and technology within the UK are secured, as well as who has access to them.

Regional, like-minded and other mechanisms

There are three main areas of activity that impact on UK export controls for biological weapons-related materials. At the regional level, the European Union has become increasingly important since the mid 1990s. At the like-minded level, the Australia Group has been in existence since the mid 1980s; more recently, the PSI has emerged as a means of enforcing the control of certain materials and equipment through interdiction of goods *en route* to a state or other entity. As indicated, under UNSCR 1540 (2004), the UK has been an active supporter of UN-mandated export controls.

The Australia Group emerged during the mid 1980s in response to Iraqi use of chemical weapons during the Iran–Iraq war (Robinson, 1986, p52). Liaison with Australia Group members is central to the effectiveness of UK export controls in the biological weapons area. In a similar vein to the increased transparency of UK export controls, public exposure and recognition of the role of the Australia Group brought increased information into the public domain (Mathews, 2004, pp1–4; Seevaratnam, 2006). The Australia Group is addressed in more detail in Chapter 10 and is not considered further here.

The Proliferation Security Initiative

One recent development is the emergence of the nascent enforcement arm of the export-control arrangements: the Proliferation Security Initiative. Launched in 2003 by the US, it is not a new treaty or a set of legally binding obligations, but aims to encourage states to use existing international and national law to prevent and interdict trafficking in weapons and materials related to nuclear, chemical and biological weapons, and ballistic missiles. The PSI consisted initially of 11 'core countries', but has expanded over time to include over 80 as of early 2007 (Davis et al, 2007, p17). Under a statement of interdiction principles, the members of the PSI, *inter alia*, agreed to 'Undertake effective measures, either alone or in concert with other states, for interdicting the transfer or transport of WMDs [weapons of mass destruction], their delivery systems, and related materials to and from states and non-state actors of proliferation concern' (White House, 2003).

The PSI maintains the kernel of an accepted enforcement arm of all the export-control arrangements. Now, at least, the opportunity exists to coordinate preventive action against the transfer of the tangible goods under the auspices of the PSI. Whether or not the PSI continues to expand remains to be seen; it has yet to become universally accepted, but neither has it been substantially challenged by any coordinated 'anti-PSI' group within the global community. As such, while there remain questions about the efficacy of the PSI, it fits neatly as one of the components in the web of prevention related to non-proliferation activities worldwide.

United Nations Security Council Resolution 1540

In 2004, the United Nations Security Council passed Resolution 1540 (2004) under which it reaffirmed that the proliferation of nuclear, chemical and biological weapons, as well as their means of delivery, constituted a threat to international peace and security. Taking a significant step forward, the Security Council decided to act under Chapter VII of its charter (action with respect to threats to peace, breaches of the peace and acts of aggression) by determining that all member states of the UN will prohibit provision of any support to non-state actors that attempt to acquire, develop or use nuclear, chemical or biological weapons, or their means of delivery. To give effect to this decision, the Security Council required each state to adopt and enforce effective laws to prohibit the manufacture, acquisition, possession, development, transport, transfer or use of such weapons or attempts to assist, finance or take part in such activities. Although focused on non-state actors, the resolution established, through the activities of its committee, standards and benchmarks for effective export controls and encouraged their adoption by all UN member states.

The European Union

With the transition of the European Community into the EU as a result of the 1993 Maastricht Treaty, the differences among the EU member states in the application and enforcement of export controls became problematic. While external pressures, such as the first Gulf War (1990 to 1991) played a part in the development of European export controls, it was the internal pressures of the transition to the single market and the prospects of economic and monetary union within the EU that forced action. In simple terms, the prospect – and objective – of free movement of goods between EU members required export controls to be based on a common standard acceptable to all member states. Thus, as Davis notes: 'the external perimeter [of the union] was only likely to be as strong as the export-control practices adopted at the weakest point of the Community' (Davis, 2002, p59).

After much haggling a European Community regime for the export of dual use goods was established in 1994 (EU, 1994). While workable, the regime was complex, and by 1998 the EU was coming to the view that the system was too complicated and only full harmonization would eliminate the problems with implementation of the regime. Negotiations on a new system occurred between 1998 and 2000, and the adoption of a new community regime for the control of exports of dual use items and technology (EU, 2000) now forms the basis of the EU-wide export-control regime. Since European law is binding on all member states, the consolidated criteria for licensing export from the UK incorporates not only the UK's primary and secondary legislation, but also the EU regime. In practice, this does not mean that export licensing from the UK is determined by decisions made in Brussels; rather, the EU-wide regime is part of European law, but each member state is required to implement it nationally under its own export-control legislation and regulations.

National boundaries on international science?

From the above it is clear that the application of export controls has altered, not least in their internalization and the growing cooperation between states. The UK, for example, relies on cross-departmental efforts to ensure the application and effectiveness of its export controls. It also bases its controls on common lists devised with its partners in the European Union and works closely with members of the Australia Group. As the net cast by export controls increases in scale and scope, a key question remains whether or not export controls are a barrier to international science, trade and development. While the focus here is on controlled items, it has to be acknowledged that the vast majority of scientific cooperation, international trade and interaction in the life sciences does not require an export licence either in the UK or, indeed, within other states. The question, as far as this volume is concerned, is whether or not export controls constitute a boundary on international science.

The answer is 'yes, but'. Export controls are a boundary on international science, international technology transfers and international trade. There is not completely free movement of goods, materials or knowledge across the globe. Whether or not export controls are deemed, or perceived, as a necessary, acceptable or legitimate boundary is a different issue. Viewed from the perspective of the UK government, based on the stated policy of the UK, the answer is likely to be that export controls are necessary because there are states and non-state actors seeking to acquire and develop biological weapons capabilities. They are legitimate because the international commitments and international law to which the UK is subject requires implementation of non-proliferation obligations. And they are acceptable because the trade in materials, equipment and technology subject to such licensing is not adversely affected by such controls.

The latter requires some clarification. There certainly are denials of export licences; but as the UK reported to the States Parties of the BWC in 2006, of the 195 licences issued to export pathogens, toxins and equipment under the UK controls between January 2002 and December 2005, only one licence was refused (UN, 2006, p59). This is not anomalous. During 2000, the UK reported that it only refused two licence requests related to biological materials (UN, 2000, p3) and figures for the total UK export licences between 1985 and 1999 point to fewer than 1.5 per cent of licence applications being denied (Davis, 2002, p140). More recent evidence has suggested a similar pattern of a small number of denials, of which 50 per cent of refusals are related to weapons of mass destruction (House of Commons, 2003a).

While the figures for export licence denials are incomplete, there is little to suggest that licence denial is routine, significant or a major barrier to trade or cooperation in science. Indeed, claims that the peaceful economic development of some states has been hampered by export controls have not been substantiated by evidence. As in the nuclear field two and half decades ago, the biggest problem appears to be that licensing affects all states and actors in order to prevent transfers of sensitive and potentially dangerous materials and technology to a very small percentage (Walker and Lönnroth, 1983, p134). The hard cases, such as Iraq during the 1980s and 1990s, and others in more recent times, drive policy responses: the impact of such policies is felt by everyone.

Building on Roberts's observations from 1998, for the majority of states, export controls are not insurmountable barriers per se but enablers: 'The export control system is most accurately described as a system that licenses, channels and renders transparent trade in dual use materials' (Roberts, 1998, p241). The question is now no longer what has to be controlled, corralled and denied to others in the interests of national security, but how can legitimate activity involving potentially dangerous materials and knowledge be facilitated and proceed without endangering the security of the UK and others? The answer here is not new: it was articulated over a decade ago. There has been a shift away from efforts to deny technology to increasing certainty about the uses to which the science and technology is put, and knowing what happens to the materials, technology and knowledge that leave one state and enter another (Moodie, 1995, p198). For example, the development of the EU regime was a necessary condition to permit free movement of goods and people across the member states: without it, trade and movement of sensitive materials and technology would have been prevented. The development of the regime therefore facilitated EU-wide activities, including science, trade and cooperation efforts. Moreover, as the EU has expanded to incorporate the former states of the Warsaw Pact in Eastern and Southern Europe, the standards and requirements for export controls have disseminated to an increasing number of states.

Without assurance of actual implementation mechanisms being in place within states, without confidence in the ability of a national government to enforce its writ and regulations on its own territory, and without the necessary level of transparency and accountability between states, it is extremely difficult to claim that exports of certain technology, materials or knowledge should occur – never mind occur freely without any controls. The risks are simply too great.

Conclusions

Proliferation of biological weapons to either states or non-state actors has been deemed a threat to international peace and security. The international community has deemed export controls a necessary undertaking to prevent proliferation of these weapons and to prevent the transfer of associated dual use materials and technology unless it is for legitimate peaceful purposes. These rules of international non-proliferation emerged as a result of a desire by key Western states to limit proliferation. Like all such rules, the mechanisms represent the special interests and values of the states that made them (Bull, 2002, p53). Over time, the sustainability of the rules became possible because of the cycle of rules being made, communicated, administered, interpreted, enforced, legitimized, adapted, and protected (Bull, 2002, p54). Both in terms of UK export licensing policy over the last two decades and the Australia Group, it is possible to identify each of the elements that Bull considered necessary for an effective set of rules to function. As a result, the net of export controls has continued to spread and gain legitimacy. Few states or outside observers now view export-control arrangements through the lens of an economic cartel on high technology dressed up in a cloak of security imperatives. In certain circumstances, export controls can act as a barrier to international science; but that barrier is needed. Perhaps more importantly, export licensing acts as an enabler of scientific, technological and economic cooperation.

Note

1   For the US, see www.exportcontrol.org/index.php/pagetype/frontpage/id/1351.html. For the UK, see www.dti.gov.uk/europeandtrade/strategic-export-control/index.html and for Australia, see www.asno.dfat.gov.au.

References

Albright, D. and Hinderstein, C. (2005) 'Unraveling the A. Q. Khan and future proliferation networks', *The Washington Quarterly,* vol 28, spring, pp111–128

Alves, G. and Hoffman, K. (1997) *The Transfer of Sensitive Technologies and the Future of Control Regimes,* Geneva, United Nations

Australia Group (2003) 'Strengthening Measures to Prevent the Spread of Weapons of Mass Destruction', Press Release, Australia Group, Public Documents, June 2003, www.australiagroup.net/en/releases/press_2003_06.htm, accessed 24 April 2005

Balmer, B. (2006) 'The UK Biological Weapons Program' in Wheelis, M., Rózsa, L. and Dando, M. (eds) *Deadly Cultures: Biological Weapons since 1945,* Cambridge, MA, and London, UK, Harvard University Press

Beck, M., Cassady, C., Gahlaut, S. and Jones, S. (2002) *Strengthening Multilateral Export Controls,* Georgia, University of Georgia

Bertsch, G. K. and Gower, E. S. (1992) *Export Controls in Transition,* London, Duke University Press

Bevan, T. (2003) 'Adapting national controls and enforcement to fight WMD terrorism', Fifth International Conference on Export Controls, Budapest, 15–17 September

Braun, C. and Chyba, C. F. (2004) 'Proliferation rings: New challenges to the nuclear nonproliferation regime', *International Security,* vol 29, fall, pp5–49

Bull, H. (2002) *The Anarchical Society,* 3rd edition, Basingstoke, UK, Palgrave

Chyba, C. F. and Greninger, A. L. (2004) 'Biotechnology and bioterrorism: An unprecedented world', *Survival,* vol 46, pp143–162

Clout, L. (2007) 'Toxins ban to beat terrorist threat', *Telegraph,* 25 January

Corera, G. (2006) *Shopping for Bombs: Nuclear Proliferation, Global Insecurity and the Rise and Fall of the A. Q. Khan Network,* Oxford, Oxford University Press

Croft, S. (1996) *Strategies of Arms Control,* Manchester, Manchester University Press

Cruise, L. (2003) 'Outreach activities by the Australia Group', Fifth International Conference on Export Controls, Budapest, 15–17 September

Davis, I. (2002) *The Regulation of Arms and dual use Exports: Germany, Sweden and the UK,* Oxford, Oxford University Press

Davis, I., Isenberg, D. and Miller, K. (2007) 'Present at the Creation: US Perspectives on the Origins and Future Direction of the Proliferation Security Initiative', BASIC Occasional Paper on International Security Policy, No 54, February

DTI (UK Department of Trade and Industry) (2007) 'Department of Trade and Industry, Europe and World Trade, Strategic Export Control', www.dti.gov.uk/europeandtrade/ strategic-export-control/index.html

Dunn, L. (2006) 'Countering proliferation insights from past 'wins, losses and draws', *Nonproliferation Review,* vol 13, November, pp479–489

Dunworth, T., Mathews, R. J. and McCormack, L. H. (2006) 'National implementation of the Biological Weapons Convention', *Journal of Conflict and Security Law,* vol 11, pp93–118

EU (European Union) (1994) Council of the European Union, Council Regulation (EC) No 3381/94 of 19 December 1994 setting up a community regime for the control of exports of dual use goods

EU (2000) Council of the European Union, Council Regulation (EC) No 1334/2000 of 22 June 2000 setting up a community regime for the control of dual use goods and technology

FCO (UK Foreign and Commonwealth Office) (2000) *Sanction Regimes, Arms*

Embargoes and Restrictions on the Export of Strategic Goods, The Consolidated EU and National Arms Export Licensing Criteria, 26 October, Hc 199-203w, London, FCO

FCO (2006) 'Active diplomacy in a changing world: The UK's international priorities', presented to Parliament by the Secretary of State for Foreign and Commonwealth Affairs by Command of Her Majesty, March, CM 6762

Feakes, D. (2001) 'Export controls, chemical trade and the CWC', in Tucker, J. B. (ed) *The Chemical Weapons Convention: Implementation Challenges and Solutions*, Washington, DC, Monterey Institute of International Studies

Gahlaut, S., Beck, M., Jones, S. and Joyner, D., (2004) *Roadmap to Reform: Creating a New Multilateral Export Control Regime*, Georgia, University of Georgia.

Goldblat, J. (1971) 'The problem of chemical and biological warfare', *CB Disarmament Negotiations 1920–1970*, vol IV, Stockholm, Almqvist and Wiksell

Gould, C. and Folb, P. I. (2000) 'The South African Chemical and Biological Warfare Program: An Overview', *Nonproliferation Review*, fall–winter, pp10–23

Grillot, S. R. (1998) 'Explaining the development of nonproliferation export controls framework, theory, and method', in Bertsch, G. K. and Grillot, S. R. (eds) *Arms on the Market: Reducing the Risk of Proliferation in the Former Soviet Union*, London and New York, Routledge

Guthrie, R., Hart, J., Kuhlau, F. and Simon, J. (2004) 'Chemical and biological warfare developments', *SIPRI Yearbook 2004: Armaments, Disarmament and International Security*, Oxford, Oxford University Press

HMSO (Her Majesty's Stationery Office) (1996) *The Right Honourable Sir Richard Scott, Report of the Inquiry into the Export of Defence Equipment and dual use Goods to Iraq and Related Prosecutions: Return to an Address of the Honourable the House of Commons dated 15 February*, HC 1995/96 115, London, 5 volumes and index (the Scott Report)

House of Commons (1999) *Defence – Fifth Special Report*, 30 June 1999, www.parliament.the-stationery-office.co.uk/pa/cm199899/cmselect/cmdfence/540/54006.htm

House of Commons, (2003a) 'International Development – Minutes of Evidence Ordered by the House of Commons to be Printed 6 May 2003', Minutes of Evidence taken before the Defence, Foreign Affairs, International Development and Trade and Industry Committees, Thursday, 27 February

House of Commons (2003b) *The Government's Proposals for Secondary Legislation under the Export Control Act*, Defence, Foreign Affairs, International Development and Trade and Industry Committees, First Joint Report of Session 2002-03 HC 620, 20 May

House of Commons (2007) 'Corrected Transcript of Oral Evidence to be Published as HC 117-iii', House of Commons, Minutes of Evidence taken before Quadripartite Committee, Strategic Export Controls, Thursday, 15 March, Right Honourable Margaret Beckett MP, Paul Arkwright and Mariot Leslie, Evidence Heard in Public Questions 205–285

Hoyt, K. and Brooks, S. G. (2003/04) 'A double-edged sword', *International Security*, vol 28, pp123–148

Joyner, D. H. (2004) 'The enhanced proliferation control initiative: National security necessity or unconstitutionally vague?' *Georgia Journal of International and Comparative Law*, vol 32, pp107–123

Karp, A. (1993) 'Controlling weapons proliferation: The role of export controls', *Journal of Strategic Studies*, vol 16, March, pp18–45

Kellman, B. (1994) 'Bridling the international trade in catastrophic weaponry', *American University Law Review*, vol 43, spring, pp755–847

Koblentz, G. (2003/04) 'Pathogens as weapons: The international security implications of biological warfare', *International Security*, vol 28, pp84–122

Lincy, V. and Milhollin, G. (2007) 'Iran's nuclear web', *New York Times*, 13 February

Lipson, M. (2005) 'Transgovernmental networks and nonproliferation', *International Journal*, vol LXI, pp179–198

Littlewood, J. (2005) *The Biological Weapons Convention: A Failed Revolution*, Aldershot, Ashgate Publishers

Mathews, R. J. (2004) 'The development of the Australia Group Export Control Lists of Biological Pathogens, Toxins and dual use Equipment', *The CBW Conventions Bulletin*, no 66, December, pp1–4

McLeish, C. and Nightingale P. (2005) 'Effective Action to Strengthen the BTWC Regime: The Impact of Dual Use Controls on UK Science', Bradford Briefing Paper, 2nd series, no 7, May

Meselson, M. (2000) 'Averting the hostile exploitation of biotechnology', *The CBW Conventions Bulletin*, no 48, June, pp16–19

Miller, D. (1996) *Export or Die: Britain's Defence Trade with Iran and Iraq*, London, Cassell

Moaiyeri, A. R. (2006) 'Statement by Ambassador Extraordinary and Plenipotentiary and Permanent Representative of the Islamic Republic of Iran before the Sixth Review Conference of the States Parties to the Convention on the Prohibition of the Development, Production and Stockpiling of Bacteriological (Biological) and Toxin Weapons and on their Destruction', 20 November, Geneva

Moodie, M. (1995) 'Beyond proliferation: The challenge of technology diffusion', *The Washington Quarterly*, vol 18, spring, pp183–202

Müller, H. (1993) 'The export controls debate in the "new" European Community', *Arms Control Today*, March

NRC (National Research Council) (2006) *Globalization, Biosecurity and the Future of the Life Sciences' Committee on Advances in Technology and the Prevention of Their Application to Next Generation Biowarfare Threats*, Washington, DC, National Academies Press

Pearson, A. (2006) 'Incapacitating biochemical weapons; Science, technology and policy for the 21st century', *Nonproliferation Review*, vol 13, July, pp151–188

Roberts, B. (1998) 'Export controls and biological weapons: New roles, new challenges', *Critical Reviews in Microbiology*, vol 24, pp235–254

Robinson, J. P. P. (1986) *Chemical and Biological Warfare Developments: 1985*, SIPRI Chemical and Biological Warfare Studies no 6, Oxford, Oxford University Press

Rood, J. C. (2006), Assistant Secretary for International Security and Nonproliferation Remarks to the Sixth Biological Weapons Convention Review Conference, Geneva, Switzerland, November 20

Seevaratnam, J. I. (2006) 'The Australia Group: Origins, accomplishments and challenges', *Nonproliferation Review*, vol 1, July, pp401–415

Smithson, A. (1997) 'Separating Fact from Fiction: The Australia Group and the Chemical Weapons Convention', Henry L. Stimson Center Occasional Paper no 34, pp1–53

Sokolski, H. D. (2001) *Best of Intentions*, London, Praeger

UN (United Nations) (2000) 'Ad Hoc Group of the States Parties to the Convention on the Prohibition of the Development, Production and Stockpiling of Bacteriological (Biological) and Toxin Weapons and on Their Destruction', Working paper submitted by the United Kingdom of Great Britain and Northern Ireland – Fulfilling the Objectives of the Biological and Toxin Weapons Convention: Resolving the Issue of Trade and Exchange of Technology, BWC/AD HOC GROUP/WP.424, 20 July 2000

UN (2001) 'Ad Hoc Group of the States Parties to the Convention on the Prohibition of the Development, Production and Stockpiling of Bacteriological (Biological) and Toxin Weapons and on Their Destruction', Working paper submitted by Australia, Austria, Belgium, Canada, the Federal Republic of Germany, Italy, Republic of Korea, Sweden, and the United Kingdom of Great Britain and Northern Ireland, BWC AHG, BWC.AD HOC GROUP/WP.443, 26 February 2001

UN (2004) Nations Security Council, Security Council Committee Established Pursuant to Resolution 1540 (2004), Note verbal dated 29 September 2004 from the Permanent Mission of the United Kingdom of Great Britain and Northern Ireland to the United Nations addressed to the Chairman of the Committee, S/AC.44/2004/(02)/3, 14 October

UN (2005) United Nations Security Council, Security Council Committee Established Pursuant to Resolution 1540 (2004), Note verbal dated 19 September 2005 from the Permanent Mission of the United Kingdom of Great Britain and Northern Ireland to the United Nations addressed to the Chairman of the Committee, S/AC.44/2004/(02)/3/Add.1, 4 October

UN (2006) *Sixth Review Conference of the States Parties to the Convention on the Prohibition of the Development, Production and Stockpiling of Bacteriological (Biological) and Toxin Weapons and on Their Destruction,* Geneva, BWC/CONF.VI/INF.4, 28 September

US Department of State (2004) *Legal Authorities for an Effective Export Control System,* Report prepared for the Department of State, Bureau of Nonproliferation, Office of Export Control Cooperation on Behalf of the Center for International Trade and Security, University of Georgia, by Dr Richard T. Cuppitt, School of International Service, American University, 23 October 2004

Walker, W. and Lönnroth, M. (1983) *Nuclear Power Struggles: Industrial Competition and Proliferation Control,* London, George Allen and Unwin

Wenger, A. and Wollenmann, R. (2007) *Bioterrorism: Confronting a Complex Threat,* Boulder, CO, and London, UK, Lynne Rienner

White House (2003) *Fact Sheet: Proliferation Security Initiative: Statement of Interdiction Principles,* Office of the Press Secretary, Washington, DC, 4 September, www.state.gov/t/isn/rls/fs/23764.htm

Wyszomirski, E. (1995) 'The CWC and barriers to chemical trade', *Chemical Weapons Convention Bulletin,* no 28, June, pp1–3

10

Chemical and Biological Weapons Export Controls and the 'Web of Prevention': A Practitioner's Perspective

Robert J. Mathews[1]

Introduction

One of the greatest contemporary security concerns facing the international community relates to the possibility of the acquisition of chemical and biological weapons (CBW) by either 'rogue states' or terrorist groups. In particular, there has been an increased awareness of the threat of biological terrorism following 11 September 2001 and the anthrax letter incidents.

It was recognized by policy-makers and their scientific advisers during the early meetings of the Australia Group in the mid 1980s that a range of measures are required to reduce the possibility of CBW proliferation, including the development of export licensing regulations for relevant dual use chemical and biological materials, equipment and technology, and outreach and awareness-raising activities to ensure that all people working with these materials (including traders) are aware of all relevant laws and regulations.

The objectives of this chapter are to describe, from a practitioner's perspective, the development and evolution of the Australia Group CBW export-control lists, and to then briefly discuss how a national export licensing system based on the Australia Group lists forms an essential component of the 'web of prevention'.

A brief history of the Australia Group

In my view, the history of the Australia Group can be best characterized through the following five fairly distinct phases:

1   genesis (March 1984–May 1985);
2   early days (June 1985–1988);
3   'getting serious' (1989–1993);
4   consolidation (1994–2000);
5   post-11 September 2001 (2001–present).

It is useful to describe the history of the Australia Group in terms of these five phases.

The genesis of the Australia Group

During 1983 and early 1984, there were several allegations by Iran to the United Nations Security Council that Iraq was using chemical weapons in the Iran–Iraq war. In response, under UN General Assembly Resolution 37/98D, the UN secretary-general initiated an investigation of use of chemical weapons in the Iran–Iraq war. The UN team contained members from Australia, Spain, Sweden and Switzerland. The UN investigation took place from 13 to 19 March 1984 and the UN team confirmed that sulphur mustard blister agent and Tabun nerve agent had been used, and that there were many chemical weapons casualties (UN, 1984).

By mid 1984, it was clear that Iraq had used large quantities of sulphur mustard blister agent and smaller quantities of Tabun nerve agent, and was increasing the use of chemical weapons against Iran. Furthermore, Iraq was seeking to acquire precursors for more toxic nerve agents (including Sarin and VX), and was obtaining at least some of its chemical weapons precursor chemicals from Western companies. At the same time, Iraq was developing a broadly based chemical industry sector using Western engineering companies, which it was judged could eventually result in an indigenous chemical weapons production capability.

In addition to the humanitarian dimension to the use of chemical weapons, Australian officials were concerned that the continued use of chemical weapons in the Iran–Iraq war would threaten the existing norms against the use of CBW (in particular, the 1925 Geneva Protocol), and that chemical weapons proliferation could spread from the Middle East to other regions, including to Australia's neighbourhood. There were also concerns that continued chemical weapons use in the Iran–Iraq war could jeopardize the Chemical Weapons Convention negotiations that were taking place in the Conference on Disarmament in Geneva.

In response, in August 1984 Australia placed export controls on eight chemical weapons precursor chemicals that Iraq was known to be seeking for chemical weapons purposes. A number of other countries – namely, Canada, Japan, New Zealand, the US and the (then ten) countries in the European Union[2] also placed export controls on a number of chemical weapons precursor chemicals.

In mid November 1984, during informal consultations in Canberra, it was recognized that despite the export controls being enacted by 15 countries on a number of chemical weapons precursor chemicals, Iraq was still obtaining the precursors it needed and producing chemical weapons. It was realized that Iraq was probably shopping around based on the variations in the different countries' control lists. In response, Australian officials suggested that it would be useful to convene an informal meeting of the 15 countries in an effort to harmonize the various national export-control lists.

Australian officials conducted informal bilateral discussions with officials of the other 14 export-control countries in early 1985. The initial proposal by Australia was for a meeting to take place in the margins of the Conference on Disarmament summer session in Geneva. However, there were concerns that a meeting on chemical weapons export controls by a group of Western countries, if publicized, could be misinterpreted by the Warsaw Pact countries and the Non-Aligned Movement (NAM) countries as a lack of interest in the Western group countries in the Conference on Disarmament to achieve comprehensive chemical weapons disarmament. To reduce this possibility, it was eventually agreed to convene a one-day meeting on 28 June 1985 at the Australian Embassy in Brussels.[3] It was further agreed that the meeting itself, as well as the substance of the meeting, would be 'confidential' to avoid the 'suppliers club' tag.

The early days (June 1985–1988)

The first meeting in June 1985 agreed that chemical weapons proliferation was a serious security issue, and the participating countries decided that there was value in exploring how their existing export controls might be made more effective. To this end, the countries agreed to meet again on 5 to 6 September 1985 in Brussels, with a session of 'chemical experts'. Because of sensitivities, it was decided that 'strict confidentiality' would be maintained on the proceedings of the meetings.[4]

There were more than 50 people participating in the third Australia Group meeting in December 1985, and it was clear that the Australia Group (which at that time was referred to as the 'Brussels Group' by Australian officials) had outgrown the small conference room at the Australian Embassy in Brussels. In May 1986, the Australia Group meeting was held at the Australian Embassy in Paris. In May 1987, the meeting became known as the Australia Group Meeting on Chemical Weapons Precursors.[5]

Between 1985 and 1987, the Australia Group developed a short core list[6] and a longer warning list[7] of chemical weapons precursor chemicals (see Mathews, 1993). There was also discussion about whether the controls should be 'destination specific' or *'erga omnes'* controls, with all countries agreeing to move towards *erga omnes* controls, especially after it was recognized that Iraq was seeking to obtain its requirements through middlemen and 'front companies'. Concerns were also expressed about Iraq's attempts to obtain dual use chemical production equipment for chemical weapons purposes. This resulted in the development of a draft dual use chemical production equipment warning list.

By early 1988, it had become clear that the Australia Group export controls on chemical weapons precursor chemicals were having limited success. The export controls had slowed Iraqi chemical weapons precursor procurement; forced Iraq to seek alternative suppliers of preferred chemicals, from either 'front companies' or non-Australia Group supplier countries; and had forced Iraq to go back to earlier stages in chemical weapons production processes or choose less efficient production routes.[8] As a result, fewer chemical weapons were being produced by Iraq and they were more expensive. But Iraq was still obtaining dual use production equipment from the West.

At this time, there were diplomatic initiatives by a number of Australia Group countries to encourage other major chemical supplier countries to implement similar export controls. This resulted in the formation of the Leipzig Group, which was the Warsaw Pact equivalent of the Australia Group. The Leipzig Group met three times between 1987 and 1989. Apparently, some Warsaw Pact countries had adopted the Australia Group control lists; however, there was apparently no attempt by the Warsaw Pact countries to harmonize their controls. During its meetings, the Leipzig Group considered and denied exports of certain production equipment.[9]

Getting serious (1989–1993)

Since early 1988, increasing concerns emerged about the proliferation and use of chemical and biological weapons following the large-scale use of nerve agent against civilians at Halabja in March 1988, evidence that 'countries of concern' were developing an interest in biological weapons programmes, and the revelations of a large-scale Libyan chemical weapons production facility being built at Rabta. These concerns led to United Nations Security Council Resolution 620, adopted on 26 August 1988, which, *inter alia*, called on all states to continue to apply, establish or strengthen strict controls on the export of chemical products serving for the production of chemical weapons.[10]

These increasing concerns led the Australia Group participants to increase the size of the chemical weapons precursor core list and warning list, and to commence development of a dual use chemical production equipment control list, as well as lists of biological agents and biological production equipment. In this respect, the Australia Group meeting in June 1991, which occurred a few months after the Gulf conflict, was a watershed. With coalition forces anticipating that they may have been attacked with Iraqi chemical and biological weapons came greater awareness, clarity and recognition of the threat posed by CBW proliferation, and greater determination of the Australia Group participants to make the measures as effective as possible in countering the CBW threat.

In recognition of the seriousness of the biological weapons proliferation threat, the Australia Group participants convened a series of biological weapons experts' meetings, which led to the development of four separate lists: one list for human and zoonotic pathogens and toxins (referred to as the *List of Biological Agents for Export Control*); a *List of Plant Pathogens for Export Control*; one for animal pathogens known as *List of Animal Pathogens for Export Control*; and a *List of dual use Biological Equipment for Export Control* (for a more detailed discussion, see Mathews, 2004).

The conclusion of the Australia Group meeting in June 1993[11] marked for the first time the adoption of a full range of lists covering precursor chemicals and dual use chemical production equipment, as well as the four lists of biological weapons-relevant items.

Consolidation (1994–2000)

The achievement, in 1993, of the various chemical and biological dual use control lists, as discussed above, was recognized as heralding a new phase in the work of the Australia Group, with the technical issues largely settled and hopefully only requiring continuing maintenance. The subsequent consolidation process included regularly reviewing the various control lists, with refinement and expansion of the biological lists, refinements to the chemical production equipment list, and agreement on rules for export licensing of 'chemical mixtures'. There was also considerable attention given to the issue of intangible technology transfer at this time.

By the early 1990s, a number of developing countries had become opposed to informal export-control arrangements, such as those of the Australia Group, because of their concerns that such export controls may inhibit legitimate trade in chemical and biological items. These concerns prompted the O'Sullivan Statement during the 'end game' of the CWC negotiations in Geneva in 1992. Delivered by Australian Ambassador Paul O'Sullivan on behalf of those countries which were participating in the Australia Group at that time, the statement included the following sentence:

> *They undertake to review, in the light of the implementation of the convention, the measures that they take to prevent the spread of chemical substances and equipment for purposes contrary to the objectives of the convention, with the aim of removing such measures for the benefit of States Parties of the convention acting in full compliance with their obligations under the convention. (O'Sullivan, 1992)*

Thus, a major activity during the 'consolidation' phase of the Australia Group was defending the group's export-control system and providing assurance to developing countries (both in the Organization for the Prohibition of Chemical Weapons PrepCom in The Hague and the BWC Ad Hoc Group in Geneva) that the group's export controls were, in fact, supporting the objectives of both the BWC and the CWC. In addition to national statements made at various meetings in The Hague and Geneva, outreach activities included regional seminars and workshops, as well as bilateral consultations in capitals.

Post-11 September 2001

In response to the increased awareness of the threat of biological terrorism following 11 September 2001 and the anthrax letters in October 2001, the different Australia Group lists have remained under regular review in an effort to further raise the barriers to chemical and biological terrorism, as well as CBW proliferation,[12] in accordance with the counter-terrorism objective that is now included in the philosophy of the Australia Group.[13] This has led to adjustments to the various control lists, including the addition of several new biological agents and new toxins to the Australia Group biological list, as well as refinements to the *List of dual use Biological Equipment for Export Control.*[14]

At the same time, Australia Group participants have recognized that the effectiveness of the various control lists derives from their collective application, especially in view of the increasing number of countries which have become potential inadvertent suppliers of relevant items as a result of the increasing globalization of the chemical and biological sciences and the chemical and biotechnology industries. For this reason, Australia Group participants are encouraging all exporting and transhipment countries to implement similar measures. In recent years, Australia Group participants have maintained a practice of briefing a large number of non-participating countries on the outcomes of their meetings. These briefings include making available lists of precursor chemicals, biological agents, and related equipment and technologies that are of proliferation concern.

So, while historically a number of developing countries had opposed informal export-control arrangements, such as those of the Australia Group (see, for example, Kervers, 2002), post-11 September 2001 and the anthrax letter incidents, a number of them have now recognized that the national export licensing measures developed by the group would raise the barriers to chemical and biological terrorism, and have adopted similar controls.

Reflections on the evolution of the Australia Group

Since the mid 1980s, we have witnessed many interesting and unpredictable changes, including:

- major changes in international relations, following the end of the Cold War;
- increased globalization of chemical and biotechnology industries;
- major discoveries and developments in the life sciences;
- a revolution in information sciences and communications technologies; and
- dramatic changes in the security environment, particularly since 11 September 2001.

Throughout this period, the Australia Group has remained an informal 'like-minded' group with the flexibility to adapt to changing international relations, science and technology, and to a varying security environment. Membership has increased from 15 to 40 countries, as well as the European Commission, and the various control lists have been developed and revised taking into account the various changing circumstances. The Australia Group has demonstrated the valuable and necessary role of 'soft law' agreements between 'like-minded' countries as a complement to the treaty-based obligations contained in the 1972 Biological Weapons Convention and the 1993 Chemical Weapons Convention.

The net result of increased concerns about chemical and biological terrorism, the adoption of UN Security Council Resolution 1540 (2004), and the Australia Group outreach activities is the acceptance amongst an increasing number of State Parties to the BWC and the CWC of the role of the lists as a means to implement their non-proliferation obligations under Article III of the BWC and Article I of the CWC. This has led to a growing acceptance of the Australia Group lists as the international benchmark in relation to export controls directed at CBW proliferation, and a number of states that are not participants in the Australia Group meeting are adopting their own national export licensing systems, using lists similar to those developed by the group.

Export licensing, web of deterrence and web of prevention

So how do the export-control lists that have been developed and refined by the Australia Group fit in with the 'web of deterrence' and the 'web of prevention'? As already discussed in this volume's introduction, the term web of deterrence was based essentially on a Cold War concept. Indeed, from entry into force of the BWC in 1975 until the late 1980s, deterrence was the primary means by which BWC States Parties met their obligation under BWC Article IV to take measures to 'prohibit and prevent' the transfer of biological weapons – the deterrence being a criminal penalty under domestic legislation. In Australia, for example, the 1976 Crimes (Biological Weapons) Act implements criminal sanctions for violations of the BWC, including the transferring of biological weapons (see Dunworth et al, 2006).

However, as discussed above, from the late 1980s, when the international community became aware that Iraq was seeking to acquire a biological weapons capability, a number of 'like-minded' states went beyond criminal legislation, with awareness-raising activities followed by the development and enactment of export-control regulations on a range of relevant dual use biological materials, equipment and technology. The operation of this export licensing system is based on a cooperative approach between various government agencies and the biological science community, including industry and traders.[15] This approach includes regular outreach and developing a cooperative relationship based on trust (Howlett, 2005). Thus, in my view, the term 'web of prevention' is a much more accurate characterization of this cooperative set of activities than the term 'web of deterrence'.

Clearly, there are a range of measures that need to be taken by all countries to ensure that they do not inadvertently support CBW proliferation or chemical and biological terrorism activities, including the enactment of criminal legislation; the development of regulations to enhance the security of relevant materials, equipment and technology; and outreach and awareness-raising activities to ensure that all people working with these materials (including traders) are aware of all relevant laws and regulations, including through codes of conduct. Some of these measures are specified in UN Security Council Resolution 1540.

Clearly, a national export licensing system based on the Australia Group dual use CBW-related materials, equipment and technology control lists should be seen as an essential part of the measures that each country adopts as part of its web of prevention.

Notes

1   The views expressed in this article are those of the author and do not necessarily reflect those of the Australian government.
2   At that time, there were ten member countries of the European Union: Belgium, Denmark, France, the Federal Republic of Germany, Greece, Ireland, Italy, Luxembourg, The Netherlands and the UK.
3   The countries invited to the first meeting were those 15 countries which had already put in place export controls on chemical weapons precursor chemicals. The European Commission was also invited to send observers, which it did (two observers). There were 33 people at the first meeting.
4   The meeting agreed that if Australia were asked about the meetings which it was convening, the press or other enquirers were to be told: 'Australia had initiated consultations with countries which had instituted controls on the export of certain chemicals with a view [to] strengthening the observance of the 1925 Geneva Protocol and in support of a [Chemical Weapons] Convention.'
5   In December 1990, the meeting became known as the Australia Group Informal Consultations on Preventing Association with Chemical and Biological Weapons Programmes; more recently, it has become known as the 'Australia Group'.
6   The core list contains those chemicals that all Australia Group participant countries agreed to place under national export control.
7   The chemicals included on the warning list, although not agreed for inclusion on the core list (i.e. common control list), were considered sufficiently important for a list to be provided to industry and traders in order that they seek guidance from government officials if they were suspicious about a particular export request of any of the listed items.
8   Indeed, by 1988, Iraq had formed an Anti-Australia Group Committee in Baghdad, tasked with keeping track of current Australia Group export-control lists and with trying to find alternative suppliers (information provided by a former United Nations Special Commission official, based on interviews conducted in Iraq in 1991).
9   Information provided by a participant of the Leipzig Group meetings.
10 UN Security Council Resolution 620, adopted on 26 August 1988, *inter alia*:

> *Condemns resolutely the use of chemical weapons ... Encourages the Secretary-General to carry out promptly investigations ... Calls upon all States to continue to apply, or establish or to strengthen strict controls on the export of chemical products serving for the production of chemical weapons ... Decides to consider immediately, taking into account the investigations of the Secretary-General, appropriate and effective measures.*

11 This was the largest meeting of the Australia Group, with more than 260 participants squeezed into the conference room of the Australian Embassy in Paris.
12 There had been regular discussion of chemical and biological terrorism issues within

the Australia Group since the Tokyo subway incident in 1995. However, chemical and biological terrorism received substantially greater attention within the Australia Group following 11 September 2001.

13 For example, at the meeting in October 2001, the Australia Group participants expressed the resolve of their governments to prevent CBW proliferation, whether by state or non-state actors, and agreed that the group has an important role to play in reducing the threat of CBW terrorist attacks. See Australia Group Document AG/Oct01/Press/Chair/24, available at www.australiagroup.net.

14 This included the reduction in the capacity of fermenters under control from 100 litres to 20 litres, reflecting the smaller scale of operation that might be employed by a terrorist group.

15 However, there is obviously still an element of deterrence in a national export-control system as there are serious penalties for exporting listed dual use biological materials, equipment and technology without an appropriate export licence.

References

Dunworth, T., Mathews, R. J. and McCormack, T. L. H. (2006) 'National implementation of the Biological Weapons Convention', *Journal of Conflict and Security Law*, vol 11, pp93–118

Howlett, B. (2005) 'Australian export controls', in Mathews R. J. (ed) *Proceedings of the Biological Weapons Convention Regional Workshop: Co-hosted by the Governments of Australia and Indonesia: 21–25 February 2005*, Melbourne, University of Melbourne

Kervers, O. (2002) 'Strengthening compliance with the Biological Weapons Convention: The protocol negotiations', *Journal of Conflict and Security Law*, vol 7, October, pp275–292

Mathews, R. J. (1993) 'Comparison of the chemicals on the Australia Group control list with those in the CWC schedules', *CBW Conventions Bulletin*, vol 21, p1

Mathews, R. J. (2004) 'The development of the Australia Group export control lists of biological pathogens, toxins and dual use equipment', *CBW Conventions Bulletin*, vol 66, p1

O'Sullivan, P. (1992) 'Statement Made on Behalf of the Australia Group by the Representative of Australia', 629th Plenary Meeting of the Conference on Disarmament, CD/1164, 7 August, Geneva

UN (United Nations) (1984) *Report of the Specialists Appointed by the Secretary-General to Investigate Allegations by the Islamic Republic of Iran Concerning the Use of Chemical Weapons: Note by the Secretary-General*, 39 UN SCOR, UN Doc S/16433, New York

United Nations Security Council Resolution 1540 (2004) Adopted by the Security Council at its 4956th meeting, 28 April, S/Res/1540 (2004)

11

How Does Secrecy Work? Keeping and Disclosing Secrets in the History of the UK Biological Warfare Programme

Brian Balmer

What control should scientists working in security-sensitive areas have over where and when, if at all, they publish their results? Whose interests are served through disclosing or withholding information? As the chapters in this book indicate, in relation to biological weapons this is a live debate today, largely focused on the potentially malign use of scientific discoveries made within non-military settings. A corollary to this discussion is an ongoing dispute over whether the state should employ contentious categories, such as 'sensitive but unclassified', as a way of regulating scientific information (NRC, 2004). The associated monitoring of scientists to prevent harmful information being made public has been flagged positively as part of a web of prevention (e.g. BMA, 1999, p90); yet the spectre of undue censorship and excessive secrecy follows rapidly in its wake.

It follows that thinking about secrecy as a component in any web of prevention at the outset involves recognizing the ambivalent role that it may play. States may demand, justifiably or unjustifiably, transparency in order to monitor the research activities of other states; yet the same states may wish to maintain a wall of secrecy around their own activities, which may be sensitive for security or commercial reasons. Likewise, the well-recognized dual use dilemma suggests that science, which has beneficial applications if disseminated, may also find itself subject to restriction should it have potential malign applications. The aim of this chapter is not directly to resolve these contemporary policy debates. Rather, this author, as a sociologically minded historian, attempts to inform these debates through an analysis of how secrecy has operated in past biological warfare research.

Issues surrounding military science, secrecy and transparency are frequently regarded as the historical preserve of nuclear research (Badash,

2003), yet are not entirely without precedent in the life sciences. By way of illustration, one exchange of views between the US, Canada and the UK, which resonates with contemporary debates, occurred in 1953 behind closed doors. In a climate of Cold War secrecy, British biological warfare researchers wanted to publish some of their work on immunization against anthrax, a move opposed by their US and Canadian collaborators. When scientific advisers in the UK discussed this matter, they soon looked beyond the scientific value of the work, noting that publishing would adversely affect relations with the US. On the other hand, they pointed out, there was no obligation to suppress the work under current security classifications. The advisers argued, moreover, that not publishing the work could imply that the UK was preparing for biological warfare.[1] Despite these considerations, the scientific advisory board was reminded by its chairman that its role was to provide only a 'technical opinion'.[2] And the board's opinion at the outcome of this discussion was that the work should not be kept secret.

The situation dragged on for three months without resolution. During this time, the director of the UK biological warfare programme, David Henderson, made personal approaches to the director of Camp Detrick in the US without any result.[3] As an additional complication, two groups in the UK programme were now working on different approaches to producing anthrax antigen. Only one of the groups needed to refer to previous US work if they were to publish, and Henderson foresaw problems with staff morale if one, but not the other, group was allowed to publish its findings. Eventually, through direct intervention by the US representative posted to the UK programme, the matter was resolved in favour of the UK. This short-lived disagreement illustrates one argument that is advanced in this chapter. A close examination of the historical record shows that classification and secrecy are not simply about the content of science. In this instance, scientific and political issues were distilled into a 'technical opinion'. Publications represented more than a means of disseminating scientific information; they were simultaneously an expression of the strength, or fragility, of collaboration between three nations.

Despite the victory for open publication in the previous example, it is difficult to exaggerate the role of secrecy in past biological warfare programmes. A number of recent historical surveys of biological warfare research have emphasized that all state-sponsored programmes, together with sub-state organized activities, were cloaked in utmost secrecy (Balmer, 2002; Guillemin, 2005; Wheelis et al, 2006). Twentieth-century state programmes have been documented in many countries, notably Canada, France, Germany, Hungary, Iraq, Japan, South Africa, the former Soviet Union, the UK and the US. In the case of the former Soviet Union, entire cities might disappear from the map or be closed off in order to conceal their military activities (Gentile, 2004; Hart, 2006). Beyond the physical security of locks, guards and gates, scientists working in secret military organizations were restricted in activities such as publication, conference attendance and patenting, thus largely divorcing them from the reward system and other social institutions of open academic science.[4]

It is fairly straightforward to suggest reasons for this secrecy. It kept enemies from knowledge of largely untried and potentially devastating weapons, and prevented them from knowing about military and political intentions regarding these weapons. Secrecy separated workers from communities advocating moral constraints that might otherwise have been felt to be binding on researchers (Colwell and Zilinskas, 2000; Balmer, 2002). Even if the moral arguments of groups on the outside had no impact on the behaviour of researchers on the inside, secrecy would have prevented any revelations that might lead to wider public censure. Finally, secrecy would have minimized the possibility of a nation being accused, whether accurately or inaccurately, of breaching international law, especially after the advent of the 1972 Biological Weapons Convention.

As well as suggesting reasons behind secrecy in biological warfare programmes, it is also possible to ask normative questions about the desirability and effects of secrecy. While some philosophers have considered when secrecy might be ethically justified in a range of situations, including military and scientific settings (Bok, 1989), the loss of accountability entailed by secrecy is frequently raised as the most telling criticism of undue secrecy, particularly in discussions about biological warfare. Guillemin (2005, 2006), in this vein, makes a forceful argument that secrecy allowed biological warfare scientists to cut loose from a 'moral compass'. This loss had practical effects – for example, at the end of World War II, it stifled possible public debate on the continuation of wartime biological warfare research into peacetime. Referring also to the US authorities' exchange of data from the Japanese biological warfare programme, in return for immunity from prosecution for its head, General Shiro Ishii (Harris, 1994), Guillemin argues that 'by keeping the dreadful secrets of the Japanese biological warfare program, the US government lent legitimacy to offensive biological warfare aimed against civilian populations' (Guillemin, 2005, p91).

Normative questions and historical reasons for secrecy both demand an understanding of how secrecy operates; to a large extent, this is the theme of this chapter, which focuses mainly on the British biological warfare programme simply because this author can claim detailed historical knowledge of secrecy here. The chapter will look at two sides of the operation of secrecy: keeping secrets in and letting secrets out. Picking up on the earlier example of research publication, it highlights how secrecy and transparency are operationalized through security classifications. As mentioned, a close look at the debates around classification reveals a series of choices that reflect wider concerns, particularly coordination and cooperation between national research programmes. Turning next to how secrets 'escape', the chapter discusses how breaches of secrecy were dealt with in the history of the UK programme. This section contrasts the controlled release of secrets through press releases and other announcements with the uncontrolled breach of secrecy exemplified by leaks. Restoring control, I argue, becomes a matter of the authorities employing various resources, including resources such as rumour and gossip that are normally seen as the province of those to whom secrets are leaked.

Keeping secrets: Security classification and the value of information

Secrecy is enacted through a range of tools and practices, not least the classification of information. Classifying, of course, is a fundamental and ubiquitous activity through which we organize an otherwise chaotic world. Yet the resultant taxonomies are far from neutral and inconsequential descriptions of the world, as sociologists Bowker and Starr (1999, pp2–3) point out in their detailed study of classification in action:

> These standards and classifications, however imbricated in our lives, are ordinarily invisible … Remarkably for such a central part of our lives, we stand for most part in formal ignorance of the social and moral order created by these invisible entities. Their impact is indisputable and … inescapable. Try the simple experiment of ignoring your gender classification and use whichever toilets are nearest; try to locate a library book shelved under the wrong Library of Congress catalogue number.

Classifications, therefore, despite their routine and mundane nature, have a powerful role in creating and reinforcing order in the world. Whatever the reality of the situations that they classify, taxonomies have very real effects. Security classifications are no less powerful at ordering the world into varieties of secrets. Arguing along similar lines, White (2000) claims that secrecy is a way of 'valorizing', or adding value to, information. With security classification, this value is encoded in a hierarchy ranging from the most valued and top secret through to the least valued and unclassified in relation to how powerful groups or individuals perceive the importance of any item of information. Turning to the historical record, there have been a number of protracted discussions about security classification and biological warfare research. Bearing in mind the observations that classification embeds values, creates order and has effects, we would be unwise to dismiss these disagreements over classification as mere bureaucracy. Instead, as we turn to the record of once-secret government documents, we can ask what else was at stake in the settlement of these disputes?

Classification and UK–US collaboration

Biological warfare security classification in the UK sat alongside a more general governmental system of security classification and vetting that had grown up since World War II.[5] A four-tiered taxonomy, which formed the basis of the system later used throughout the Cold War, was adopted on 1 July 1943 – namely, most secret, secret, confidential and restricted.[6] As the then Cabinet Secretary Sir Edward Bridges recalled nine years later, the term top secret soon replaced most secret. According to Bridges, this ostensibly minor change facilitated a more fundamental collaborative alignment between the UK and the US, which had operated with just secret, confidential and restricted:

If my recollection is right, we had prolonged discussion with the Americans and found great difficulty in coming to terms with them. It appeared that their greatest objection was to the use of the term 'Most Secret', which – to their way of thinking – implied that papers which were called 'Secret' were not really secret at all.[7]

Bridges further explained that Most Secret 'referred so to speak to the papers which were kept in the top drawer of the cupboard in which the secret files were kept'.[8] The replacement term top secret apparently appeased the US by suggesting that secret files were, indeed, secret, and that top secret further denoted the 'top layer of secret papers'.[9] Although Bridges's anecdote suggests a trivial change in nomenclature, there was a more serious underlying agenda: to coordinate work on both sides of the Atlantic.

Biological warfare security classification remained on the UK agenda into the Cold War, again as a means of controlling information and coordinating research with the US. During the early 1950s, an extended discussion took place between the two countries as they attempted to keep their research programmes coordinated even as the US changed their classification schemes. During this time, secrecy had been given greater salience as atomic secrets were betrayed. The Harwell physicist Klaus Fuchs was arrested in 1950 and shortly afterwards fellow physicist Bruno Pontecorvo escaped to the USSR (Vincent, 1998; Turchetti, 2003). Hunting for spies had equally become a commonplace security activity in the US (Badash, 2003). Against this backdrop, one historian of Whitehall secrecy characterized the atmosphere in the UK in the following terms:

The conviction grew that those who consented to work in secret had secrets of their own to hide. The glad confidence in the value of science to the citizens of the welfare state was replaced by a less trusting and respectful attitude to those charged with discovering the hidden mysteries of nature. (Vincent, 1998, p202)

Since the end of World War II, the UK had shared classification schemes with the US in just two areas: biological warfare and atomic matters.[10] In April 1951, the US Chiefs of Staff notified their UK counterparts that the biological warfare security classifications that had held since 1948 were to be revised.[11] To illustrate the scheme, they provided a list of examples of what would now fall under each of the four categories from top secret downwards, so that the whole document ran to several pages in length.[12] Within a month, the UK Air Ministry voiced objections, specifically to four of the proposed classification changes (see Box 11.1).[13]

The UK Air Ministry argued that access to the first two items would help an enemy develop countermeasures; that revealing rosters and organizational tables would leave any named individuals vulnerable; and, finally, that an unclassified rating of material for training purposes would sacrifice control by leaving this information outside the reach of the Official Secrets Act. A further

---

Box 11.1 *Proposed changes to the security classification scheme for biological warfare agreed between the US and the UK*[14]

'The fact that specific living agents or their toxic derivatives, identified by name, code name and/or description have been selected for or are being manufactured for offensive military use', to be downgraded from TOP SECRET to SECRET.

'Full details of the processes involved in the manufacture of BW agents for offensive purposes' to be downgraded from TOP SECRET to SECRET.

'Rosters and tables of organisation of BW installations and organisations' to be downgraded from CONFIDENTIAL to RESTRICTED.

'Information concerning methods of employment and tactical use of BW agents as necessary for defensive purposes' to be downgraded from RESTRICTED to UNCLASSIFIED, although with the omission of the word 'tactical' and addition of the term 'for instruction and training in measures of defence against BW'.

Source: quoted from TNA, WO 188/665, BW(51)34 Chiefs of Staff Biological Warfare Sub-Committee. BW Security Classification (27 June 1951)

---

report for the high-level Chiefs of Staff's Biological Warfare Sub-Committee followed in November, in which these changes were now described as 'a considerable relaxation of Security Classifications'.[15] The report itself revealed important differences between the secrecy cultures of the two nations. To begin with, and echoing the discussions described earlier during World War II, it noted that the:

> *USA tend to be much more sparing with the allotment of TOP SECRET classification than the UK … They [USA] tend to bracket TOP SECRET and SECRET together as a group well above the other Security Classifications, limiting TOP SECRET classifications to the minimum. The UK tendency, however, is to place TOP SECRET on a pinnacle apart and group SECRET and CONFIDENTIAL more together. As a result it is felt that SECRET has a higher significance in the USA than in UK.*[16]

The differences, once again, amounted to more than trivial discrepancies in bureaucratic practice. Classification acted out different national policies and research priorities. In this respect, the report noted that American pressure to relax security classification around biological warfare came from increasing numbers of people needing access to information as the US programme geared itself up for production:

> *USA are far nearer to the potential production stage of BW agents than in the UK. Once this stage is reached it is virtually impossible to maintain an*

unduly high Security Classification without imposing crippling handicaps on production planning.[17]

In the ensuing discussion among the UK Chiefs of Staff, this difference was repeatedly stressed and various officials pointed out that matters, such as the names of specific agents selected for biological warfare, should remain top secret as long as possible, even if this entailed divergence from the US.[18] The 'need-to-know' position of the UK was summarized by the chairman of the Biological Warfare Sub-Committee, Lieutenant-General Sir Kenneth Crawford:

We felt in general over the whole BW field that the amount of information given out should be the minimum and to as few people as possible, and that items should remain classified as highly as possible until it was absolutely necessary to downgrade them for production.[19]

Three years later, in 1954, further coordination problems were flagged as the US decided to drop the term 'restricted' entirely. Consequently, information classified in the UK as restricted would, on arrival in the US, be classified upwards to confidential and therefore have a smaller distribution than intended by UK scientists and policy-makers. In response, the Chief Scientist at the Ministry of Supply, Owen Wansborough-Jones, pointed out rather wearily that the UK should simply go its own way as 'little would be gained by having a long and tedious argument with the US. It would always be difficult to decide what classification to give any piece of information.'[20] The view of the US Chemical Corps representative, present at the same meeting, differed on the grounds that 'since there was a great deal of information passed between the US and UK, it was very desirable that similar subjects were accorded the same security protection in the two countries'.[21]

The following year, when a draft of the *US Chief Chemical Officers Guide to Security Classifications* was put before the UK Chiefs of Staff for comment, they reiterated their position on divergent classificatory schemes. Their discussion reveals that while the differences were thought to have little practical effect, they nonetheless reflected deeper assumptions about the role and aims of the UK scientific programme compared with the US. Security classification was different in the UK, according to the Chiefs of Staff and their scientific advisers, because the UK was pursuing more fundamental research:

We appreciate that the position in the USA regarding research, development and production in the BW field is very different from that in this country where our effort is concentrated mainly on fundamental research. For this reason we realise that many of the examples given in the guide are governed by local conditions ... The differences in the programmes and conditions in our two countries are such that there are bound to be differences in the detailed application of policy for security classification ... For this reason we believe that any attempt to seek agreement on a guide as detailed as the one under comment would be neither desirable or possible [sic].[22]

A short contribution by the Canadians to this debate also revealed a different problem created by a divergence in classificatory regimes. The fact that the US was collaborating with Canada in its biological warfare research was proposed as an unclassified matter in the US; yet this would have had severe political repercussions for the Canadians who declared:

> *Canadian policy does not permit the designation 'Unclassified' for Canadian work in the offensive field of BW agents primarily because of political considerations. This, of course, has no direct bearing on the statements in the document [draft Guide] as written but does mean that statements by the USA that they are participating in offensive BW work with Canada could not be considered 'Unclassified' by Canada.*[23]

The Canadian concerns reinforce my main point: that far more was at stake in assigning and harmonizing security classifications than the exercise of bureaucracy. For the US, collaboration with Canada was unexceptional. On the other hand, Canada, with no offensive programme of its own but close collaboration with the US programme, could not afford for that information to be anything but hidden.

Security classification and invisible categories

A final point to make regarding the effects of classification schemes is that security classifications are powerful tools, not only for organizing but equally for thinking. Some things are far easier to conceptualize within some classificatory schemes; conversely, some things may be extremely difficult or even impossible to conceptualize using other schemes. In other words, beyond the silence of secrecy imposed by a classification scheme, the architecture of the scheme may create other ways of stifling information. This point is exemplified in the way in which dual use (the potential for science and technology to be used for peaceful or military purposes) was sidestepped in a 1952 US security classification system. In this system, only matters deemed directly related to biological warfare were given a classification, whereas under 'unclassified' was listed:

> *Technical and research data which are not of direct or anticipated military application, but are of interest and use to the arts, science, and public health. Subject to the agency having prime cognizance and other properly designated authority, such data may be published in technical and scientific journals, giving the name of the author and the name of the establishment or establishments where the work is done. For example, data presented as having been gathered in the normal course of non-military scientific research, unclassified military research, and data dealing with problems concerning natural forms of disease may be submitted for publication.*[24]

This classification, which cleaves apart sensitive biological weapons research and work with no immediate military application, highlights a classificatory tension identified by Bowker and Starr (1999, pp10–11). The categories of an idealized classification scheme, they argue, are mutually exclusive; in the real world, however, this ideal is hardly ever realized. Again, any classification scheme does not simply describe reality; it actively creates (and silences) categories with which to work. The classification scheme for biological warfare security attempts to make an 'either–or' choice for scientific and technical knowledge. It is, according to the quote, either a security problem or it is of benign interest to the 'arts, sciences and public health'. In this scheme, any dual use science that is at once unclassified *and* top secret would, to use Bowker and Starr's terminology, be a 'monster' transgressing the neat bureaucratic categories of the scheme. Or, put more prosaically, the classification scheme sidesteps the problem of dual use by classifying a world in which 'the dual use problem' is simply assumed not to exist and, through the lens of the scheme, is rendered invisible.

Letting secrets out: Orderly and disorderly release of knowledge

Just as the state and its agents used security classification to order the world into a hierarchy of knowledge, such orderly, controlled release of information has also been directed at a wider public through occasional press releases. One example of this type of announcement reveals how different assumptions are embedded within the text of a press release. Shortly after the end of World War II, the UK Chiefs of Staff considered a general public announcement about biological warfare, intended to be made with the US and Canadian authorities. In a report to the Chiefs of Staff Committee, advisers stated three reasons for making an announcement:

> *(i) It would allay any anxiety on the part of the public through uncontrolled leakages;*
> *(ii) It would provide authority for the release of scientific information of value in industrial, agricultural and medical fields;*
> *(iii) It would assist in the integration of post-war biological research with Allied scientific studies.*[25]

What was there to know? Primarily, during World War II, the UK developed a rudimentary anthrax weapon for use against livestock and successfully tested an anti-personnel anthrax bomb (Carter and Pearson, 1999; Carter, 2000; Balmer, 2001). Towards the end of the war, close collaboration with the US and Canada resulted in the UK ordering, though never actually receiving, mass-produced anthrax bombs from the US. The public announcement on biological warfare read very differently. It explained that shortly after the fall of France, 'it was decided that experiments should be carried out to assess with greater accuracy the possible effects of German secret weapons of this nature and to design defences'. The announcement also reported that after 1942, collaboration with the US and Canada was initiated in order to devote more resources to the work and 'to protect the country against any weapons containing bacteria which the enemy might produce'.

Here, the release of information is equally an effort to exercise control over secrets, with only carefully selected information made public. The announcement reveals assumptions made by its authors about the relationship between those who are party to secrecy and those outside. As the first point in the public announcement makes clear, it assumes a trusting public who would become undesirably anxious if they were contaminated with uncontrolled information leakages.

The second justification for a public announcement about biological warfare was to enable the free flow of information. The announcement, it was argued, would provide 'authority' for the release of information to a wider audience. This authority presumably would arise from a general public awareness, not only that biological warfare research had taken place, but also that it had serendipitously given rise to peaceful applications. In the words of the public announcement:

> These researches [into biological warfare] have resulted in the accumulation of much knowledge concerning fundamental problems in micro-biology, including new techniques applicable to the study of preventative medicines and of value to agriculture. It is the intention of His Majesty's Government to make the results of fundamental studies available to scientific workers generally, and arrangements for publication to learned societies and in appropriate scientific journals are now in progress.

The 'authority' for the information release was also bolstered by presenting a case for the necessity of the wartime and post-war biological warfare research programme. Taking in the third benefit of the announcement, easing the Allied collaborative effort, the announcement stated that UK, Canadian and US research had 'revealed new techniques and new methods of approach which might constitute a potential danger to a country unprepared'. Consequently, the UK was to continue its biological warfare research programme because:

> This is essential in order that means of defence against this form of war can be adequately planned and prepared, and action taken in the event of this form of warfare materialising.

Although the particular course of action to be taken remained unspecified in the document, shortly after the public announcement was drafted the UK laid plans to develop a strategic anti-personnel capability in biological warfare that would be equivalent to their nascent atomic bomb (Balmer, 2001, 2006).

Letting secrets out: Leaks

Press releases allowed for controlled secrecy, not in the marked contrast between classified and open knowledge, but essentially as propaganda that contained carefully selected and worded information about the rationale and activities of the UK programme. In further contrast to this orderly release of information and corollary regulation of secrecy, past biological warfare programmes, along with other secret weapons programmes, have faced unplanned breaches of secrecy. In a close analysis of recent spying allegations in the US nuclear research programme, Masco observes that secrecy and the resultant fragmentation of information, where no one has the whole picture, contributes to an atmosphere of rumour and fear. In his words (Masco, 2001, p451):

> *Secrecy, however, is also wildly productive: it creates not only hierarchies of power and repression, but also unpredictable social effects, including new kinds of desire, fantasy, paranoia and – above all – gossip.*

At Los Alamos during the late 1990s, the accusations of Chinese spying and theft of information generated just such an atmosphere. Masco argues that this atmosphere was followed up with what he terms 'hyper-security measures', with the introduction of unprecedented and baroque controls (e.g. elaborate rules about who could associate with whom, or novel uses for technologies such as lie detectors) designed to either repair the breach in secrecy or at least allow managers to be seen to be managing the situation. Turning to biological warfare, Masco's observations can be extended by looking at two examples from the history of the UK research programme.

The UK biological warfare research programme was born in exemplary secrecy. Even Churchill and his War Cabinet, together with the most senior advisory committee on biological warfare, were not party to the initial decisions to found a research group at Porton Down in Wiltshire (Balmer, 2001). Once under way, the work was carried out behind the physical security of guards, gates and fences provided by the military research establishment. Records of the work, minutes of meetings, correspondence and memoranda were generally classified. Indeed, to the detriment of the historical record, but to the profit of security, much discussion and decision-making about biological warfare that took place in Whitehall and at Porton, at least until the end of the war, was carried out by word of mouth.[26]

By 1942, the physical protection of secrets offered by Porton Down was insufficient for the ambitions of the research programme. Progress towards a working anti-personnel weapon, the anthrax-charged 'N bomb', had reached the stage where scientists wanted to undertake outdoor trials beyond the bounds of Porton. The subsequent clandestine trials on the remote Scottish island of Gruinard are well documented (Carter and Pearson, 1999; Carter, 2000; Balmer, 2001; Willis, 2004). Some months following the trials, security was threatened by an outbreak of anthrax affecting around 30 to 50 sheep and other assorted domestic animals on the nearby mainland. Paul Fildes, the head of the research programme, and his deputy David Henderson visited the site and attempted to stem the outbreak, apparently by setting fire to heather in the vicinity of the infections.[27]

Fildes later noted to his superiors that the initial method for disposing of dead sheep from the trial, placing them with an explosive charge so that they would be buried under rocks, had gone awry. Too much charge was used and one or two sheep were blown into the sea, later to be washed onto the mainland shore, about three-quarters of a mile away. Rumours followed, but not entirely arising from public gossip. To begin with, the security services had been tasked with spreading a rumour that the outbreak had originated from a carcass that had dropped from a Greek ship at a nearby convoy assembly point. The rumour apparently took root because it was soon followed up by a compensation claim to the Ministry of Agriculture. Fildes was informed of the claim and protested that allowing it would constitute a security breach. The Ministry of Agriculture representative concurred, proposing to decline the claim 'on the grounds that we are not responsible for animals thrown overboard from Greek ships'.[28] Eventually, the compensation was granted along with an explanation that a settlement for the sum between Greece and the UK would most likely be made after the war.

A decade later and, once again, outdoor trials with potential biological warfare agents led to a compromise in security. The events, described in detail elsewhere (Balmer, 2004), occurred during *Operation Cauldron*, which took place off the coast of Scotland, between May and September 1952. The trials had been protected with the usual high levels of secrecy. Prior to the trials, Prime Minister Churchill had intervened to ensure that no public statement was made about the trials and a press release, prepared in the event of being forced to reveal information, was stripped of substantive content. Local fishermen received notice of the trials from the UK Admiralty in the form of a chart of the danger area and a warning that 'special trials' would be taking place from May to September. The notice informed fishermen that they were to steer clear from the 5 mile radius of the danger area when a red flag was flying. Although there was no hint whatsoever that the trials involved biological agents, the commanding officer of the trial vessel still recommended that the warning was 'couched in as strong language as possible in conformity with the requirements for security'.[29]

On the final day of the trial, a fishing vessel, the *Carella*, strayed into the danger zone around the trial shortly after a test bomb had been detonated. The *Carella* ignored warnings and the ship's crew was exposed to a cloud of plague. The authorities' response was to tail the trawler over the next 21 days without notifying the crew and to listen for a distress call. Medics aboard the tailing vessels were instructed, in the event of receiving a distress call, to board the ship and inform the crew that they were treating their stricken crew members for pneumonia. In the meantime, back on shore, UK Admiralty staff were instructed to approach the owners of the *Carella*. They were told to obtain the names and addresses of the trawler crew, plus details of any changes of personnel that might have occurred. The trawler's owners were told a cover story, 'that the trawler was in a forbidden area and that the men may have seen secret equipment which it was particularly desired that they should not'.[30] When it eventually transpired that the crew was unaffected by plague, the *Carella*'s owners were informed that there had, after all, been nothing of interest for the fishermen to accidentally spot.

In the context of this discussion of secrecy, these two incidents demonstrate how secrecy operates in a slightly different way from that proposed by Masco.

In the Los Alamos case, Masco describes a security breach in a secretive atmosphere that generates rumour and gossip; this is then followed up by social control through the establishment of hyper-security measures. This leaves rumour and gossip in the province of those on the outside of the secret. A rhetorical division is forged between the rational, calming intervention of the authorities and the irrational, ill-informed set of ignorant outsiders prone to panic and gossip. Alternatively, the Gruinard and *Carella* incidents show how rumour and gossip actually meld with hyper-security. In both cases, rumours were deliberately created by those in authority in order to control information and manage the situation. This is not merely a feature of biological warfare. Rumour and gossip are resources that were used by the authorities in the Manhattan Project. For example, there were attempts to spread a rumour in Santa Fe that an electric rocket was being built at Los Alamos (Serber, 1998, pp78–79).

At a broader level, this use of rumour and gossip alerts us to assumptions embedded in contemporary debates about security and the governance of biological weapons. In these discussions, while rumour, gossip and paranoia are often depicted as inherent attributes of 'others' (Williams, 2004) – an ignorant or irrational public, for example – the examples from the historical record suggest that rumour and gossip can equally be construed as governance tools for keeping those 'others' ignorant.

Conclusions

The pervasiveness of secrecy in the history of biological warfare tends to work against attempts to understand how secrecy works in practice. At first glance, all that can appear to be said from examining the historical record is that programmes were secret, full stop. Of course, this message can then be used as a springboard to asking why secrecy was paramount and also to ask normative questions about its desirability. This chapter has taken a slightly different approach to secrecy and has paused to reflect on the operation of secrecy in the UK biological weapons programme. Security classification, in this case, reflected how British biological weapons scientists and advisers viewed the status of their own programme, both on its own terms – as having reached a particular stage of development and as pursuing fundamental research – and in relation to its allies, particularly its standing with respect to the US. Secondly, the chapter pointed out that the release of secrets by the state is often accompanied by strong controls over just what is or is not revealed. While this observation is unexceptional, the chapter further argued that in cases where this control is lost, we witness the authorities using tools not always immediately associated with governance – including rumour and gossip – to restore order and maintain a grip on secrecy. Throughout, the chapter has emphasized that although the publication or otherwise of scientific information is important, more than just this fate can be at stake when keeping and revealing secrets.

Notes

1   If the work remained secret, it is not clear who would be able to make such a construal. The UK scientists were, at this time, working towards an anti-personnel biological bomb (Balmer 2001).

2   The National Archive (hereafter TNA), WO188/668, AC12384/BRBM29, BRAB, 29th Meeting (12 June 1953).

3   Camp Detrick was the key site of the US army biological warfare programme.

4   This phenomenon has largely been analysed in relation to other Cold War military scientific programmes (see Westwick, 2000; Gusterson, 2003).

5   Although the following account supports the general (and widely accepted) picture of a UK government machine obsessed with secrecy, it is worth noting that a wider and contrasting debate about secrecy took place throughout Whitehall in parallel with these discussions. The chief concern expressed by senior civil servants in this debate was the apparent proliferation of over-classification, which it felt led to an undermining of the special status of top secret information.

6   TNA, CAB 21/1659 Security Classification of Official Documents (11 June 1943).

7   TNA CAB 21/2836 Memo EEB to Sir Norman Brook (1 April 1952).

8   TNA CAB 21/2836 Memo EEB to Sir Norman Brook (1 April 1952).

9   TNA CAB 21/2836 Memo EEB to Sir Norman Brook (1 April 1952).

10 TNA, WO 188/666 BW(54)5 Chiefs of Staff Committee Biological Warfare Sub-Committee, BW Security Classification (2 March 1954).

11 TNA, WO 188/665, BW(51) 34 Chiefs of Staff Biological Warfare Sub-Committee, Security Classification of Biological Warfare Information, Report by Wing Commander G. M. Wyatt and Major D. M. C. Prichard (26 November 1951).

12 TNA, WO 188/665, BW(51) 34 Chiefs of Staff Biological Warfare Sub-Committee, BW Security Classification (27 June 1951).

13 TNA, WO 188/665, Annex, Copy of a letter received from DDI (ORG&S) dated 25/7/51 addressed to Wing Commander A. W. Howard, Ministry of Defence (25 July 1951).

14 TNA, WO 188/665, BW(51) 34 Chiefs of Staff Biological Warfare Sub-Committee, BW Security Classification (27 June 1951).

15 TNA, WO 188/665, BW(51) 34 Chiefs of Staff Biological Warfare Sub-Committee, Security Classification of Biological Warfare Information, Report by Wing Commander G. M. Wyatt and Major D. M. C. Prichard (26 November 1951). On the general apparatus for biological warfare policy-making in the UK, see Balmer (2001).

16 TNA, WO 188/665, BW(51) 34 Chiefs of Staff Biological Warfare Sub-Committee, Security Classification of Biological Warfare Information, Report by Wing Commander G. M. Wyatt and Major D. M. C. Prichard (26 November 1951).

17 TNA, WO 188/665, BW(51) 34 Chiefs of Staff Biological Warfare Sub-Committee, Security Classification of Biological Warfare Information, Report by Wing Commander G. M. Wyatt and Major D. M. C. Prichard (26 November 1951).

18 TNA, WO 188/665 BW (51) 4th Meeting, Chiefs of Staff Committee, Biological Warfare Sub-Committee (2 November 1951).

19 TNA, WO 188/665 BW (51) 4th Meeting, Chiefs of Staff Committee, Biological Warfare Sub-Committee (2 November 1951).

20 TNA, WO 188/666 BW(54) 5 Chiefs of Staff Committee Biological Warfare Sub-Committee, BW Security Classification (2 March 1954).

21 TNA, WO 188/666 BW(54) 5 Chiefs of Staff Committee Biological Warfare Sub-Committee, BW Security Classification (2 March 1954).

22 TNA, WO 188/666, COS(C)(55) 61 from J. H. Gresswell, Joint Secretary, BW Sub-Committee to the Secretary, BJSM, Washington (26 May 1955).
23 TNA, WO 188/666, BW(55) 9 Chiefs of Staff Committee Biological Warfare Sub-Committee, BW Security Classifications (27 June 1955).
24 TNA, WO 188/666 BW(52) 6 Chiefs of Staff Committee Biological Warfare Sub-Committee, BW Security Classifications (21 April 1952), Annex, Policy Governing Classification of Matter Concerning Biological Warfare.
25 TNA, CAB 80/51, Chiefs of Staff Committee, Public Announcement on Biological Warfare: Report by the Inter-Services Sub-Committee on Biological Warfare (7 November 1945).
26 More recently, word of mouth was also a way of maintaining secrecy and avoiding (later) accountability in the South African biological warfare programme (Gould and Hay, 2006).
27 These activities were reported by locals who still recalled the events some years later (Willis, 2004)
28 TNA, WO 188/654, Letter Fildes to Duff Cooper (14 April 1943).
29 TNA, ADM 1/25255 from Commanding Officer HMS Ben Lomond to Flag Officer, Scotland, Cauldron – Operational Trials Area – Warning to Fishermen (14 May 1952).
30 TNA, ADM 1/26857, Letter Noble to R. A. Butler MP (18 September 1952).

References

Badash, L. (2003), 'From security blanket to security risk: Scientists in the decade after Hiroshima', *History and Technology* vol 19, pp241–256

Balmer, B. (2001) *Britain and Biological Warfare*, Basingstoke, UK, Palgrave

Balmer, B. (2002) 'Killing "without the distressing preliminaries"', *Minerva*, vol 40, pp57–75

Balmer, B. (2004) 'How does an accident become an experiment? Secret science and the exposure of the public to biological warfare agents', *Science as Culture*, vol 13, pp197–228

Balmer, B. (2006) 'The British program', in Wheelis, M., Rózsa, L. and Dando, M. (eds) *Deadly Cultures: Biological Weapons Since 1945*, Cambridge, MA, Harvard University Press, pp47–83

BMA (British Medical Association) (1999) *Biotechnology, Weapons and Humanity*, Amsterdam, Harwood

Bok, S. (1989) *Secrets: On the Ethics of Concealment and Revelation*, New York, Vintage

Bowker, G. C. and Starr, S. L. (1999) *Sorting Things Out*, Cambridge, MA, MIT Press

Carter, G. B. (2000) *Chemical and Biological Defence at Porton Down 1916–2000*, London, TSO

Carter, G. B. and Pearson, G. (1999), 'British biological warfare and biological defence, 1925–45', in Geissler, E. and van Courtland, Moon, J. E. (eds) *Biological and Toxin Weapons*, Oxford, Oxford University Press, pp91–126

Colwell, R. and Zilinskas, R. (2000) 'Bioethics and the prevention of biological warfare', in Zilinskas, R. (ed) *Biological Warfare*, Boulder, CO, Lynne Rienner, pp225–245

Gentile, M. (2004) 'Former closed cities and urbanisation in the FSU: An exploration in Kazakhstan', *Europe–Asia Studies*, vol 56, pp263–278

Gould, C. and Hay, A. (2006) 'The South African Biological Weapons Program', in Wheelis, M., Rózsa, L. and Dando, M. (eds) *Deadly Cultures*, Cambridge, MA, Harvard University Press, pp191–212

Guillemin, J. (2005) *Biological Weapons: From the Invention of State-Sponsored Programs to Contemporary Bioterrorism*, New York, Columbia University Press

Guillemin, J. (2006) 'Scientists and the history of biological weapons: A brief historical overview of the development of biological weapons in the twentieth century', *EMBO Reports*, vol 7(SI), ppS45–S49

Gusterson, H. (2003) 'The death of the authors of death', in Biagioli, M. and Galison, P. (eds) *Scientific Authorship*, New York, Routledge, pp281–307

Harris, S. (1994) *Factories of Death: Japanese Biological Warfare 1932–45 and the American Cover-Up*, London, Routledge

Hart, J. (2006) 'The Soviet Biological Weapons Program', in Wheelis, M., Rózsa, L. and Dando, M. (eds) (2006) *Deadly Cultures*, Cambridge, MA, Harvard University Press, pp132–156

Masco, J. (2001) 'Lie detectors: Of secrets and hypersecurity in Los Alamos', *Public Culture*, vol 14, pp441–467

NRC (National Research Council) (2004) *Biotechnology Research in an Age of Terrorism*, Washington, DC, National Academies Press

Serber, R. (1998) *Peace and War*, New York, Columbia University Press

Turchetti, S. (2003) 'Atomic secrets and governmental lies', *The British Journal for the History of Science*, vol 36, pp389–415

Vincent, D. (1998) *The Culture of Secrecy: Britain 1832–1998*, Oxford, Oxford University Press

Westwick, P. (2000) 'Secret science', *Minerva*, vol 38, pp363–391

Wheelis, M., Rózsa, L. and Dando, M. (eds) (2006) *Deadly Cultures: Biological Weapons Since 1945*, Cambridge, MA, Harvard University Press

Williams, S. J. (2004) 'Bioattack or panic attack?', *Social Theory and Health*, vol 2, pp67–93

Willis, E. (2004) 'Contamination and compensation', *Medicine, Conflict and Survival*, vol 20, pp334–343

White, L. (2000) 'Telling more: Lies, secrets and history', *History and Theory*, vol 39, pp11–22

12

Reflecting on the Problem of Dual Use

Caitríona McLeish

The problem of biological weapons has been described as the 'most important under-addressed threat' facing today's global environment (UN, 2006). Biological weapons do, indeed, deserve special attention: although they resemble other weapons in that they attack life, advances in the life sciences coupled with advances in associated technologies could eventually make it possible to disrupt and manipulate any life process that keeps us functioning as human beings (Meselson, 2000). If that were to happen, then the nature of conflict would be radically changed, opening up unprecedented opportunities for violence, coercion, repression or subjugation.

One approach to address the threat that bioweapons pose is the creation of a robust and resilient multilayered array of integrated policies aimed at convincing a potential user of biological weapons that the risks of detection and retribution far outweigh any possible benefits. As noted in the introduction, this approach recognizes that there is no 'silver bullet' solution to the problem of biological weapons and that to be truly effective, a response needs to include governance measures and initiatives from complementary policy domains that contribute to the overall aim of preventing the use of biological weapons (Pearson, 1993, p151). As developed in this book, such a 'web of prevention' should connect policies and commitments 'stretch[ing] from the individual to the international' (Littlewood, 2004, p3). This would include international treaties such as the 1972 Biological Weapons Convention and the 1993 Chemical Weapons Convention, which codify the long-established norm of non-use, as well as complementary activities, such as the coordination of national export controls among groups of like-minded countries; United Nations Security Council action, as in resolution 1540, to universalize national legislation implementing the 1972 and 1993 treaties; and new pluri-lateral measures, such as the US-led Proliferation Security Initiative. Self-governing initiatives from the scientific community regarding its work practices are also necessary.

In some way, each of these governance measures addresses the issue of dual use. This concept – the idea that a technology can have multiple purposes, which in the biological warfare environment, in particular, include purposes that are not easily separated – is central to how the biological weapons problem is understood. It assists us, for example, in understanding why societal vulnerability to these weapons exits and identifies some of the causes of that vulnerability. This, in turn, lends itself to analysis of how and why the perceived threat of biological weapons is framed in a particular way and why certain policies then become generated. As argued in this chapter, to a large extent, what determines the nature and scope of the web of prevention in the biological weapons environment is how the concept of dual use is understood, and how its characteristics are applied to the relevant stages of the technological innovation process. If the concept is understood too narrowly, then new opportunities for additional governance along an innovation path will be missed and opportunities for synergistic relations with other policy domains will go unexplored. If the concept is understood too broadly, then the web becomes unsustainable for the simple reason that it will disrupt the acquisition and exploitation of these technologies for beneficial purposes (NAS, National Academy of Engineering and Institute of Medicine, 1982; Robinson, 1997; Breithaupt, 2000; Atlas, 2001, 2002; Gaudioso and Salerno, 2004; NRC, 2004; McLeish and Nightingale, 2005).

This chapter reflects on how the concept of dual use is currently understood. It shows that multiple conceptual understandings of the term currently exist that are impinging on the generation, and therefore prioritization, of governance initiatives. Given the importance of conceptual understandings, it is essential that an intellectual space is provided where the term dual use can be critically examined and where embedded assumptions that may influence governance initiatives can be unpacked. The chapter begins to consider the contribution that might be made by framing the issue of controlling dual use technologies as a technology governance problem. Some relevant literature from science and technology studies and technology innovation is therefore introduced. More than being an interesting intellectual exercise, critical examination of the concept of dual use, and the introduction of stakeholders with relevant contributions to the policy dilemma that dual use creates, can strengthen the web of prevention: sustainability can be increased by improving conceptual underpinnings and removing potentially harmful conceptual competition; by introducing insights from framings such as technology governance, new opportunities for additional governance along the innovation path are likely to arise.

The role of 'dual use' in biological weapons threat framings

In the 1997 *Proliferation Threat and Response* report by the US Department of Defense, it was argued that 'advances in biotechnology and genetic engineering may facilitate the development of potentially new and more deadly biological warfare agents'.[1] The report went on:

The ability to modify microbial agents at a molecular level has existed since the 1960s, when revolutionary new genetic engineering techniques were introduced, but the enterprise tended to be slow and unpredictable. With today's more powerful techniques, infectious organisms can be modified to bring about disease in different ways. Many bioengineering companies (both US and foreign) now sell all-in-one kits to enable even high school-level students to perform recombinant DNA experiments. The availability of free online gene sequence databases and analytic software over the Internet further simplifies and disseminates this capability. It is now possible to transform relatively benign organisms to cause harmful effects. (US Department of Defense, 1997)

Although the same report the year previously had also paid heed to how advancing science and technology might be employed to overcome 'product deficiencies in the classic agents and toxins normally addressed in such discussions',[2] the 1997 report presented new levels of concern about the threat posed by the potential misuse of life science research and technology.

Since then, publicly accessible biological weapons threat assessments have placed the issue of dual use technologies at the heart of their bio-threat frameworks (see, for example, Wilkening, 1999; Sands, 2002; Director of Central Intelligence, 2003, 2006; Lehrman, 2006; NRC and the Institute of Medicine, 2006; UN, 2006). Common to these assessments is, as one group of experts commented, the assumption that as the life sciences and associated technologies advance and pertinent knowledge and technology become increasing available, accessible and affordable:

... it is not at all unreasonable to anticipate that biological threats will be increasingly sought, threatened and used for warfare, terrorism and criminal purposes and by increasingly less sophisticated and resourced individuals, groups or nations. (NRC and the Institute of Medicine, 2006 p52)

Although this concern is not new, and is partially supported by the historical record (see, for example, Rosebury, 1947; SIPRI, 1972), it is recent unease about the potential to use advancing science and technology to create and produce new biological agents and weapons that has secured centre stage for the issue of dual use within bio-threat frameworks. For example, many authors (including Block, 1999; BMA, 1999; Dando, 1999, 2001; Nixdorff et al, 2000; Rappert, 2003, and van Aken and Hammond, 2003) argue that advancing science and technology in the fields of immunology, virology, genomics, proteomics and the study of pathogenesis and zoonosis are potentially opening up categories of biological weapons agents (other than pathogenic micro-organisms and toxic molecules) that work by reducing the efficiency of the human immune system or by evading natural detection and treatment. While these commentators stress the relevance of advances in scientific understanding, others note that technological advances over the last 20 years have made the production of biological weapons less technically challenging and capital inten-sive (Collier et al, 2004, p3).

For those working towards preventing diseases being put to a hostile use, the dual use issue is the central issue making design and implementation of effective solutions problematic. Policies and initiatives designed to constrain the acquisi-tion and exploitation of technologies for biological weapons purposes can also potentially disrupt 'legitimate' scientific and technical activities with corre-sponding and potentially substantial social costs. As well as social costs, the inability to easily separate the socially beneficial and legitimate uses of these biological technologies from socially detrimental and illegitimate uses means that the threat from biological weapons cannot be removed entirely: as long as technologies with relevant dual uses exist and continue to proliferate through legitimate technology development and research activities, the potential for misuse exists, and as new technological opportunities for misuse open, percep-tion of the potential biological weapons threat and societal vulnerability will increase. Such are the current levels of perceived threat and vulnerability that mainstream discussions about the biological weapons threat tend to use the word 'when' rather than the word 'if'.

Deconstructing the concept of 'dual use'

So what is 'dual use'?

Essentially, the concept describes the ability of any technology to be put to a purpose other than that which it was originally intended for. Within the biolog-ical weapons environment, the dual use issue is particularly acute, with much of the knowledge, tools and techniques needed to develop and produce biological weapons having legitimate uses in activities such as scientific research, drug and vaccine production, agriculture and industrial processing. Consequently, attempts to create policies to reduce the likelihood of the misuse of dual use biological technologies need to balance encouragement and promotion of the socially beneficial uses with successfully preventing opportunities to divert those same technologies into illegal, illegitimate or hostile applications.

How one understands the dual use issue within the biological weapons envi-ronment stems from how biological weapons themselves are conceived. One definition of biological weapons is that these weapons use disease to cause harm to humans, animals and plants. Direct harm is caused to the host either by the virulence of the chosen pathogenic micro-organism (including viruses) or by the host's response to that particular pathogenic micro-organism. Understanding biological weapons in this manner means that what is known about disease, disease-causing mechanisms and the disease-fighting mechanisms of humans, animals and plants also has the potential to be of interest to those wishing to pursue the use of disease for hostile purposes. As well as specific disease-related information, scientific knowledge of a more general kind, as well as manufactur-ing technologies and processes used to create or enable the development of preventive and therapeutic measures, may also be of interest.

Understanding the problem of dual use in these terms seems sensible; but it is in no way the agreed method. In expert discussions, multiple understandings are presented and terms such as 'dual use', 'dual purpose', 'multipurpose' and even 'dual intention' are used interchangeably without explanation as to their differences. Multiple understandings are also present in expert literature. The 2004 US National Academies Fink Report, for example, presented dual use 'in the language of arms control and disarmament' – that is, as 'technologies intended for civilian application that can also be used for military purposes' (NRC, 2004, p18). In another National Academies report two years later, an extended understanding of dual use was used where different categorizations of use were included alongside the capacity and potential of both tangible and intangible biological technologies to be misused (NRC and the Institute of Medicine, 2006). This extended definition considered use in terms of harmful or peaceful purposes; but other subcategories of use can also be considered, such as 'legitimate' and 'illegitimate'.

Highlighting multiple presentations and/or interchangeable terminology may seem trivial; but it suggests important conceptual inadequacies that could undermine efforts to prevent biological weapons from being used. Depending upon which presentation of dual use is employed, different influences will be brought to bear on policy generation and, therefore, prioritization. For example, in the common use of the term, which the Fink Report assigned to the language of arms control and disarmament, the problem of dual use is understood in terms of technology transfer, which leads to policies that focus on the movement of technology from one sector to another. An extended understanding of dual use which includes sub-categorizations of use ('harmful/peaceful' and 'legitimate/illegitimate') accommodates intra-sector technology transfers, as well as transfers between sectors.

The need to accommodate intra-sector transfers within dual use definitions can be further strengthened when issues of right and wrong uses of technology emerge. These can occur within, as well as across, sectors. The 2006 National Academies report captured the importance of unpacking the term 'use' when it described a continuum of potentially dangerous activities. Using multiple terms with different understandings that are largely distinguished on the basis of the intent of the user, the report noted that:

> ... the use of technology without the intent to cause harm but with unanticipated dual use consequences, including experiments or other activities conducted with inadequate oversight or without an awareness of the consequences of certain outcomes, would be considered inappropriate use, while the deliberate use of technology for the creation, development, production or deployment of biological weapons is considered malevolent or malicious use, with malevolent indicating the intent to cause death or serious injury, and malicious a lesser degree of intended damage. (NRC and the Institute of Medicine, 2006, p29)

When deciding where effort is to be applied, extended understandings of how technology can be used and misused permit the generation of policies that emphasize the user and their social contexts, rather than the physical location of the technology (see, for example, McLeish, 2002).

Understanding dual use in terms of policy solutions

When the term dual use first entered the technology policy literature, its conventional employment highlighted the benefits that a nation could expect from exploiting civilian technologies to develop and produce military technologies (Alic et al 1992; Alic, 1993; Reppy, 1999; Molas-Gallart, 2000, 2002; on technology transfer more generally, see Bozeman, 2000). However, from the late 1970s, the term began to take on negative associations, referring instead to the potential of technologies with legitimate civilian uses to aid the proliferation of prohibited military technologies (UN General Assembly, 1977; Roberts, 1995; Molas-Gallart, 1996).

The centrality of the dual use issue to the problem of biological weapons was recognized by the negotiators of the 1972 Biological Weapons Convention when they provided that each State Party should never in any circumstance:

> ... *develop, produce, stockpile or otherwise acquire or retain microbial or other biological agents, or toxins whatever their origin or method of production of types and in quantities that have no justification for prophylactic, protective or other peaceful purposes; and weapons, equipment or means of delivery designed to use such agents or toxins for hostile purposes or in armed conflict.*

In this prohibition, the entire biological weapons innovation process, except research, is covered, and member states also undertake not to help 'any State, group of States or international organizations' to do the same. Measures in addition to the BWC which can also be included within the web of prevention seek to strengthen these prohibitions. Because the weapons themselves are outlawed by the BWC, these additional measures focus on the technological subcomponents of the weapons systems. Within these measures, however, competing understandings of dual use are found; so what follows is a descriptive account of three of those different understandings of dual use, which are presented for the purposes of illustration as three separate and distinct understandings.

Model 1: A context-driven understanding of dual use

Increased attention began to be given to the biological weapons problem at the end of the Cold War when international security threats were redefined. In 1992, for example, the summit session of the United Nations Security Council highlighted weapons of mass destruction as the greatest threat to international peace and security and outlined a course of action involving 'the members of the Council [committing] themselves to working to *prevent the spread of technology related to the research for or production of* such weapons and to take appropriate action to that end' (UNSC, 1992, emphasis added).

Placing the duality problem at the heart of their proposed course of action, the words emphasized above reflect an understanding of the dual use problem as being acquired. Rather than the technology itself being inherently dangerous, this understanding regards the context of technology to be potentially danger-ous. Within this context-driven model of dual use, then, policy solutions are based on what social scientists would regard as a deterministic belief that posses-sion of technologies will lead to the realization of the misuse potential. Consequently, policy solutions are created around ideas of technology transfer – that is, not allowing technology to be possessed in particular contexts.

Export controls are a classic policy within the context-driven model and are considered in depth in Chapter 9 in this volume. These controls depend upon the identification and listing of critical technologies associated with the produc-tion and development processes of undesirable end products – in this case, biological weapons. Exports of technologies listed as critical are only allowed after a judgement has been passed about the legitimacy of the request to trans-fer and the intent of the requesting party. Transfer will only occur if the recipient is not judged to be a cause for concern (Defense Science Board, 2000).

Examples of export-control systems include the Australia Group, which is described in Chapter 10. The Australia Group was set up during 1984 to 1985 in response to evidence that Iraq had sourced precursor chemicals and materi-als for its chemical warfare programme through legitimate industrial channels (Robinson, 1992; Zilinskas, 1999). The group later turned its attention to biological agents and relevant dual use manufacturing and dispersal equipment, also after evidence was uncovered about diversions of dual use materials to biological weapons programmes.

The central objective of the Australia Group (to use licensing measures to ensure that exports of certain chemicals, biological agents, and dual use chemi-cal and biological manufacturing facilities and equipment do not contribute to the spread of chemical and biological weapons[3]) adheres to a context-driven understanding of dual use in that members agree to:

> ... *limit the risks* of proliferation and terrorism involving chemical and biological weapons *by controlling transfers of technology that could contribute to chemical and/or biological weapons activities by states or non-state actors [emphasis added].*[4]

Although the potential malevolent users are defined, what is emphasized is the connection between reducing the risks of proliferation and/or terrorism and the transfer of technology from a legitimate to an illegitimate domain.

Other export-control regimes recognize the distribution of dual use technolo-gies via intangible methods of transfer. The Wassenaar Arrangement on Export Controls for Conventional Arms and dual use Goods and Technologies, for example, has since 2000 included non-physical technology transfers routes, such as oral conversation (including telephone conversations), facsimile transmissions and other electronic transfers (e.g. the internet), in its control measures. In doing this the Wassenaar Arrangement goes beyond a simple artefact definition of technology to one that includes specific information necessary for the 'development', 'production' or 'use' of an artefact. This includes technical data such as blueprints, formulae, diagrams or tables, and technical assistance such as instruction, skills, training, working knowledge and consulting services.[5] These intangible elements of technology reflect a social science understanding of technology as comprising not just the artefact but also:

> ... *the ability to recognise technical problems, the ability to develop new concepts and tangible solutions to technical problems, the concepts and tangibles developed to solve technical problems, and the ability to exploit the concepts and tangibles in an effective way. (Autio and Laamanen, 1995)*

Model 2: A user-driven understanding of dual use

A second understanding of the dual use problem can be found when examining some of the new national biosecurity controls governing dual use activities in terms of what can be done, with what technologies and by whom. Much effort has, for example, been spent in identifying, listing and then constructing controls around certain critical pathogens and toxins identified as having the potential to be especially threatening to humans, animals or plants. In the UK, such a list is found in Schedule 5 of the 2001 Anti-terrorism, Crime and Security Act. Updated and extended in January 2007 to reflect scientific advances, the list now contains 45 viruses, 5 rickettsiae, 21 bacteria, 13 toxins and 2 fungi, and extends to the genetic material of these pathogens and to genetically modified organisms containing a sequence of a listed agent (UK, 2007). Special legal obligations are placed on those wishing to use these agents: for example it is a legal obligation for the occupier of any premises to notify the Secretary of State prior to keeping or using any of the agents, and should there be reasonable grounds for believing that security measures are inadequate, the secretary of state can require the occupier to dispose of any or all parts of the substance. Likewise, the act also empowers the Secretary of State to prevent an individual from having access to dangerous materials and/or parts of premises where these materials are kept (United Kingdom of Great Britain and Northern Ireland, 2001; for an assessment, see McLeish, 2004).

A similar list exists in the US. The 2001 USA Patriot Act places special restrictions on 81 viruses, bacteria, fungi and toxins, as well any genetic modifications thereof, any nucleic acids that can produce infectious forms of any of the viruses, and any recombinant nucleic acids that can encode for the functional forms of any toxin if the nucleic acids can be expressed *in vivo* or *in vitro*, or are in a vector or recombinant host genome and can be expressed *in vivo* or *in vitro*.[6] The act forbids what it calls 'restricted persons' to possess, transport or receive these listed agents (2001 USA Patriot Act). To ensure this requirement is met, the 2002 Public Health Security and Bioterrorism Preparedness and Response Act requires all individuals wishing to access, possess, use, work with or transfer any of the select agent to undergo registration. Registration includes undergoing a security assessment conducted by the Federal Bureau of Investigation before being approved by either the Centers for Disease Control and Prevention or the US Department of Agriculture's Animal and Plant Health Inspection Service.

Both the UK's Schedule 5 list and the US's select agent rules emphasize the role of the user in the dual use problem. Rather than seeing dual use as an inherent characteristic of certain technologies, these controls focus on the externalities of the technology – in this case, users. Like the first model, critical technologies are also listed; but in this understanding of dual use, the focus of policy is not the act of transfer or its means, but rather the individuals who have access to that technology. This second model can therefore be thought of as user-driven understanding of dual use.

This shift in the focus away from emphasizing transfer and its means towards emphasizing the role of the user is particularly evident in the US select agent controls. The USA Patriot Act denies the right of possession and the right to transport or receive select agents to what it calls 'restricted' persons. In doing this, the act categorizes the users of select agents into two categories: 'restricted' and (by implication) 'not restricted'. A restricted person is defined as an individual who:

- is under indictment for a crime punishable by imprisonment for a term exceeding one year;
- has been convicted in any court of a crime punishable by imprisonment for a term exceeding one year;
- is a fugitive from justice;
- is an unlawful user of any controlled substance (as defined in section 102 of the Controlled Substances Act (21 USC 802));
- is an alien illegally or unlawfully in the US;
- has been adjudicated as a mental defective or has been committed to any mental institution;
- is an alien (other than an alien lawfully admitted for permanent residence) who is a national of a country to which the Secretary of State has made a determination (that remains in effect) that such country has repeatedly provided support for acts of international terrorism; or
- has been discharged from the US armed services under dishonourable conditions.

The act correlates the potential risk of misuse with an assessment of the users' character. The implied calculation is that if the potential user falls into one of these eight categories, he is not fit to possess, transfer and receive select agents without causing unnecessary risk to national security. However, if the user does not fall into one of these eight categories, he is fit to possess, transfer and receive select agents because he does not pose an unnecessary risk to national security.

Standing as a hybrid of the context-driven understanding of dual use and the user-driven understanding are those governance efforts which emphasize both the future contexts of users and the transfer of intangible elements of technology, such as knowledge. The ability to recognize and solve technical problems and to exploit those solutions requires specialist knowledge and skills that are located in people, rather than things or contexts (see Molas-Gallart, 1997). Governance efforts that concern themselves with this element of the dual use problem include those which vet scientists from certain countries wishing to study particular scientific disciplines relevant to the production and development of any of the weapons of mass destruction.

The UK has run such a governance effort since 1994 after it had become apparent that a number of state proliferators had exploited scientists who had received their educational training in the UK. In order to prevent (potential) proliferators of weapons of mass destruction from taking courses that would help them to acquire *the knowledge necessary to assist with the production or manufacture (proliferation) of WMDs* within their home country that might one day threaten the UK's national security,[7] universities and higher education colleges were able, on a voluntary basis, to seek the government's advice about whether an application should be regarded as a proliferation risk based on the country of origin of the applicant and the subject they wish to study.

At the time of writing, plans have been announced by the UK government to re-launch the scheme as a compulsory measure affecting the applications of any post-graduate student from outside the European Union coming to UK universities to study scientific disciplines that are considered relevant to the development of WMDs or their delivery systems (see, for example, Gilbert, 2007; Asthana, 2007).

Model 3: Understanding dual use as an inherent characteristic of technology

Whereas the governance efforts of the previous models (including the hybrid model) have emphasized externalities, the final set of governance initiatives to be discussed present dual use as an inherent characteristic of technology. Although advocates of this view acknowledge that interaction with a user is needed for the technology to be misused, they deem the potential of misuse to be so high and the outcome of any potential misuse so grave as to warrant implementing controls covering all users, in all contexts. Recent governance initiatives on the communication and dissemination of scientific results reveal just such a viewpoint.

Explaining, in an article written for *Nature*, the basis of their decision to draw up preliminary guidance for additional peer review for security-sensitive information, the 34 members of the Journal Editors and Authors Group (2003) stated that the 'prospect of bioterrorism has raised legitimate concerns about the potential abuse of published information'. In this new environment, the group proposed that the journal editor be allowed to judge whether 'the potential harm of publication outweighs the potential societal benefits' (Journal Editors and Authors Group, 2003). If the journal editor does conclude that potential harm outweighs potential gain, the group proposed that the paper is either modified or not published.

A similar presentation of dual use was given in the Fink Report, *Biotechnology Research in an Age of Terrorism: Confronting the dual use Dilemma* (NRC, 2004). Although the committee did acknowledge the difficulty of making 'useful distinctions between permitted and prohibited purposes at the level of basic research' (NRC, 2004, p19), it recommended a number of actions that ought to be considered to minimize the potential for misuse. These recommendations included pre-publication review of manuscripts with particular scrutiny given to publications describing experiments that would:

- demonstrate how to render a vaccine ineffective;
- confer resistance to therapeutically useful antibiotics or antiviral agents;
- enhance the virulence of a pathogen or render a non-pathogen virulent;
- increase transmissibility of a pathogen;
- alter the host range of a pathogen;
- enable the evasion of diagnostic detection modalities; or
- enable the weaponization of a biological agent or toxin (NRC, 2004 p5).

The committee identified and highlighted these seven 'experiments of concern' as possessing certain characteristics which made them especially dangerous given current scientific and technological possibilities. The committee recommended that this identification process be performed again in the future so that the 'experiments of concern' reflected future threat realities (NRC, 2004, p6).

As well as recommending pre-publication review for these 'experiments of concern', the committee also advocated implementing additional general safety and security oversight, which is described in some detail in Chapter 7. It believed that this additional oversight should take place at the institutional level by expanding the remit of the Institutional Biosafety Committees so that they could evaluate the potential benefits of conducting one of these experiments against the potential risks before the experiment takes place, and designate the project either as able to move forward or as raising concerns that need further consideration at a higher level (NRC, 2004, p7).

What can be learned about the concept of dual use?

The understandings of dual use presented above represent some, but not all, of the multiple understandings of the concept that can be found when examining current policy solutions and governance initiatives. For the purposes of illustration, they have been presented as three distinct understandings; but as shown by the hybrid model, there is much overlap. The three models have been chosen to highlight how different understandings of the concept of dual use can lead to different focuses in the policies and government initiatives that they elicit.

Although much is written about the problem of dual use and about policies to govern dual use technologies, there is a notable lack of critical examination of the concept. This is surprising given the centrality of the issue to framing of the biological weapons threat and the impact that different conceptual understandings have on policy generation and prioritization of efforts. More worrying, though, is the potential impact that competing understandings can have on the sustainability of the web of prevention. Lack of conceptual clarity in the governance process can, for example, heighten the tendency towards initiating inadequate and/or short-term policy responses to the long-term anti-proliferation goal. Furthermore, empirical work has shown that if subjects of regulatory controls do not fully understand the underlying assumptions of the controls, including conceptual understandings, they resist implementing them (for more on this, see McLeish and Nightingale, 2005).

The differences between the three understandings of dual use outlined above centre on competing conceptualizations about what constitutes technology, and what is the relationship between technology and function and the innovation process. These differences are, in part, a product of dual use being dynamic in character. The fact that dual use is a dynamic concept should be obvious and not in dispute: it must necessarily embrace changing understandings about the nature of the locations within which science and technology are being generated and/or used, as well as embracing shifting understandings about the biological weapons problem, including changes in understandings about the threat posed by these weapons, the actors involved and concepts of use.

As in any discussions involving dynamic concepts, there is a tendency towards conceptual ambiguity in discussions about the dual use problem. However, if one's objective is a sustainable web of prevention with well-formed governance measures, then such ambiguity is not appropriate. Rather, one is required to examine and, if necessary, unpack the core concepts of the web and the appropriateness of any understandings that guide policy. This is not an easy undertaking; but this ought not to mean that the task goes undone.

Opening up the conceptual framework to critical examination

In and of itself, an examination of the conceptual framing of dual use will not provide definitive answers on how to manage the problem of biological weapons; but, as Moodie (2004) argues, intellectual infrastructures are important because:

> ... concepts shape our constructs of reality, and they can prompt a sense of new opportunities with respect to what can be done to address major challenges. In other words, it both opens up new policy options and promotes either the identification of new policy tools or the application of existing tools in novel ways.

If one were to attempt to ameliorate the conceptual differences described above, it seems necessary to accept that the dual use issue is not just a security issue. To this end, and given the legal status of biological weapons, understanding the dual use issue within a technology governance framework should be given careful consideration. This requires opening the issue beyond traditional security actors to a non-traditional security audience who are experts in innovation studies and technological pathways, as well as in science and technology studies.

As a starting point in considering how technology governance might inform the dual use debate and potentially open new opportunities to address the problem of biological weapons, it is interesting to note that within science and technology studies, technologies are not considered to be neutral objects to which actions are done. Rather, technologies are viewed as having 'encoded politics', which by accentuating different elements allows for different conceptualizations. Whichever of these conceptualizations of technology is used will directly affect what is thought of as appropriate governance. Mitcham (1978, 1994), for example, assigns differing articulations of the term 'technology' to two major professional groups: engineers and social scientists. To engineers, he assigns a view of 'technology' that is limited to 'direct involvement with material construction and the manipulation of artefacts', while to social scientists he assigns an extended understanding where 'all making of material artefacts, the objects made, their use, and to some extent their intellectual and social contexts' are included (see McLeish, 2006, pp218–220).

Based on empirical research, there is general agreement amongst science and technology policy scholars that a definition of technology must include three interacting parts:

1 *the physics of the artefact* that objectively determines how the technology behaves;
2 *an imposed function* that both guides people's interactions with the technology and determines how the technology should behave; and
3 *a technological regime* in which the artefact interacts with its social and physical environment in order to achieve its function.

While the physics of the artefact refers to its structure, technology scholars regard the imposition of functions on that artefact as determining how it is understood and supposed to work, as perceived by the user. Interestingly, whether the function works or not, the identity of the technological artefact remains the same. For example, a safety valve on a pipe has the function of stopping the build-up of pressure so that an explosion can be averted. However, as Searle (1995) notes, the identity of the safety valve remains true for the user even if it malfunctions and fails to stop a pressure build-up causing an explosion; in such cases, the users say that 'the safety valve didn't work'.

The role played by the imposition of function in determining technological identity and in determining how that technology is supposed to work permits technology studies to accommodate the idea of multiple functions being imposed at any stage after invention. For example, the function of a CD, as intended by its inventor, is to store information. However, a CD can also have other functions imposed upon it if a change occurs in the context of use and the wider socio-technical regime: a CD could be used as a coaster for a coffee cup or tied to a fruit tree to scare off birds. Although the physics of the CD is unaltered and its original function continues to be a relevant use, alternative functions are made possible by a change in the context of use, a change in the intention of use and (possibly) a change in the user (see McLeish, 2004).

In technology policy, therefore, it is not unusual or controversial to consider technologies as having multiple uses because these uses are created by changes in contexts, changes in user, changes in user intention, and changes in the relationship of that technology to other technical and social systems. Choosing between multiple functions is not seen as something that is determined by the physics of the artefact because function is not perceived as an inherent characteristic of technology. Rather, function is seen as being primarily dependent upon what is most appropriate to the user in the given context.

In this chapter's presentation of the three different understandings of dual use, the context-based understanding of dual use regards the function of a technology as being fixed and intrinsic, whereas in the user-driven understanding of dual use, multiple functions in multiple environments are expected and therefore accommodated. This latter understanding is more modern and in line with the body of knowledge produced within a technology governance framework (see, for example, Freeman, 1982; Rosenberg, 1982; Searle, 1995; Pavitt, 1999; Nightingale, 2004) where the functions of technology are understood to be based on people's intentional understanding of function, while how well technologies perform these functions depends upon the intrinsic properties of the technology and its interactions with the wider environment, which typically includes other socio-technical systems.

Understanding innovation is also central to the differences between the three framings of dual use. Particularly where dual use is regarded as an inherent property of the technology, innovation is portrayed as primarily about an inventive occurrence that creates a technology with a fixed function that is then diffused in a relatively costless fashion. Such a linear model of innovation that oversimplifies the relationship between science and technology within this process can be traced to observations made in the 1945 Bush report, *Science: The Endless Frontier*, which examined post-war US science. According to Brooks (1994, p477):

> *Over time, this report came to be interpreted as saying that if the nation supported scientists to carry out research according to their own sense of what was important and interesting, technologies useful to health, national security and the economy would follow almost automatically once the potential opportunities opened up by new scientific discoveries became widely known to the military, the health professions and the private entrepreneurs operating in the national economy.*

The linear model of innovation, when applied to biological weapons, can, in a similar manner, be interpreted as saying that a new generation of biological weapons will follow almost automatically once the potential opportunities opened up by new scientific discoveries become widely known to entrepreneurial proliferators and/or terrorists.

Critics of this model of innovation dismiss the idea that there is a straightforward progression from the generation of scientific knowledge to the development of a technology (e.g. Rosenberg, 1974; Freeman, 1982; Nightingale, 2004). Additionally, critics say that the linear model underestimates the costs of technological development compared to research and the technical difficulties involved in developing an artefact, as well as overlooking the non-scientific knowledge that has to be integrated in order to develop technology.

Like the advocates of the user-driven understanding of dual use, critics of the linear innovation model present innovation as a process that is complex, rather than an event. The complexity is achieved from the necessary indirect interactions that take place between autonomous bodies of scientific and technical knowledge, which are then mediated through social choices and institutions. Policies using the linear model of innovation are therefore thought likely to overestimate the benefits of controls and to underestimate their costs (see McLeish and Nightingale, forthcoming). Moreover, conceptualizing innovation as a complex process calls into question ideas that diffusion of scientific papers and/or possession of certain technology equates to the accumulation of technological capabilities.

Conclusions

If one accepts that the dual use problem is dynamic rather than static in character, then the continual and critical examination of what is meant by dual use becomes an essential governance activity.

Much is currently written 'about' dual use, and although writing about it and analysing governance initiatives is an important activity that needs to continue, it is reactive. Conceptual assumptions have already been incorporated within the chosen governance solution, and if these assumptions are based on ill-formed conceptualizations, then the resulting policy solutions are likely to be inadequate.

To be proactive, there needs to be an exploration at the conceptual level of the nature of the problem of dual use given the impact that conceptual understandings have on the generation, and therefore prioritization, of governance initiatives. This does not seem to be occurring and is notably absent in discussions about how best to govern dual use technologies Perhaps the reason for the lack of discussion is that the multiple understandings about dual use, technology and the innovation process, currently evident in biological weapons policy generation, are the very best possible. However, even the briefest of glances into the technology studies and innovation literature show that this is unlikely. Definitions, models and understandings about technology, the relationship between science and technology, and the technological innovation process have changed over time. Yet often quoted in writings about dual use is a 12-year-old definition of technology – without examination at the conceptual level, we will not know whether this definition of technology remains the most appropriate definition to capture the entirety of the innovation process and, therefore, the potential opportunities for diversion into misuse.

Because of the centrality of dual use to the biological weapons problem, and the importance it has to the web of prevention, it is essential that this sort of proactive examination takes place. Opening an intellectual space in which meaningful and innovative exploration of the dual use issue can take place is necessary, and by focusing on the conceptual underpinnings of the dual use problem there is a real opportunity to move understandings beyond their current framing. If conceived as a technology governance issue, as well as a security issue, then observations and insights from actors not normally associated with security, such as science and technology scholars, experts in technology life cycles and innovation pathways, as well as economics generally and industrial economics specifically, can be usefully included in the generation of dual use governance measures. Their inclusion would also provide new opportunities for synergistic relations with other policy domains.

In widening the conceptual framework to a full range of intellectual stakeholders, those in the security community who are willing to engage are likely to discover new opportunities for additional governance along the innovation path. If such an interaction were to happen, governing dual use technologies could move from the reactive to the proactive, in this way strengthening the web of prevention by further increasing the difficulties involved in diverting technologies from legitimate to illegitimate applications.

Notes

1   See www.defenselink.mil/pubs/prolif97/annex.html#technical.
2   See www.defenselink.mil/pubs/prolif/access_tech.html.
3   See www.australiagroup.net/en/agobj.htm.
4   See www.australiagroup.net/en/guidelines.html.
5   See www.wassenaar.org/controllists/16%20-%20WA-LIST%20%2804%29%202% 20-%20DEF.doc.
6   Correct as of June 2006; see www.hms.harvard.edu/orsp/coms/BiosafetyResources/ Bioterrorism/Select-Agent-Listing.doc.
7   For more information, see www.fco.gov.uk/Files/kfile/VVS.doc.

References

van Aken, J. and Hammond, E. (2003) 'Genetic engineering and biological weapons: New technologies, desires and threats from biological research', *EMBO Reports*, vol 4, pp57–60
Alic, J. (1993) 'Technical knowledge and technology diffusion: New issues for US government policy', *Technology Analysis and Strategic Management*, vol 5 pp369–383
Alic, J., Branscomb, L., Brooks, H., Epstein, G., Carter, A. (1992) *Beyond Spinoff: Military and Commercial Technologies in a Changing World*, Harvard, Harvard Business School Press
Asthana, A. (2007) 'Tighter checks on students from overseas', *The Observer*, 28 January
Atlas, R. M. (2001) 'Bioterrorism before and after 11 September', *Critical Reviews in Microbiology*, vol 27, pp355–379
Atlas, R. M. (2002) 'National security and the biological research community', *Science*, vol 298, pp753–754

Autio, E. and Laamanen, T. (1995) 'Measurement and evaluation of technology transfer: Review of technology transfer mechanisms and indicators', *International Journal of Technology Management*, vol 10, no 7/8, p647, cited in Molas-Gallart, J. (1996) *Developing dual use Technology Transfer Methodologies: Taxonomy of Policy Alternatives*, report prepared for the National Engineering Laboratory, Brighton, SPRU, July

Block, S. (1999) 'Living nightmares: Biological threats enabled by molecular biology', in Drell, S., Sofaer, A. and Wilson, G. (eds) *The New Terror: Facing the Threat of Biological and Chemical Weapons*, Stanford, Hoover Institution Press

BMA (British Medical Association) (1999) *Biotechnology, Weapons and Humanity*, Amsterdam, Harwood Academic Publishers

Bozeman, B. (2000) 'Technology transfer and public policy: A review of research and theory', *Research Policy*, vol 29 pp627–655

Breithaupt, H. (2000), 'Toxins for terrorists: Do scientists act illegally when sending out potentially dangerous material?', *EMBO Reports*, vol 1, no 4, pp298–301

Brooks, H. (1994) 'The relationship between science and technology', *Research Policy*, vol 23, pp477–486

Bush, V. (1945) 'Science: The Endless Frontier', Report to the President by Vannevar Bush, Director of the Office of Scientific Research and Development, July, www.nsf.gov/od/lpa/nsf50/vbush1945.htm

Collier, S., Lakoff, A. and Rabinow, P. (2004) 'Biosecurity: Towards an anthropology of the contemporary', *Anthropology Today*, vol 20, p3

Dando, M. (1999) 'The impact of the development of modern biology and medicine on the evolution of offensive biological warfare programs in the twentieth century', *Defense Analysis*, vol 15, pp43–62

Dando, M. (2001) *The New Biological Weapons: Threat, Proliferation and Control*, London, Lynne Rienner Publishers

Defense Science Board (2000) *Protecting the Homeland: Report of the Defense Science Board*, Washington, DC, Defense Science Board

Director of Central Intelligence (2003) *Acquisition of Technology Relating to Weapons of Mass Destruction and Advanced Conventional Munitions, 1 January through 30 June 2002*, Unclassified Report to Congress, Washington, DC, DCI

Director of Central Intelligence (2006) *Acquisition of Technology Relating to Weapons of Mass Destruction and Advanced Conventional Munitions, 1 January–31 December 2004*, Unclassified Report to Congress, Washington, DC, DCI

Freeman, C. (1982) *The Economics of Industrial Innovation*, 2nd edition, London, Pinter

Gaudioso, J. and Salerno, R. M. (2004) 'Biosecurity and research: Minimizing adverse impacts', *Science*, 30 April, vol 304, p687

Gilbert, N. (2007) 'All postgraduate visas to require security vetting', *Research Research*, 24 January, www.researchresearch.com

Journal Editors and Authors Group (2003) 'Statement on the consideration of biodefence and biosecurity', *Nature*, vol 421, p771

Lehrman, T. (2006) 'Building Transformational Partnerships to Combat WMD Terrorism', Remarks at the US Military Academy, Washington, DC, 7 November

Littlewood, J. (2004) *Managing the Biological Weapons Problem: From the Individual to the International*, no 14, Stockholm, Weapons of Mass Destruction Commission.

McLeish, C. (2002) 'Accommodating Bio-Disarmament to Bio-Technological Change', DPhil thesis, University of Sussex, Brighton, SPRU

McLeish, C. (2004) 'A background note on dual use technologies: Can technology studies inform the dual use debate?', paper presented at 21st Pugwash CBW Workshop: The BWC New Process and the Sixth Review Conference, Geneva, Switzerland, 4–5

December

McLeish, C. (2006), 'Science and censorship in an age of bio-weapons threat', *Science as Culture*, vol 15, pp215–236

McLeish, C. and Nightingale, P. (2005) *The Impact of Dual Use Controls on UK Science: Results from a Pilot Study*, SWEPS 132, Brighton, SPRU

McLeish, C. and Nightingale, P. (forthcoming) 'Biosecurity, bioterrorism and the governance of science: The increasing convergence of science and security policy', *Research Policy*

Meselson, M. (2000) 'Averting the hostile exploitation of biotechnology', *CBW Conventions Bulletin*, no 48, pp16–19

Mitcham, C. (1978) 'Types of technology', *Research in Philosophy and Technology*, vol 1, pp229–294

Mitcham, C. (1994) *Thinking through Technology: The Path between Engineering and Philosophy*, Chicago, University of Chicago

Molas-Gallart, J. (1996) *Developing dual use Technology Transfer Methodologies: A Taxonomy of Policy Alternatives*, report prepared for the National Engineering Laboratory, Brighton, SPRU

Molas-Gallart, J. (1997) 'Which way to go? Defence technology and the diversity of "dual use" technology transfer', *Research Policy*, vol 26, October, pp367–385

Molas-Gallart, J. (2000) 'dual use technologies and transfer mechanisms', in Schroeer, D. and Elena, M. (eds) *Technology Transfer*, Aldershot, Ashgate, pp3–21

Molas-Gallart, J. (2002) 'Coping with dual use: A challenge for European research policy', *Journal of Common Market Studies*, vol 40, pp155–165

Moodie, M. (2004) 'Confronting the biological and chemical weapons challenge: The need for an "intellectual infrastructure"', *The Fletcher Forum of World Affairs*, vol 28, winter, pp43–56

NAS (National Academy of Sciences) National Academy of Engineering and Institute of Medicine (1982) *Scientific Communication and National Security: A Report Prepared by the Panel on Scientific Communication and National Security Committee on Science, Engineering and Public Policy*, Washington, DC, US National Academy Press

Nightingale, P. (2004) 'Technological capabilities, invisible infrastructure and the unsocial construction of predictability: The overlooked fixed costs of useful research', *Research Policy*, vol 33, pp1259–1284

Nixdorff, K., Brauburger, J. and Hahlbohm, D. (2000) 'The biotechnology revolution: The science and applications', in Dando, M., Pearson, G. and Tóth, T. (eds) *Verification of the Biological and Toxin Weapons Convention*, NATO ASI Series, I. *Disarmament Technologies 32*, Dordrecht, The Netherlands, Kluwer Academic

NRC (National Research Council) of the US National Academies of Sciences, Committee on Research, Standards and Practices to Prevent the Destructive Application of Biotechnology (2004) *Biotechnology Research in an Age of Terrorism: Confronting the dual use Dilemma*, Washington, DC, US National Academy of Sciences

NRC and the Institute of Medicine of the US National Academies, Committee on Advances in Technology and the Prevention of Their Application to Next General Biowarfare Threats (2006) *Globalization, Biosecurity and the Future of the Life Sciences*, Washington, DC, National Academies Press

Pavitt, K. (1999) *Technology, Management and Systems of Innovation*, Cheltenham, UK, Edward Elgar

Pearson, G. (1993) 'Prospects for chemical and biological arms control: The web of deterrence', *The Washington Quarterly*, vol 16, pp145–162

Rappert, B. (2003) 'Biological weapons, genetics and social analysis: Emerging responses, emerging issues – I', *New Genetics and Society*, vol 22, pp169–181

Reppy, J. (1999) 'dual use technology: Back to the future?', in Markusen, A. and Costigan, S. (eds) *Arming the Future: A Defense Industry for the 21st Century*, New York, Council on Foreign Relations Press

Roberts, B. (1995) 'Rethinking export controls on dual use materials and technologies: From trade restraints to trade enablers', *The Arena*, no 2, June

Robinson, J. P. (1992) 'The Australia Group: A description and assessment', in Brauch, H., van der Graaf, H., Grin, J. and Smit, W. (eds) *Controlling the Development and Spread of Military Technology: Lessons from the Past and Challenges for the 1990s*, Amsterdam, VU University Press

Robinson, J. P. (1997) 'Controlling dual use biotechnology: The crucial role of national measures', paper presented to the *8th Pugwash Study Group on Implementation of the CBW Conventions Workshop*, Geneva, Switzerland, 20–21 September, Brighton, SPRU

Rosebury, T. (1947) *Experimental Air-Borne Infection*, Microbiological Monographs, Society of American Bacteriologists, Baltimore, Williams and Wilkins Company

Rosenberg, N. (1974) 'Science, invention and economic growth', *The Economic Journal*, vol 84, March, pp90–108

Rosenberg, N. (1982) *Perspectives on Technology*, Cambridge, Cambridge University Press

Sands, A. (2002) 'Deconstructing the Chem-Bio Threat', Testimony for the US Senate Foreign Relations Committee, 19 March

Searle, J. (1995) *The Construction of Social Reality*, London, Allen Lane

SIPRI (Stockholm International Peace Research Institute) (1972) *The Problem of Chemical and Biological Warfare: Vol 2. CB Weapons Today*, New York, Humanities Press

UK (2007) *The Schedule 5 to the Anti-terrorism, Crime and Security Act 2001 (Modification) Order 2007*, Statutory Instrument 2007 No 929 and *Explanatory Memorandum*, www.opsi.gov.uk/si/dsis2007.htm

United Kingdom of Great Britain and Northern Ireland (2001) *Anti-terrorism, Crime and Security Act*

UN (United Nations) (1972) *Economic and Social Consequences of the Armaments Race and Its Extremely Harmful Effects on World Peace*, report of the Secretary-General, A/32/88, 12 August

UN (2006) *Uniting against Terrorism: Recommendations for a Global Counter-Terrorism Strategy*, report of the Secretary-General A/60/285, 27 April

UN General Assembly (1977) *Economic and Social Consequences of the Armaments and its Extremely Harmful Effects on World Peace and Security*, report of the Secretary General, A/32/88, 12 August

UNSC (United Nations Security Council) (1992) *Note by the President of the Security Council*, S/23500, 31 January, UNSC

US Department of Defense (1997) *Proliferation Threat and Response, 1997, A Report by the Secretary of Defense*, 2nd edition, William S. Cohen, 25 November 1997, www.ciaonet.org/book/cohen02/index.html

Wilkening, D. (1999) 'BWC attack scenarios', in Drell, S., Sofaer, A. and Wilson, G. (eds) *The New Terror: Facing the Threat of Biological and Chemical Weapons*, Stanford, Hoover Institution Press

Zilinskas, R. A. (1999) 'Iraq's biological weapons: The past as future?', in Lederberg, J. (ed) *Biological Weapons: Limiting the Threat*, Cambridge, MA, MIT Press

13

Governing Dual Use Life Science Research: Opportunities and Risks for Public Health

Emmanuelle Tuerlings[1]

Health is defined by the World Health Organization as 'a state of complete physical, mental and social well-being and not merely the absence of disease or infirmity'. The WHO constitution also establishes links between health and security by stating that 'the health of all peoples is fundamental to the attainment of peace and security and is dependent upon the fullest co-operation of individuals and States'. Linkages between health and security can take many forms. Issues linked to international security include emerging diseases, such as SARS and avian influenza, HIV/AIDS, environmental change, economic stability, or accidental or deliberate biological events; they illustrate the impact that public health can have on international security (WHO, 2007a). In a highly interconnected and interdependent world, the risks to health must be addressed in a collective and responsible manner, as exemplified by the 2007 World Health Day theme on international health security, with the following global message: 'Invest in health, build a safer future.'

The issue under discussion in this book illustrates one linkage between health and security. The tremendous advances in life science research[2] will most certainly lead to both improved health and well-being – for instance, through new diagnostic tools, treatments and vaccines to treat infectious diseases – and to enhanced responses to disease outbreaks, which particularly affect developing countries. Biomedical research and international partnerships are considered essential starting points to achieve the United Nations Millennium Development Goals (MDGs) (Juma and Yee-Cheong, 2005). Health research similarly plays a critical role in improving public health. Yet recent research has shown that only 10 per cent of the global amount spent on health research every year was used for health problems that affect 90 per cent of the world's population – the '10/90 gap' (Global Forum for Health Research, 2004; WHO, 2004). Although recent data tend to indicate that overall resources for health research have risen, many challenges still remain – not least that of reducing inequalities in health conditions among populations.

Yet opportunities may also be accompanied by risks that cannot be ignored. The risks posed by life science research can express themselves, for instance, through a laboratory accident or through deliberate misuse. New knowledge and technologies are powerful and evolve quickly, with important and sometimes controversial implications that have been highlighted in studies of bioethics and of equitable access to life sciences research, particularly with regard to resource-poor countries. This book specifically underlines the related complementary implication of international health security.

Because of what is usually called the dual use dilemma,[3] the governance mechanisms that have been suggested for managing the risks associated with the accidental or potential misuse of life science research and development (R&D) could also affect the development of a science that has much to offer for the benefit of public health. At the same time, public health is concerned with the protection and promotion of health and therefore considers that it is responsible for safeguarding communities against the potential risks posed by life science research. As a result, a fine balance must be struck between furthering the public health benefits of research and development in the life sciences and limiting its potential risks – a balance that allows the flowering of new techniques and knowledge and also gives all actors involved with life science research useful guidance on how to manage the associated risks (WHO, 2005). Because of its significance for public health, it is important to view research in the life sciences from a public health perspective. Indeed, strong public confidence must be maintained in science – communication and international collaboration are essential for scientists to work in productive environments in order to provide policy-makers with evidence-based advice that will ultimately strengthen international health security. The WHO project on Life Science Research and Development and Global Health Security takes this approach, and aims to raise awareness from a public health viewpoint and to provide information and guidance to its member states on this topic.

As part of this project, a scientific working group recently met under the framework of the WHO to discuss the implications of life science research for international health security (WHO, 2007b). The group was a mix of public health workers, academicians, researchers, policy-makers, security experts and representatives from international organizations. The working group had commissioned five working papers to explore the various linkages between public health, life science research and security – these papers were intended to guide the discussions of the scientific working group.

The commissioned documents brought out various suggestions and conclusions. They reviewed the links between nuclear physics and chemistry to examine the links between life science research and security issues. They highlighted the importance of ethics and considerations of human behaviour in raising awareness about the potential misuse of the life sciences. Capacity development in health research was deemed a priority in ensuring the proper use of life science research and in minimizing misuse. Investments in health systems and health systems research, together with international cooperation in health research, are essential in this regard. The papers and the discussions that followed also emphasized the need to address these issues across a bio-risk spectrum, different risks being allocated to naturally occurring diseases (both infectious and non-communicable), to accidental outbreaks and to deliberate outbreaks. This approach is essential for the prioritization of various health risks and for purposes of resource distribution and funding. The need was also raised for a multifaceted and international solution, based on a complex foundation of education, raising awareness and building health capacity.

The scientific working group recognized that these issues are complex and challenging for public health, and 'paid special attention to the needs and vulnerabilities of developing countries'. It underlined 'the need for the global community to respond to these challenges in a manner that is sustained and comprehensive', and identified five priority areas for which action is needed:

1   *education and training for life science students and researchers, and, ultimately, even for high school students, journalists and the public;*
2   *preparedness for a possible major outbreak of disease resulting from the intentional or inadvertent misuse of biological agents by preparing for natural disease events;*
3   *development of risk assessment methods;*
4   *engagement of all stakeholders in the life science community, and development with and through them of guidelines for oversight; and*
5   *thoroughgoing capacity-building at country level, including ethics, clinical practice, laboratories and research. (WHO, 2007b)*

Regional activities with WHO member states will further discuss these five areas and hopefully provide guidance on this issue from a public health perspective, particularly from developing countries.

The security and health of people are interdependent. Recognizing these links is therefore essential in order to strengthen international health security. The public health community must be aware of this issue and of the proposed governance mechanisms, particularly if these affect its work. Policy-makers and the security communities should similarly be encouraged to think about the public health implications of such governance measures. The scientific working group agreed that finding and maintaining the right mix of policies so that the benefits of life science research can be maximized while risks are kept to a minimum will require considerable effort on the part of both the life science and security communities. Addressing this issue requires a complex and dynamic process, calling for a multifaceted solution, international coordination and sustained engagement.

A public health approach underscores that greater awareness of the risks posed by life science research should go together with a greater capacity for health research to face local and national diseases and health conditions. Such an approach will strengthen international health security and promote the message: 'Invest in health, build a safer future.'

Notes

1   The author is a staff member of the World Health Organization. The author alone is responsible for the views expressed in this publication and they do not necessarily represent the decisions or the stated policy of the World Health Organization.
2   'The life sciences comprise all sciences that deal with living organisms, including human beings, animals and plants. It is a broad field that encompasses biology, biotechnology, genomics, proteomics, bioinformatics, pharmaceutical and biomedical research and techniques'. WHO (2005).
3   'Knowledge and technologies that result from life science research and used for legitimate research and technology development may also be appropriated for illegitimate intentions and applications'. WHO (2007b).

References

Global Forum for Health Research (2004) *The 10/90 Report on Health Research, 2003–2004*, Geneva, Global Forum for Health Research

Juma, C. and Yee-Cheong, L. (2005) 'Reinventing global health: The role of science, technology, and innovation', *The Lancet*, vol 365, pp1105–1107

WHO (World Health Organization) (2004) *World Report on Knowledge for Better Health: Strengthening Health Systems*, Geneva, WHO

WHO (2005) *Life Science Research: Opportunities and Risks for Public Health*, Geneva, WHO, (WHO/CDS/CSR/LYO/2005.20), www.who.int/csr/resources/publications/deliberate/WHO_CDS_CSR_LYO_2005_20.pdf/, accessed in April 2007

WHO (2007a) *Invest in Health, Build a Safer Future: Issues Paper*, Geneva, WHO, www.who.int/world-health-day/2007/issues_paper/en/index.html/, accessed in April 2007

WHO (2007b) *Scientific Working Group on Life Science Research and Global Health Security: Report of the First Meeting*, Geneva, Switzerland, *16–18 October 2006* (WHO/CDS/EPR/2007.4), www.who.int/csr/resources/publications/deliberate/WHO_CDS_EPR_2007_4n.pdf/, accessed in April 2007

Index